VISUAL
IMPACT

VISUAL IMPACT

CREATIVE DISSENT
IN THE 21ST CENTURY

LIZ McQUISTON

CREATIVE DISSENT IN CONTEXT: TECHNOLOGY AND CHANGE

CREATIVE DISSENT IN CONTEXT: TECHNOLOGY & CHANGE

The terrorist attacks of 9/11 provided a brutal wake-up call that launched the twenty-first century. Two jets hijacked by Al-Qaida terrorists crashed into the twin towers of the World Trade Center in New York City; another came down in the fields of Pennsylvania; and the last crashed into a wing of the Pentagon in Washington, DC. Within minutes, this twenty-first century disaster, resulting in nearly 3,000 deaths, was brought to our eyes by the world's media.

The total destruction of such a symbol of global capitalism – with collapsing buildings and clouds of billowing dust – heralded a new era of change. Unlike the instabilities of the 1990s – embodied by declining empires, weakening ideologies (both capitalist and communist) and conflicts initiating migrating populations – the changes of the new century were charged with certainties, actions and aggressions, albeit often flawed or misguided. These have included collapsing financial markets and economies; the fall of dictators bringing chaos rather than longed-for democracy; global terrorism driven by retaliation or fanaticism; and drawn-out wars the product of plunging into conflicts with no sound reasoning, strategy or exit plan.

Visual Impact explores how artists and designers, professional and otherwise, have responded to, or protested against, events caused by these overarching certainties. These creative activists have produced extraordinary projects, interventions or demonstrations using a variety of media, and a number of shared, key issues underpinning the breadth of the work have emerged.

One is the crossing or blurring of boundaries between creative fields of practice, particularly when dealing with social or political messages of dissent. Classic formats remain as strong as ever, in the form of posters, paintings, photographs, films, performances and so on. However they are now just as likely to be viewed in a gallery as on the side of a building. Images are as likely to be part of a march as they are to be shared on the internet or viewed on TV. All these settings offer space for exposure, shock and subversion. With such shifting platforms, media and scale, professional labels such as fine artist, graphic designer, photographer, filmmaker and so on start to lose their relevance, and terms such as artist, activist or social commentator start to become more meaningful.

Another key issue important to *Visual Impact* is the way in which emergent technologies have impacted on creative dissent since the start of the twenty-first century. Global networking through emails and websites defined the activism of the 1990s; the development of broadband, smartphones and 'sharing' via social media defined activism in the 2000s. By the end of the first decade most mobile phones were web-enabled and equipped with cameras, thus sites such as

YouTube, Facebook, Twitter and Flickr were set to play leading roles in the revolutions of the Arab Spring and the Occupy movement.

Mobile technology, with its ability to capture and disseminate events as they happen, has also allowed the world to bear witness to bad behaviour and atrocities, and to interact with people making courageous stands wherever they are. It has introduced new methods of exposure such as 'citizen journalism' and added another dimension to 'whistle-blowing' by unleashing iconic imagery, such as the photograph of the standing Iraqi prisoner undergoing torture in Abu Ghraib prison. It has also brought activists a cloak of anonymity, as demonstrated by collectives producing poster comments on subjects ranging from the Syrian conflict to the use of drone warfare that have been uploaded onto social media.

However, emergent technologies also point towards a world of increasing transience, where messages and captured images can be as easily deleted as uploaded – in much the same way that graffiti or street art can be painted over with lightning speed. Thus art, actions, events and history are obliterated. In this sense technology has become a major battlefield in the present and future fight for freedom of speech. A recent example was the Chinese government's censorship/deletion of renowned artist-activist Ai Weiwei's blog in 2009 around the time of his 'Citizen Investigation' into the Sichuan earthquake and the deaths of thousands of school children.

Viewed from another angle, online activism offers the experience of the collective. One way that artists and designers can show solidarity for an issue or cause is by producing work for a themed website or blog as part of a fund-raising campaign or 'subvertizing' competition. In this way, the collection of work in *Visual Impact* goes a long way towards answering that well-worn question: 'Is the poster dead?' The poster, as can be seen here, is very much alive, in many sizes, scribbled or printed, electronic and aided by mobile technology, and still performing its most important role as impactful and immediate carrier of political expression. Online image banks (see Voces con Futura, page 54–55) have also emerged, archiving and displaying uploaded posters generated by the mobilization of a protest movement, natural disaster or other crisis. Viewing them is akin to hearing the shouts in a demonstration or being immersed in an urgent

conversation. The viewer feels their anger … even if unable to read the language.

Visual Impact aims to explore examples of visual dissent and protest since 9/11 in both the cyber and real worlds, and the artworks are therefore pre-

sented within a framework of historical and political events during the years 2000 to 2015. However, no book-sized exploration could hope to provide coverage of all the important movements and events of the past 15 years. Nor could it cover every aspect of global politics or embrace every country in the world. Instead *Visual Impact* focuses on particular lines of activity and enquiry, presenting a snapshot of recent dissent using a wide range of media. It includes work produced by a variety of practitioners – from graphic designers, fine artists and street artists, to photographers and filmmakers – as well as unnamed members of a crowd, anonymous graffitists and sign-scribblers.

Each chapter begins with an introduction intended to contextualize the creative projects within it. The projects are then examined individually in greater detail throughout the chapter. In order to apply an accessible narrative to the content it has been necessary to shape it into subsections, even though it is evident that some of the content could easily fit into two, or perhaps even three, of the chapters. Similarly, many different movements or issues share particular concerns, interests and voices, and thus there are natural points of overlap.

Visual Impact begins with a brief history chapter concerning the visual legacy of the 1990s. The massacre of Tiananmen Square and the graphic art it inspired casts a long shadow that stretches to the present. Although occurring in 1989, its legacy can be seen in the output of current artists such as Ai Weiwei. Cyberactivism also began in the 1990s with the worldwide networks of the anti-globalization movement; and subvertizing was the weapon of choice for attacking multinationals and their branding, as well as politicians. The first Gulf War of 1991 brought anti-war protests and the Balkan Wars produced a wide range of artistic statements documenting the hell and horror of citizens caught up in the crossfire.

Chapter One examines the creative outpouring of work from the events that came to be grouped under the Arab Spring banner, as well as the protests against austerity measures from the global Occupy movement, spreading from Wall Street to Europe and beyond. Anti-

Putin feelings brought Russia's brazen performance artists to worldwide attention and the Turkish prime minister's authoritarianism was confronted in Istanbul's Taksim Square. Brilliant posters pasted up in Brazil's rapidly expanding major cities showed how creativity could speak out against appalling poverty and Chinese artists became social commentators. This chapter also demonstrates how emergent technologies played a crucial role in the organization and documentation of all of the above.

The wars in Afghanistan and Iraq are the subject of Chapter Two, where anti-war protest materials are to be found alongside artistic reactions to the Abu Ghraib scandal. There are also examples demonstrating how the 'War on Terror' became embedded in popular culture, and analyses of heroism, casualties and death are made through photographs, toy soldiers and sensitively presented postage stamps. Other projects exploring the documentation of war range from court sketches from the 9/11 military tribunals at Guantanamo Bay to a hand-written transcript of an interview with a British trauma surgeon volunteering in war-torn Syria.

Chapter Three presents work that explores divided countries – the Israeli-Palestinian conflict, North and South Korea – as well as some of the cultural divisions of our time that exist across countries and societies. These include visual comments relating to the veil, particularly those that give rise to its many conflicting meanings and interpretations in modern life. The legalizing of same-sex marriage produces artistic celebrations in some countries and anti-gay protests in others, while feminist art is shown to be more daring than ever, as well as having a lethal sense of humour.

Chapter Four confronts environmental disasters, both natural and man-made. Hurricane Katrina inspired projects researching government rescue

mismanagement, inherent racism, out-of-control violence and other disturbing issues. The BP Oil Spill brought suffering to America's Gulf Coast and anti-corporate activism from the design world. And a collaborative, photographic and ecological research project conducted on Louisiana's 'Cancer Alley' presents a beautiful but haunting visual experience of a possible toxic future.

In short, the visual projects contained in this book show that over the past fifteen years the emergent technologies have become integral to image capture, image making and image dissemination. Creative disciplines are merging and the individual has greater strength through connectivity – the smallest protest can now be captured

and broadcast to the entire planet. And within this melange of experience, a powerful visual history will continue to build up and take stock of current political concerns and activism ... and rush them forward to future generations.

Page 8. *Action Half-Life, Episode 16*, digital collage by AES+F. Russia 2003. The Moscow-based mixed media art group AES+F create subversive visual narratives exploring 'the values, vices and conflicts' of contemporary culture. This is one of a series of images created in the style of a futuristic 3D computer game, where young teenagers take on heroic poses with heavy weaponry and wear costumes of pure white as if modelling for an advertisement (they are invincible, no pain or suffering can possibly befall them). Of the many interpretations that may be derived, one of the most shocking is the continual perpetuation – now and into the future – of the glorification of heroism and war. For, however it may be coated in modern-day glitter or gloss, each generation continues to send its children to fight new wars.

Page 9. *Inside Out Project: Russian Embassies Across Europe*, 51 portraits are held by a group standing up against homophobic treatment of LGBT groups in Russia. A project facilitated by the artist JR. France 2011 to present. Photo by Chad Meacham.

Page 10. Left: T-shirt bearing one of the most popular images on twitter, when Barack Obama was campaigning for a second term in the 2012 Presidential election. Obama was known for his strategic use of social media and targeting young people in his election campaigns. USA 2012. Right: One of the many digitally-manipulated Conservative Party election posters uploaded to the mydavidcameron.com website, during the UK general election campaign of 2010. (David Cameron was Head of the Conservative Party.)

Page 11. Left: *Hot Shots*, portrait of the Russian performance art duo the Blue Noses. Russia 2003. Top right: Front cover of *Empire: Nozone IX*, edited by Nicholas Blechman. A compendium of work by artists, designers, photographers and writers interrogating and protesting the condition of America after '9/11'. Front cover illustration, *Deadly Alliance* by Knickerbocker. USA 2004. Below Right: *Israel Palestine 2004*, poster by Yossi Lemel. Israel 2004. A comment on the relentless inconclusiveness of the Israeli-Palestinian conflict.

Page 12. *Twilight Avenger*, single screen installation, high definition video with stereo sound by Canadian artist Kelly Richardson. UK 2008. The setting is a dark, mysterious, fairy tale-like forest; suddenly a heroic stag walks into view, surrounded by a menacing, spectral glow – as if the victim of a past nuclear accident or other toxic experience, returning to avenge the damage imposed on nature. Or is it a premonition of the future? Richardson's concerns for the human and industrial impact on the environment are never blatant, but embedded in haunting, ambiguous (and often immersive) visual experiences that force viewers to conceive their own interpretations.

Page 13. *Bread Martyr*, the first person to be shot by government snipers in Homs, Syria while shopping for bread. An electronic poster by anonymous poster collective Alshaab Alsori Aref Tarekh (The Syrian People Know Their Way), 2011–12.

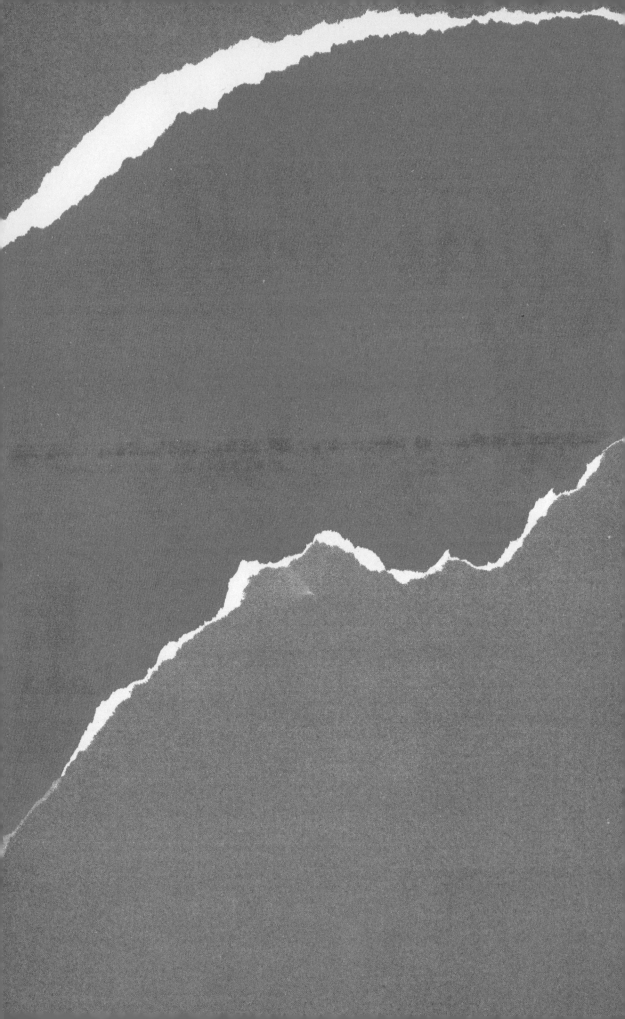

GRAPHIC HIGHLIGHTS OF THE DIGITAL AGE: THE VISUAL LEGACY OF THE 1990s

GRAPHIC HIGHLIGHTS OF THE DIGITAL AGE: THE VISUAL LEGACY OF THE 1990s

The vast possibilities for spreading political protest through emerging technologies became manifest in May 1989 during a series of pro-democracy demonstrations held in Tiananmen Square in Beijing, China. Right under the nose of a hardline communist regime, images of banners, paintings and a statue of the 'Goddess of Democracy' (a figure not dissimilar to America's *Statue of Liberty*) filled live television coverage. Fax and telex machines sent messages around the globe – and the world responded in solidarity.

French magazine *Actuel*, along with 16 other magazines, published the solidarity manifesto 'Fax for Freedom' accompanied by a long list of fax numbers belonging to Chinese offices and institutions. Readers were then encouraged to bombard the institutions with faxes to cause chaos – however short-lived. British style magazine *The Face* urged its readers to take part in the protest-by-fax with the headline: 'You have the technology to change history'. The interaction between the protest and the rest of the world was dynamic and instantaneous, aided by developments in news media and technology.[1]

Then, suddenly, it all came to an abrupt stop. On 4 June 1989 the government ordered troops to open fire on the protesters, leaving over 2,000 dead. The photographs of bloody protesters and bicycles crushed by tanks reverberated round the world. The following day an image of a lone protester with shopping bags standing in front of a column of tanks, shouting defiantly and stopping them in their tracks became an enduring symbol of the pro-democracy spirit.

The brutality of the massacre continued: within three weeks the 'tank man' was reported to have been executed[2] and others thought to be connected with the protests were pursued viciously by the authorities for years afterward. Attempts were made to bury memories of the massacre for generations. (On pursuing the subject, a colleague working in a language school in Shenyang, northeast China, in the early 2000s was surprised to hear talk of a great 'gas leak' that happened in June 1989, followed by the words 'one of the most important days in Chinese history'. There was no further conversation. The repeated use of

this exact phrase suggested that either the speakers used a coded language in fear of surveillance and reprisals, or that there was a genuine lack of awareness.)[3]

The desire for change that led to the Tiananmen Square protest had also been building up for at least a decade among Chinese artists. The personality cult of Chairman Mao Zedong, the revered leader of the People's Republic of China, had long been sustained artistically by the stiff propaganda of Socialist Realist art. Yet following Mao's death in 1976 a generation of young avant-garde artists, who had also begun to engage with art movements in the West, brazenly started to produce work that challenged the dominant culture. One distinct method, as seen in the work of Wang Guangyi, was the production of subversive versions of Mao's portrait: a practice that still has currency today. The now world-famous Ai Weiwei also made an early jab at authority in *June 1994*, taken under the sombre portrait of Mao in Tiananmen Square. Despite the tragedy of Tiananmen Square, or perhaps because of it, China could no longer close its doors to the world. However harsh the response from the authorities, artists persisted in producing social or political critiques and, in the event of a crackdown, became equally skilful in going underground or becoming invisible. This ability to exist despite the watchful eye of the authorities ensured that irreverent art would stubbornly continue to occupy a place in the cultural framework.[4]

GLOBALISM, CAPITALISM AND ECO-CRIMES = CYBERACTIVISM

Calls for change in the 1990s also came in the form of the far-reaching anti-globalization move-

ROAD RAGING
Top Tips for
Wrecking Roadbuilding

March 1997 – reprinted October 1997

ment, decrying the inadequacies and failures of a global economy involving 'free trade' (not 'fair trade') regulated by international agencies such as the International Monetary Fund (IMF), the World Trade Organization (WTO) and the World Bank. It had anti-corporatism and anti-capitalism at its heart, and was particularly critical of the power wielded by multinational corporations, represented by highly visible brand names. The concerns of the movement were not new and had been growing for decades before the explosion of actions in the 1990s, and it has been in evidence ever since. It has no leaders, but many spokespeople (such as Naomi Klein and George Monbiot) and activists who have made full use of emerging digital technology as a means of connecting and mobilizing its many participants.

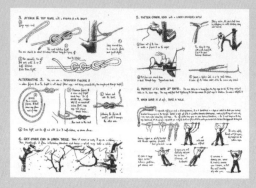

At this time the anti-globalization movement also joined up with a new and urgent form of environmentalism. Far from fuzzy, cheerful people 'going green' the 1990s saw eco-warriors and activists of all ages and occupations, tired of lobbying governments and determined to make an impact. In Britain this was seen in a series of dramatic anti-road protests, usually involving stalling bulldozers brought in by contractors to clear the ground in preparation for building a highway or by-pass, often planned through forests or other areas of natural beauty. Protesters would use highly inventive, even drastic, methods of direct action such as locking themselves to trees, living in treehouses or tree communities, and, in some cases, lying in self-made tunnels in order to stop the bulldozers. Arrests were common, and the protests rarely, if ever, stopped the road building. But they did postpone it, sometimes for long periods of time – and at substantial cost. The protests also demonstrated the ability of the determined few to stand up against the power of big business, which in turn gave encouragement to the mass protests against globalization.[5]

Both movements used networking through emails and websites, phone calls or texting as tools for mobilizing, organizing and protesting. Greenpeace established a website in the mid-1990s (and to this day claim it predated most multinational corporations' websites) and used it to help its supporters follow campaigns and actions. Online networking through websites was also used to organize mass protests against globalization, but largely in conjunction with a variety of direct-action methods: from street demon-

strations, carnivals or 'critical mass' bike rides, to graffiti and the publishing of alternative news letters or journals. Demonstrations and marches often took on a carnival atmosphere with large-scale puppets, costumes, mobile sound systems, tents or guerrilla gardening – but equally many protesters carried masks or scarves in case the atmosphere turned ugly and tear gas prevailed.

All these actions operated hand-in-hand with conventional forms of protest graphics. Images on websites relating to the organization of eco-actions or anti-globalization protests included maps showing agencies or offices deserving 'special attention' or a demonstration on their doorstep; posters and flyers were used to announce events; books or booklets on protest tactics (such as how to survive in a protest camp) were produced; alternative newsletters such as the weekly *SchNews* were circulated (online or off) alongside newspaper spoofs such as *Financial Crimes*.

There were also a wide variety of developments in media activism such as internet hackers, radio pirates, digital photojournalists and reporters communicating updates via text. In addition lightweight camcorders allowed video activists such as the Undercurrents collective to

produce alternatives to mainstream news which often depicted protesters as thugs and never seemed to capture the brutality of the police or security guards.

The need for online organization and media activism became greater as the protests got bigger – and rowdier – towards the end of the decade. 'The Carnival Against Capital: International Day of Action' on 18 June 1999 saw photographs and website reports pouring in from protests and festivals in twenty-seven countries. The London event involved more than 10,000 protesters in festivities that later erupted into riots. The 'Battle of Seattle' (30 November 1999), a massive protest against the IMF and the WTO, involved 50,000 to 100,000 protesters from all over the world, and was famed for the ensuing riots, the large amounts of tear gas and pepper-spray used, and the shutdown of the World Economic Summit being held in the city. In April 2000 clashes between protesters and police shut down Washington, DC for six hours. In July 2001 the G8 Summit turned Genoa, Italy, into a battlefield for three days, with reports of police

brutality and the fatal shooting of a protester. Protests around environmental and social justice issues would continue, but the sudden events of 9/11 channelled protesters' energies into another direction: the upcoming conflicts of the War on Terror that many believed to be driven by corporate interests.[6]

Direct action on other environmental issues included PETA campaigns for animal rights, and work from a wide range of activist groups as well as professional designers on anti-genetically modified food, global warming (the StopEsso campaign), pollution of air and water, and poverty. Some of the most vibrant anti-corporate comments came from designers in Latin America. In Mexico, they produced visual statements that were anti-government and pro-rights of indigenous people. In Argentina, protesters fought back against poverty, producing solidarity projects alongside neighbourhood-driven 'assemblies' of self-management after the Argentine economy, crippled by debt, plummeted into bankruptcy in 2001. Some blamed the government; others blamed the IMF.

What's wrong with McDonald's?

Everything they don't want you to know.

SUBVERSION AND SATIRE

During the 1990s demonstrating resistance to global corporations and multinationals, or politicians and governments, became one of the favourite activities of graphic design activists. Opposition to the tobacco industry brought polished, biting parodies that subverted the image of Marlboro and the Marlboro Man; whilst challenges to the fast-food corporation McDonald's gener-

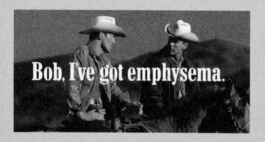

Bob, I've got emphysema.

ated an entire culture of campaign graphics, some of them extremely ghoulish. The decade also saw the rising star of *Adbusters* and their methods of 'culture jamming' and 'subvertizing' as ways of diminishing the power of global brands.

This included altering or manipulating corporate logos in order to change their meaning and other anti-consumerism activities such as their annual 'Buy Nothing Day'. All activities were communicated and their followers mustered via their busy website, with further solidarity provided by their magazine. *Adbusters* also gave visual artists

and designers the opportunity to revolt against the system creatively, and continues to do so.[7]

Visual satire aimed at politics and politicians produced scathing, and at times hilarious, attacks on US President George W. Bush and UK Prime Ministers John Major and Tony Blair. A quieter but more sour form of satire came from Post-Soviet Central and Eastern Europe, where the 1989 pro-democracy revolutions that swept communism aside left social and economic struggles in their wake. The break-up of Yugoslavia brought conflicts that developed into the Balkan Wars (1991–2000), inspiring anti-war graphics by Balkan artists and designers who documented the devastation while daring to hope for a better future. Meanwhile the fall of the Berlin wall and the dismantling of the Soviet Union heralded a new political era. President Mikhail Gorbachev was deposed after the failure of his Western-friendly economic reforms and replaced by the seemingly ineffectual President Boris Yeltsin, while the country sank into a savage war with the breakaway republic of Chechnya. Yeltsin's successor Vladimir Putin achieved fame for his execution of a brutal military campaign that crushed the Chechen rebellion, which allowed the former KGB officer to glide into the presidency in 2000.

WAR GRAPHICS
AND ANTI-WAR PROTESTS

The fall of the Berlin Wall in 1989 brought hopes for a new era of peace and international reconciliation – but it didn't last long. In August 1990 Iraq invaded Kuwait and the first Gulf War began, leading to Operation Desert Storm on 17 January 1991. It was waged against Iraq by a UN-backed coalition of thirty-six countries and led by the US military. It also became known as 'the information war' for it produced coloured war maps for step-by-step briefings, diagrams and

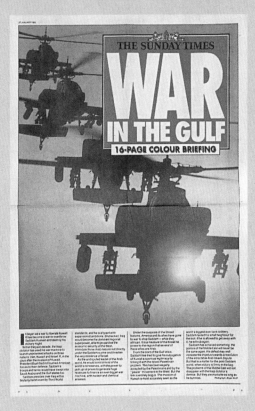

charts showing arrays of hardware, video footage of airstrike wizardry and other highly censored images of high-tech, bloodless, sanitized warfare. All of which fed the image of a videogame conflict to the folks watching on TV at home. While accompanying high-tech terminology brought us worrying phrases such as 'collateral damage' (unintended civilian casualties or damage to property), 'surgical strikes' (air attacks of pinpoint precision) and deaths or injuries inflicted by 'friendly fire' (attacks by one's own side or allies).

The grassroots-based, anti-war protests that followed were also information-led and produced in a variety of conventional print formats: posters, flyers, stickers, billboards, cartoons and comics. They challenged myths about 'smart' weaponry; demonstrated the failings of the US administration in power and investigated some of the

possible hidden motives behind the war, such as the pursuit of oil. Protest marches were frequent but rarely reported in the news. Protest imagery, particularly posters, challenged the sanitized image of war by bringing reality – images of blood, death and horror – back into people's minds, although

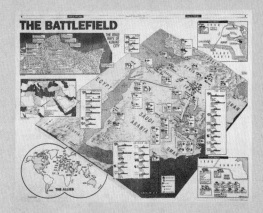

many of the images had to be drawn or painted because heavy censorship ensured a lack of photographs. The war ended on 28 February 1991, but the anti-war protests continued for a long time after and the bombing of Iraqi targets and sanctions against Iraq continued for more than a decade. Thus began a deep mistrust of mainstream media (often felt to be the vehicles for official propaganda) and the unsettling notion that graphics in the media had played a seminal role in maintaining the entertainment value of the war, while purporting to provide information.[8]

The theatre of war soon turned to the Balkans, where media reports of civil wars, ethnic and religious conflicts, and nationalistic tendencies brought confusion rather than clarity. Eventually the fog dissipated and blame was directed towards Slobodan Milosevic of Yugoslavia. In his desire to construct a Greater Serbia, he attacked Slovenia unsuccessfully and then engendered conflict in Croatia, Bosnia and Kosovo (and its resident Albanians) by fanning the already-present flames of nationalism as well as waging war through the use of his own Serbian Army and militias. Chaos reigned on a grand scale, with nationalistic groups asserting power, the purging of unwanted ethnic groups and the wilful displacement of populations to refugee camps in neighbouring countries in order to de-stabilize them. All the countries involved produced powerful imagery throughout to document the devastation.

Despite the viciousness of the Serb-Croat War (1991–92), the reputable Croatian graphic design community, well known for their international exhibitions, produced sophisticated posters of devastation and loss with regard to human life, the environment and buildings of

Enjoy
Sarajevo
1994

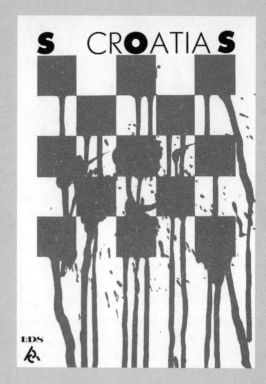

S CROATIA S

EDS

LET THE GAME START NOW!

SARAJEVO '94

Design "Trio" Sarajevo

– especially when help is needed. The postcard format suited shortages in paper and ink, and ensured an international reach since they could be easily carried in suitcases and passed on.

Kosovo bore the brunt of Milosevic's failure to achieve territorial expansion via the wars in

religious and cultural heritage.

The Bosnian War (1992–96) saw the city of Sarajevo under siege for almost four years, from April 1992 to February 1996. During that time, exceptional graphic work was to be found in the international design press from the Sarajevo-based design group Trio, consisting of founders Bojan and Dalida Hadzihalilovic (and Leila Hatt-Mulabegovic, who emigrated to Switzerland early on) plus other associates and helpers including Bojan's father, Fuad. Trio ran their 'War Studio' as a commercial office throughout the siege – as and when electricity supplies allowed.

Their best-known work is a series of postcards displaying their trademark black humour, and using the theme of Sarajevo's plight mixed with reworked pop and cultural icons.

This included the Winter Olympic Games in Sarajevo (1984), which in their hands became a sardonic symbol of how a city can be in the world spotlight one minute, then forgotten the next

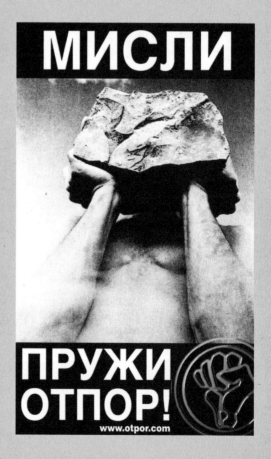

МИСЛИ

ПРУЖИ ОТПОР!

www.otpor.com

The approach to, and crossover into, the twenty-first century never seemed to move off a 'war footing' despite the efforts of extraordinary poster-makers and protests that were long-standing or engaged millions. Both David Tartakover and Yossi Lemel have created exceptional posters throughout the 1990s and beyond in support of peace and bringing an end to the Israeli-Palestinian conflict. Yet the conflict still rolls on, despite the erection of the Separation Wall (or Separation Barrier) from 2000 onwards.

The terrorist attack of 11 September 2001 stunned America and brought President George W. Bush's declaration of a 'War on Terror'. Within two years, the US had engaged itself – along with other countries – in wars in both Afghanistan (2001) and Iraq (2003). The wars would last over ten years, despite massive protest marches around the world. London's protests produced Karmarama's iconic 'Make tea not war' poster with Tony Blair carrying a gun and sporting a tea-cup helmet (see page 111) and David Gentleman's 'splashes of blood' graphic, which appeared in many protests on posters and flyers (page 108).

A glimmer of hope had come in the mid-1990s from South Africa. For years, protests had

Croatia and Bosnia. He launched successive military campaigns against the republic (1998–9), facilitating the brutal 'ethnic cleansing' of Kosovo Albanians to refugee camps in surrounding countries, thereby destabilizing those nations. As for the Kosovo Albanians themselves: some went to the refugee camps but were then ordered back home; some fled to the mountains; some were sent abroad; some just disappeared.

Milosevic however found fierce resistance at home in Belgrade. The student movement Otpor! (Resistance!) aimed to topple Milosevic by voting him out. They grew dramatically in numbers throughout Serbia and operated a highly efficient marketing strategy reinforced by strong graphics and merchandizing. By the year 2000, they had become The People's Movement, Otpor! and their 'He's Finished!' campaign helped to ensure Milosevic was voted out in the federal and presidential elections of September 2000.

Another group campaigning for change was Gradanske Inicijative (Civic Initiatives), an NGO dedicated to the democratization of Yugoslavia. Their posters and pre-election campaign materials were designed by Miljenko Dereta (executive director of the group), Ivan Valencak and Saki Marinovic and capture the forceful call for change, which would eventually vote Milosevic out on 24 September. He didn't go quietly, but a popular revolt forced him out of power on 5 October. By the end of the year he was on his way to the International Criminal Tribunal for the former Yugoslavia in The Hague.[9]

raged worldwide over South Africa's practice of apartheid, the state-sanctioned policy of white minority power over the black majority, involving racial segregation and the denial of basic human rights to blacks, Indians and people of mixed race. Nelson Mandela, black leader of the African National Congress or ANC and hero to many, had been imprisoned since 1963. During his incarceration, he had become a central point of focus for the international anti-apartheid movement. His release in 1990, and the unbanning of the ANC, marked the beginning of the end of apartheid.

In 1994, Mandela was victorious in the first democratic elections in South Africa, marking the beginning of the new South Africa. And although there were difficulties to confront, such as

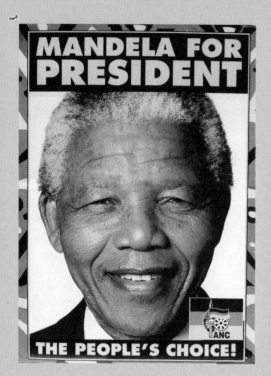

challenging the devastation of HIV and AIDS, the design community remained defiant and produced memorable graphics of South African identity, culture, strength and, above all, optimism. One example of such defiance was the highly subversive *Bitterkomix*, which produced some of the most hard-hitting, irreverent images both during and

after apartheid. Another example was the Durban studio, Orange Juice Design, headed by Garth Walker. In 1995 it published *i-jusi* (Zulu for 'juice'), a magazine intent on developing a design language rooted in the new South African experience, while promoting South African graphic design worldwide. Both were examples of the incredible inventiveness and optimism of that time.

Page 16. *Mao Zedong: Red Squares No. 1*, painting by Wang Guangyi. China 1988. One of the early provocative, satirical treatments of Mao's image. This close-up portrait was overlaid with a grid, derived from the underlying (hence invisible) grids used during the Cultural Revolution to enlarge photos into colossal, heroic paintings. But here the grid is visible, and acts as a prison or cage.

Page 17. Left: Front page of UK newspaper *Today*, 5 June 1989, showing the previous day's massacre, when China's hard-line regime had ordered troops to open fire on the Tiananmen Square protesters. Right: *June 1994*, black and white photograph by Chinese artist Ai Weiwei, taken on the fifth anniversary of the Tiananmen massacre. The photo shows his wife, Lu Qing, lifting her skirt under the gaze of the portrait of Mao in Tiananmen Square, while two patrolling soldiers have their backs turned.

Page 18. Left: Front cover from *Road Raging: Top Tips for Wrecking Roadbuilding* by Road Alert! UK 1997. *Road Raging* was an illustrated resource manual on how to construct an environmental protest camp and deal with the difficulties that ensued (violence by security guards, arrest and so on). Right: Double page spread from *Road Raging: Top Tips for Wrecking Roadbuilding* by Road Alert! UK 1997.

Page 19. Left: Front cover of the *SchNews Annual*, a collection of the free, online weekly information sheet (Dec 1996–Jan 1998) that provided 'the news the mainstream media ignores'. Published by the Brighton group Justice?. UK 1998. Top right: US riot police stand guard at the entrance to Nike Town; one of the iconic images from the mass protest known as the 'Battle of Seattle' in November 1999. Photograph by Andy Clark. Below right: *Boycott Esso*, poster by artist David Gentleman for the StopEsso campaign. UK 2001. The poster wasn't used after 9/11 due to a possible visual association with the burning twin towers.

Page 20. Left: Image from an anti-smoking campaign using Marlboro Man ad parodies, created by ad agency Asher and Partners (art director Nancy Steinman, photographer Myron Beck, writer Jeff Bossin) for the California Department of Health Services. USA 2000. Right: Front of the leaflet,

distributed by London Greenpeace (1986–90) that eventually led to the McLibel Trial. Fast food corporation McDonald's took two UK activists to court for libel over the contents of their leaflet, resulting in the longest running civil libel case in British history.

Page 21: Left: Cover page from *The Sunday Times*, 'War in the Gulf, 16-page Colour Briefing', 27 January 1991, UK. Special section on the Gulf War machine, including people, places (maps) and technology (equipment). Right: Spread from *The Sunday Times*, 'War in the Gulf, 16-page Colour Briefing'.

Page 22. Top and below left: Two of the many postcards produced on the plight of Sarajevo using reworked cultural icons by Trio design group (Bojan and Dalida Hadzihalilovic and associates). Bosnia 1993–94. Top right: *SOS Croatia*, poster by Ranko Novak. Croatia 1991. The poster makes use of the pattern of Croatia's heraldic emblem: a red-and-white checked medieval shield. Below right: *Think – Resist!*, leaflet by the student resistance movement, Otpor!. Yugoslavia 2000.

Page 23. Left: *If not elections, then what?* poster by Miljenko Dereta, Ivan Valencak and Saki Marinovic of Civic Initiatives, an NGO dedicated to the democratization of Yugoslavia. Yugoslavia 2000. Photograph by V Miloradovic. Right: *United Colors of Netanyahu*, poster by David Tartakover. Israel 1998. A Benetton pastiche referring to Binyamin Netanyahu, Prime Minister of Israel 1996–99, shown with enough bodyguards or 'suits' to fill a fashion catalogue – and known to have an aggressive attitude towards the idea of an independent Palestinian state. Photograph by David Karp.

Page 24. Top left: *Mandela for President*, poster by the African National Congress (ANC)/Unwembi Communications. South Africa 1994. Below left: *Happy 80th Birthday Madiba!*, badge produced by Mother City Queer Projects (Cape Town). South Africa 1998.

Page 25. Front cover of *i-jusi* No. 8, the magazine created in 1995 by Durban-based Orange Juice Design. Cover design by Garth Walker, showing different aspects of racial segregation (apartheid) as manufactured products of previous generations. South Africa 1999.

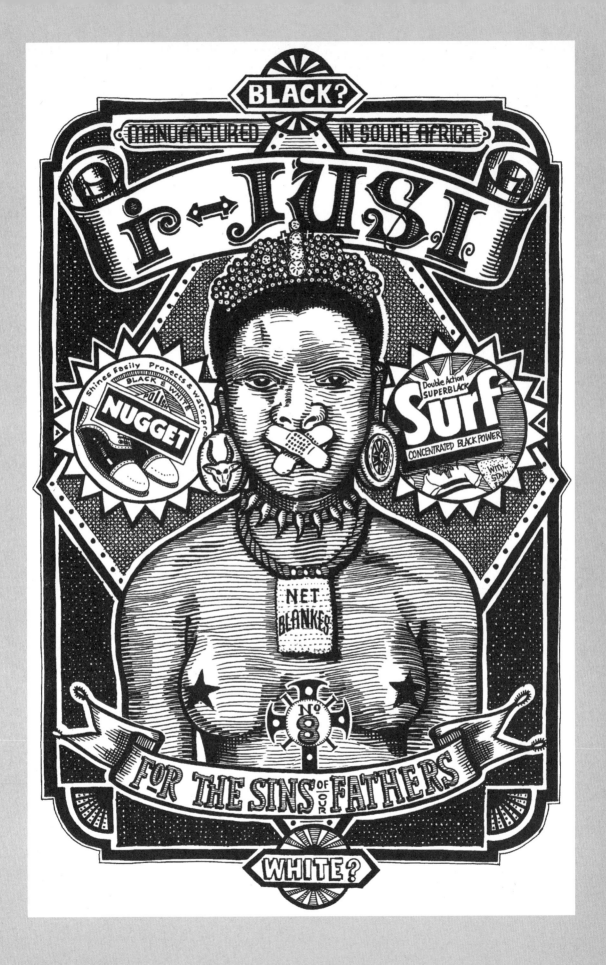

DISCONTENT AND UPRISINGS: ECONOMIC AND POLITICAL UNREST

النظام جثة تتفسخ
فادفنوها وادفنوا معها أمراضها

الشعب السوري عارف طريقه

Capitalist-based globalization brought political stability, economic wealth and immense power to the West and its multinationals throughout the 1980s and 1990s, particularly to American interests. Yet the period was also one of massive change: pro-democracy revolutions swept through Central and Eastern Europe and the dismantling of the Soviet Union was followed by various conflicts in the Balkans. In addition, many countries struggled to meet their commitments to Western regulators such as the International Monetary Fund (IMF), the World Trade Organization (WTO) and the World Bank.

Then two critical events exposed the vulnerability of America's superpower status and rocked Western economic stability. The terrorist attacks on America that occurred on 11 September 2001 shook the country to its roots, and placed the US on the path to wars in Afghanistan and Iraq that would destabilize the entire region. Politicians, economists and conflict analysts are still studying the fallout of these actions to this day.

The second event was the economic crash of 2008 when the world stood still and held its breath as the New York stock market went into free fall and America went into recession. The interconnectedness of the world's economy meant that other markets soon followed causing global recession. A number of over-extended European economies began the long journey towards economic collapse, and severe austerity measures inflicted on already beleaguered citizens brought anger against politicians and rioting in the streets. In a number of countries in the Middle East and North Africa, where immense power and wealth were controlled by long-standing dictatorships, uncaring of the poverty and indignities being suffered by their people, revolution began to brew. It ignited at the beginning of 2011, the so-called 'Year of Revolutions'.

Yet with crisis, comes creativity. This chapter is not a catalogue of all the discontent, rioting and revolutions that took place, but an exploration of some of the protests through graphic symbols, street art, posters and other visual manifestations of dissent. For many, but not all, social media played a significant role in their creation and distribution.

THE ROLE OF MOBILE TECHNOLOGY AND SOCIAL MEDIA

Global networking through emails, websites, pagers and mobile phones (and text messaging toward the end of the decade) was a normal tool for protest throughout the late-1990s. However, as good as it seemed at the time, dial-up internet connections were slow. Mobile phones could browse the web but not at speed, texting was preferable and widely used.

It took the rollover into the twenty-first century to bring the developments in technology, particularly mobile technology, that would really make a difference. Massive take up of broadband services occurred in 2002 and by the middle of the decade connectivity had been optimized for speed. New generation mobile phones soon allowed easy internet browsing as well as image/video capture and uploading ability. (Sending and receiving email whilst on the move became easier too, but texting remained a quicker and cheaper alternative for many.) 'Citizen journalism' was a new term used by mainstream news media after the start of the Iraq War (2003) to describe their use of material uploaded by ordinary people on the ground in conflict zones, or taken from civilians' blogs.[1]

Upload and download speeds increased over the following years, smartphones arrived and social media took hold, along with the concept of 'sharing' and stating preference through 'likes' and in negative comments. Facebook (launched 2004), YouTube (2005), Twitter (2006) and other applications all helped to reconfigure the mobile phone as a mobile communications device. The success of Barack Obama's 2008 campaign for the US Presidency was attributed to the clever use of social media, particularly aimed at young voters. More and more countries developed their own uses for new technology and 'sharing'; for example domestic broadband was fairly uncommon in Egypt in 2011, but the country's young population had fully embraced social-media sites through internet cafés or other public computers. Perhaps even more significantly, almost sixty-seven per cent of the population were mobile phone users.[2]

The global technology revolution was ready to play an important role in the protests that followed. Social media would form a crucial partnership with actions in the streets, and together they would change the face of activism. Cheaper phones could capture and broadcast sights and sounds that would never have surfaced before – communications and images from conflicts were no longer the province of corporate news media. Phones became the weapon for projecting causes or events (both joyful and horrific) and for organizing a call to arms.[3] However it was still the courage of citizens answering those calls and protesting in the streets that led to revolution.

THE ARAB SPRING (OR ARAB AWAKENING)

Mohamed Bouazizi was a twenty-six-year-old Tunisian who sold fruit from a street cart. He had suffered continual harassment from trading officials (allegedly for refusing to pay them bribes). On 17 December 2010, after further humiliation, he was beaten and his goods and scales were confiscated. Bouazizi approached both the municipal and governor's offices to retrieve his property, but was ignored. Feeling that he had suffered the final indignity, Bouazizi set fire to himself in the street. He died on 4 January 2011, as protests inspired by the incident were spreading throughout Tunisia, with photographs and videos uploaded to YouTube and Twitter for international viewing. With anger and unrest escalating, President Zine el Abidine Ben Ali fled, seeking refuge in Saudi Arabia on 14 January.

The fever spread to Egypt where a day of revolution erupted on 25 January 2011. Thousands of people took to the streets and Tahrir Square in Cairo became the spiritual heart of the protest. Many accounts of the events noted the variety of protesters involved: Christians, Muslims, old, young, men, women (with hijabs and without). As demonstrations progressed over the next three weeks, the regime's response escalated from an internet shutdown to tear gas and gunfire, and an incident of armed Mubarak supporters, mounted on horseback and camels, ploughing through the Square to dispel the demonstration. Further protests and violence raged throughout the country finally forcing President Hosni Mubarak out of office on 11 February.[4]

Pictures emerging from the protests showed technology-savvy crowds holding up handwritten signs to the world's media and using smartphones to upload images and video to the internet. Much of the violence was captured in this way – documenting events and alerting the world to the gravity of them. A further surprise was an explosion of street art that memorialized martyrs through portraits, recounted devastating events, caricatured unpopular officials and expressed the new sense of power felt by the protesters. The work – painted, drawn or stencilled onto many different surfaces – also provided a record of what had taken place from many perspectives. It had qualities of strength and immediacy, but also an inherent fragility – since paint and chalk can be quickly cleaned off or painted over.

'DAYS OF RAGE': THE UNREST CONTINUES

Revolution spread to Jordan, Bahrain, Morocco, Yemen and Algeria. Libya saw all-out conflict in its attempts to oust leader Muammar Gaddafi. The rebel forces armed ordinary, untrained civilians and eventually gained the upper hand, executing Gaddafi on 20 October 2011. Photographs of his body went viral.

In Syria, protests against President Bashar al-Assad turned to outright conflict that still rages in 2015. An extraordinary visual record of events – cries of solidarity, protestations and representations of appalling cruelties – has emerged from the war. The travelling exhibition *Culture in Defiance: Continuing Traditions of Satire, Art and the Struggle for Freedom in Syria* arrived in London in 2013, demonstrating the incredible wealth of visual and written material produced by Syrians in extreme danger or under duress within their own country, as well as refugees, political exiles and the diaspora. Much of the work was done by anonymous collectives and posted online for broader viewing and use by others. For example the fifteen-member collective, Alshaab Alsori Aref Tarekh (The Syrian People Know Their Way) created and posted dynamic political posters on Flickr and Facebook ready for activists to download. Citizen-photographers documented the destruction using any equipment available and then posted their work on Facebook using the tag 'Lens Young' followed by the name of their city or another identifier. The collective Comic4Syria posted comic strips and editorial cartoons on their Facebook page documenting life during the war. Another collective, Masasit Mati, used hand puppets to produce biting, five-minute videos, including the absurdist satirical series *Top Goon: Diaries of a Little Dictator* (2011). In all, numerous illustrators, graffiti artists, poets, writers and musicians have made attempts to describe, explain and lament the situation in their country.[5]

FLASHBACK: THE GREEN REVOLUTION OF 2009

Iran's 'Day of Rage', Tehran's Green Revolution, occurred in 2009, and might now be viewed as a harbinger of things to come. In June of that year, frustration and anger at the re-election of hardline President Mahmoud Ahmadinejad (in a vote that protesters believed to be fixed) drew thousands to the streets in protest. Young Iranian opposition supporters engaged in violent clashes with the police for weeks thereafter, using their phones to upload video and images to Twitter and YouTube that underlined the ferocity of the riots. Their efforts achieved unprecedented global coverage across traditional news networks and drew outpourings of solidarity via digital media – the memorably bright visual identity of the opposition led to the 'Green Revolution' appellation.

The Green Revolution failed but still acts as an important reference point for movements that challenge authority against all odds. It is also a reminder of the high percentage of young people existing in the Middle East and North Africa, who may still try to redefine their future at a later point.[6] Five years later, the protests still represent the revolution that tried but failed, and a generation that refused to be isolated from the world due to the political image created by its leaders.

In our world of connectivity and 'sharing' through social media, it is difficult for any modern community to remain isolated for long. Evidence of the desire to keep communication lines open despite political differences can be found in the popular 2012 TEDx talk 'Israel and Iran: A love story?'. In this presentation Israeli graphic designer Ronny Edry discusses his efforts to promote a dialogue between the two countries by sharing a poster of himself and his daughter on Facebook with the message 'Iranians... we [heart] you'. He received an overwhelming response and further Facebook communities grew to include 'Israel loves Iran', 'Iran loves Israel' and 'Palestine loves Israel'.

15 May 2011: a one-day march in Madrid, Spain, brought thousands of people to the city's main square, the Puerta del Sol plaza. They called themselves Los Indignados (The Outraged) and marched against an ineffectual government and a future of unemployment, poverty and desperation. Spain was on the way to bankruptcy and in need of a bail out from the European Union. Los Indignados formed a camp in the plaza and protests also spread across the country. The movement acquired a distinctive visual identity in black, yellow and red with stencil-style type. In addition, a substantial number of posters and other visual material were produced and stored online in an image bank entitled Voces con Futura (Voices of the Future). The images represented the visual voice of the protests, a mixture of the satirical, the humorous, the impatient and the strong.[7]

Greek protesters drew inspiration from Los Indignados, with Athenians setting up camp in the city's Syntagma Square. However Greece had already been through three years of severe economic depression, and austerity measures levied by successive governments following bailouts from the European Union had left the public in dire straits. Protests and rioting had occurred in 2008 following the fatal shooting of fifteen-year-old Alexis Andreas Grigoropoulos by police. Major riots ensued periodically, enflamed by the renowned heavy-handedness of the police, and by 2011 there was still no end in sight (see page 56). In addition the violent actions of Golden Dawn, a Greek right-wing extremist group, had become well known both inside and outside of the country.

By the summer of 2011, young Israelis had also caught the fever and began pitching tents in Rothschild Boulevard in Tel Aviv to protest the high cost of living, lack of jobs and political corruption. The movement spread throughout Israel.

August saw unrest in London when riots were triggered by the police shooting of twenty-nine-year-old Mark Duggan (the police claim that Duggan was armed remains hotly contested). Violence spread to other cities and fires grew out of control, as did the looting. In the aftermath, media analyses contemplated the causes – unemployment, poverty and disillusionment – while the police continued to pursue the looters for months afterwards, using news footage and pictures shared on Twitter to identify them. Even local newspapers carried pictures of alleged looters and solicited the public's help in identifying them. The practice of identifying even peaceful

protesters in demonstrations through media photographs was already in place, but it grew during the riots and led to police now carrying cameras as part of their regulation equipment.

Then it was America's turn to revolt. In late July a group of activists gathered in New York City to discuss the ways and means of challenging corrupt politicians and corporate rule against the background of a broken US economy. Thus the notion of 'Occupy Wall Street' was born and a protest camp was established in nearby Zuccotti Park. At the same time they created the crucial slogan 'We are the 99%', a response to reports that only one per cent of the US population own a very large proportion of the country's wealth.

Adbusters magazine ran a poster-invitation encouraging its readers to occupy Zuccotti Park on 17 September. The poster remains one of the most romantic images to emerge from that period: a vulnerable, barefoot ballerina poses confidently on top of the *Charging Bull* statue near Wall Street. Hence a figure of calm, fearless resolve (leading a line of protesters in the background) conquers a heavy symbol of American financial might. (The statue is a depiction of the term 'bull market', referring to a period of aggressive acquisition, heavy buying and a rising stock market. A 'bear market' implies the opposite in which investors are nervous and share prices are falling.)

As the Occupy movement spread to other cities in the USA, social media made yet another image legendary. On 18 November, two police officers at University of California, Davis, casually used pepper-spray directly in the faces of a line of protesters who were seated on the ground and refusing to move from their peaceful demonstration. Bystanders uploaded videos to YouTube and an image of Lieutenant John Pike, one of the officers involved, went viral. Pike was Photoshopped into a multitude of different contexts, and the 'Pepper-Spraying Cop' became one of the favourite internet memes of the year.[8]

Away from the Occupy movement: other renowned practitioners of social critique were producing grim, graphic comments about American society in the Obama era. Illustrator Ross MacDonald and graphic designer James Victore produced 'a loving parody' of the classic *Dick and Jane* reading primers for children. Sometimes humorous, sometimes sad, it depicts an America of guns, drugs and mass consumerism, where small-town traditions of trust and friendliness are on the wane and most adults are spaced-out or suspect. Intentionally packaged as sweet and innocent, it holds a mirror up to society and, in a call-to-action for parents, asks 'Is this where you want your kids to grow up?'

Kara Walker's work digs deep into the American past in order to expose and challenge racist attitudes that still exist today. Some of her best-known work uses stylized, black paper cut-outs, similar to genteel Victorian silhouettes, that tend to depict plantations and other scenes reminis-

cent of the 'ole South'. But the actions of the characters can be playfully vicious or tragic, and the sexual acts depicted exaggerated and cruel in a landscape of twisted racial stereotypes. (For example, a girl jumps into the air, her back arched, possibly in sexual ecstasy. At second glance it is clear she is brandishing a razor and her wrists are bleeding.) Walker is out to make the viewer uncomfortable; the way such distressing acts jar the viewer is no less relevant than the shock delivered by some of the racial attitudes that still exist in America today, shown for example by the obsession with US President Obama's birthplace, religion and skin colour earlier in his term of office.[9]

PUTIN VS PUSSY RIOT, BLUE NOSES AND OTHERS

Vladimir Putin's desire to return Russia to the former glory of the Empire makes him popular at home, but also requires him to keep a firm grip on the state, in which outbursts of dissent and opposition are met with brutal severity. He also knows how to hang on to power, serving as Prime Minister from 1999 to 2000, then as President from 2000 to 2008. He then returned to the position of Prime Minister until 2012 during Dmitry Medvedev's presidency (although many argued this was solely to provide a gap for formality's sake). Putin was elected President again in 2012, amid murmuring of electoral fixing.

In spite of, and in reaction to, the severe nature of his 'reign', there have been protests in the streets over human rights and challenges to the authority of the state. Furthermore, a number of artists have risked arrest and persisted in producing anti-authoritarian comments and performances over the years, some of them outrageously anti-Putin.

The activist group Pussy Riot sprang to life in 2011 as a reaction to Putin's possible return to power for a third Presidential term. Balaclava-ed members of the group performed *A Punk Prayer* in Moscow's Cathedral of Christ the Saviour (a powerful icon of Russian Orthodoxy) in February 2012. They were arrested and charged with 'hooliganism motivated by religious hatred'. Social media assured them worldwide support during the ensuing trial and varying terms of incarceration, and their coloured balaclavas became the global symbol of their solidarity movement.[10]

Artists such as the Blue Noses Group (formed in 1999) and Alexander Kosolapov also make an appearance as representatives of a larger group of daring image-makers, while Egor Zhgun makes calmer, but equally biting, statements online.

Protests against the World Cup were present throughout the run-up to the event, and were quickly removed at its start from the eyes of television viewers around the world – but not from prying eyes on the web. Nevertheless, as Rio remained centre stage and the world's reporters and camera crews explored the creativity of the favelas (shanty towns) and the street art of São Paulo, it was impossible not to notice the backdrop of incredible poverty and overcrowding in the city.[12]

PROTESTS IN TURKEY AND BRAZIL

The encroaching authoritarianism of Turkey's Prime Minister, Recep Tayyip Erdogan, was confronted and put to the test in June 2013. Mass protests took place ostensibly to save central Istanbul's Gezi Park from demolition, but the demonstrations were also driven by the people's desire to assert their rights. Despite police brutality, the protesters managed to take over Taksim Square and occupied the nearby Gezi Park with food stalls, a library and a stage, while social media alerts brought many other activists to join them. A police crackdown was ordered and anti-government protests raged in sixty cities throughout Turkey. Tear gas and water cannons filled the photographs that emerged from Istanbul, as well as images of the protesters' home-made gas masks cut out of plastic water bottles.[11]

Brazil's hosting of the World Cup in 2014 and the Olympics in 2016, and the building of new stadiums and other projects, seemed a tall order for a country suffering from overcrowding, weakened social services and low living standards in its main cities. So when bus and metro fares were increased in São Paulo in June 2013, mass protests broke out against the government and, in particular, President Dilma Rousseff.

OCCUPY LONDON

The activist group Occupy London Stock Exchange landed on a site of great significance for their protest camp. On 15 October 2011, they set down on a relatively small space of pavement in front of St Paul's Cathedral in London. Not only is St Paul's one of the most significant seats of the Church of England, it is considered to be highly symbolic of the heart and durability of the British people. Miraculously it was barely touched during the bombings of London in World War II, despite heavy damage around it. Moreover it sits within the historical 'City of London' that forms the corporate and financial heartland of the capital.

Within twenty-four hours a senior Church official appeared welcoming the protesters and expressing the view that Jesus would have done the same. Not long after, a yet more senior member of the Church hierarchy grudgingly agreed that the protesters could remain – but only for a short while. In the following days of soul-searching, arguments raged within the Church. The first official resigned over the Church's seemingly negative attitude to the protesters. The Church itself suffered a crisis of identity as heated debates over its current role filled the national news. Unable to cope with the media focus, the cathedral closed to public access for a week. The second official, faced with chaos in the church community, resigned. When the cathedral finally opened again, the protesters had been given notice and a deadline for their eviction.[13]

Meanwhile, the camp itself was well organized, with scheduled meetings and lectures, a library, a kitchen and occasional performances. And it had *The Occupied Times of London* newspaper, created and published by a collective, which was nominated for a major design award. But after four months and a number of legal battles along the way, the protesters could no longer extend their stay and were finally evicted from St Paul's on 28 February 2012.

An earlier period from London's recent history is shown in Laura Oldfield Ford's post-punk zine *Savage Messiah* (2005–09, with additional reflections in 2012 and 2013). It deals with the period when 'Cool Britannia', consumerism and the dreaded march of global coffee-shop-brand regeneration were devouring London to feed Blairite neo-liberalism. It is fiercely political in its relaying of survival and loss, and visually dynamic as it tours London's old tower blocks and estates, while protesting against the changes brought by the 2012 Olympic Games.

Other imagery is shown here relating to Eton-educated politicians vs 'the rest of us' – election campaigns, the riots of August 2011, issues of racial identity and economic foibles – that all point to a divided Britain. The gap between the haves and have-nots seems to be wider than ever.

CHINA'S SUBVERSION AND SATIRE

Lastly, the emerging economy of China surges forward while dragging old-style authoritarianism along with it. And however hard the government tries to keep its cultural elements under control, an avant-garde of artists, writers and other creatives has persisted in producing and disseminating challenging and anti-authoritarian work.

One of the most famous thorns in the government's side is the artist Ai Weiwei. Although a hugely important figure in global contemporary art, Ai Weiwei still causes deep irritation to the Chinese authorities because of his public pursuance of injustice. The tenacity with which he has investigated the damage to school buildings during the 2008 Sichuan earthquake is demonstrated through a number of heavily researched projects. The earthquake caused 6,898 school buildings to collapse and over 5,000 schoolchildren were killed. In the aftermath it was alleged that government corruption had allowed substandard construction of the schools. Parents were silenced: neither the government nor anyone else has as yet provided reasons as to why many of the surrounding buildings that were not part of school campuses were untouched by the earthquake. Ai Weiwei has produced at least three different artworks based on the incident that have toured the world.[14]

Although Ai Weiwei is unable to leave China since the authorities revoked his passport, his followers on social media are more than happy to come to him. He has been a dedicated blogger, and loves to use Twitter for its immediacy and ability to deliver to the masses, even though he lives in a country obsessed with intimidation, surveillance and watching the web. In 2011, he was detained by the government for two-and-a-half months, incarcerated on his own, and watched at all times by two military police (one on each side of him).[15]

Artists Qiu Jie and Sheng Qi deal with the pain of China's past as well as the shadows of the present. Qui Jie joins the number of artists who have dared to play with the monumental portrait of Mao Zedong, and its inherent and very present feelings of surveillance. While Sheng Qi has, over the years, used a harrowing symbol of the Tiananmen Square protest to construct a memorable and deeply personal portrait of modern China.

Against the background of China's industrial advances, hard-line politics and intolerance of dissent, the ghost of the 1989 Tiananmen Square massacre has risen again. This time the mass protest took place in Hong Kong. The Umbrella Revolution of 2014 shouted demands for universal suffrage, and inevitably failed to make the Beijing authorities listen. There was no massacre (thankfully) and there was no closure, only the feeling that although a battle had been lost, the war of nerves would continue for a very long time.

LOOKING BACK, LOOKING FORWARD

It could be said that most if not all of the revolutions mentioned in this chapter have failed. After all, the Arab Spring didn't secure democracy for the countries involved. It ousted dictators and, more often than not, lifted the lid on a mass of religious, ethnic and cultural power struggles that simmered beneath, leading to further clashes. The European countries in question are to date no better off. The fierce energy of the Occupy movement has dissipated, although for how long is not known, and emerging economies such as Brazil and China struggle to hold on to global economic status despite the fragility and unpredictability of their infrastructures.

But the revolutions *have* succeeded in forcing a change in a number of twenty-first-century mind-sets – for example, our view of the once stable but now shifting political and geographic spheres of the world, the difficulties in our current models of capitalism, and the blatant imbalances those models cause with regard to quality of life and the environment. And this turbulence is bound to continue for some time. Instead of seeing one powerful global economic and political model, we now see a shifting mosaic of concerns fighting for attention.

The role of technology and social media has been significant in that it has brought all of these issues closer to us. It has generated many new conversations, and through the constant development of new platforms it has provided original ways of conducting those conversations. Even more, it has made it more difficult for officialdom or 'the powers that be' to hide information or events from us. Hence it has become far more difficult for the powerful to control the public, or its many online 'friends' around the world.

But as this chapter shows, emerging technology works hand in hand with the actions of activists and protesters. Bringing all the information and images right to our keyboards or touchscreens certainly helps to start shifting the thinking of the collective consciousness – but to give that consciousness a big push, it will be necessary to face the real world, join with other people, and get out into the streets.

Page 28. Electronic poster by anonymous poster collective Alshaab Alsori Aref Tarekh (The Syrian People Know Their Way), showing President of Syria, Bashar al-Assad, with a vulture on his head. The poster reads: 'The regime is a rotting corpse. Bury it with its diseases.' Syria 2011.

Page 30. Left: Tahrir Square in Cairo, Egypt, 9 February 2011. Right: Protesters with smartphones and a baby in Tahrir Square, end January/early February. Egypt 2011. Photograph by Mia Gröndahl.

Page 31. Left: *Democracy Is Coming!*, mixed-media collage by Egyptian artist Huda Lutfi. Egypt 2008. Right: A demonstration in Istanbul against the Iranian poll results of 2009 that brought Mahmoud Ahmadinejad back to power; the placards show injured protesters in Iran. Photograph by Bulent Kilic, AFP/Getty.

Page 32. Left: Los Indignados street protest. The banner reads: 'Without a job, without a house, without a pension. YOUTH WITHOUT FEAR. Recovering our future! This is our one principle.' Spain 2011. Right: 'Mob Rule', front page of *The Independent* newspaper, Tuesday 9 August 2011, displaying the uniform and kit that were de rigueur for rioting in London. UK 2011.

Page 33. Left: *Richest 400, Bottom 150,000,000*, one of a set of hand-stamps bearing messages about the disparity of wealth in the USA, which were used to stamp dollar bills as accompaniment to the Occupy protests. The designs were placed on the internet for use by all. Designed by artists Ivan Cash and Andy Dao (Occupy George). USA 2011. Right: Three members of the Pussy Riot feminist collective were arrested for performing their 'punk prayer'

in the Cathedral of Christ the Saviour, Moscow in 2012. Their subsequent imprisonment, trial and sentencing generated international media attention, support groups and demonstrations.

Page 34. Left: 'Free Pussy Riot', three protesters bearing Amnesty International logos on their arms, deliver a petition to the Russian Embassy in London. UK 2012. Photograph by Kerim Okten/EPA. Right: Mural painting by São Paulo street artist Paulo Ito of a starving child eating a football; in the run-up to the World Cup (May 2014) the image went viral. Brazil 2014.

Page 35. Top left: 'No Rights, No World Cup', protest in São Paulo against Brazil's hosting of the 2014 World Cup despite ongoing poverty and political corruption. Brazil 2014. Photograph by Miguel Schincariol/

AFP. Below left: 'Caring is everyone's business', banner at Occupy London camp at St. Paul's Cathedral. UK 2011. Photograph by Tzortzis Rallis. Right: Umbrella Revolution support graphic by Herby Alcosta, 2014.

Page 37. Photograph by Mia Gröndahl of a café in downtown Cairo, showing a wall of portraits of martyrs to the revolution accompanied by (in English) a popular chant of the Arab Spring. Egypt 2011–12.

TAHRIR SQUARE: 18 DAYS OF EGYPTIAN REVOLUTION

News of the self-immolation of twenty-six-year-old street vendor Mohamed Bouazizi following continual police harassment brought four weeks of protests in Tunisia. Demonstrations peaked when scenes of brutality and images of dead protesters were uploaded to Facebook and YouTube: within days Tunisian President Zine el Abidine Ben Ali had fled the country.

Inspired by these events and sick of corruption within its own government, Egypt began to prepare for its 'Day of Revolution'. A Facebook page and other media sounded the alarm and huge crowds gathered in Cairo's Tahrir Square on 25 January 2011 calling for regime change.

Over eighteen days, the world watched through news and social media as a wide range of people, both young and old, came to protest. Demonstrators camped in tents in the square, reportedly creating a festival atmosphere and setting up a field hospital, information and food centres, and more. Euphoric protesters held flags, banners and handwritten signs sending messages to the media or urging President Hosni Mubarak to resign. The regime responded to the protesters with escalating force, ranging from tanks and tear gas to rubber and real bullets. However by 4 February the army tanks withdrew and on 11 February, after thirty years of oppression, Mubarak stepped down.[16]

Accounts of events in Egypt also noted the important (and heretofore unusual) presence of women at the demonstrations, who accounted for around a third of the protesters. Some came in hijabs, some without, some in jeans or Western dress. They participated both in demonstrations and in the resistance to government shows of force, determined to ensure their rights in the new Egypt.[17]

Protests spread to cities all over the country. Tens of thousands of people found their way to Tahrir, over 800 died and around 6,500 were injured in the protests there. A monument for the dead was constructed in the square to memorialize the 'Young Martyrs of the Tahrir Revolution'.[18] A happy outcome did not immediately present itself. In Mubarak's absence, Mohamed Morsi of the Muslim Brotherhood was elected leader. Yet within months of his arrival, he was considered by many to be abusing his powers. Further protests took place, and the army ousted him and took control to maintain the peace, amid accusations of a coup.

The Tunisian protests may be seen as the spark that lit the powder keg of the series of revolutions in the Middle East and North Africa known as the 'Arab Spring' or 'Arab Awakening', but Tahrir Square will always be remembered as the heart and soul of the Arab Spring, symbolically and visually.

1. Street art: woman in niqab with stencil graffiti. Egypt 2012. Photograph by Mia Gröndahl.

2. After Hosni Mubarak was ousted, protests continued. Mohamed Morsi was elected democratically on 24 June 2012. But a year of further instability followed. This photo appeared in Le Monde on 27 June 2013, showing a vendor with Egyptian flags in Cairo, ready for the nationwide protest against Morsi held on 30 June 2013. The poster in Arabic says: 'WANTED – (Mohamed Morsi) Escaped from Wadi Natroun prison on 29 Jan 2011'. The military deposed Morsi on 3 July 2013. Photograph by Amr Nabil/AP.

1.

2.

THE ARTISTIC EXPRESSION
OF EGYPT'S REVOLUTION

The Egyptian protests brought media attention to the visual or written expression of people's demands, desires and emotional experiences. Written messages appeared on banners and signs in Tahrir Square, or were stencilled and graffitied on walls and other surfaces in the city. This form of protest was a rarity under the heavy hand of Mubarak's regime and its appearance was seen as a courageous outburst of creativity brought on by visions of a new era of freedom.[19]

Protest street art presented a wide range of experiences and at times offered a 'close-up' view that the news media couldn't capture. The pictorializing of martyrs was prevalent, as was the demonizing of key members of the regime – which is understandable after thirty years of seeing Mubarak gloriously represented in giant portraits on hoardings and the walls of public buildings everywhere. Stories of particularly brutal actions were also depicted, such as the direct shooting of protesters or the work of snipers. One widely known symbol of resistance was the stencilled 'blue bra woman', recreating the story of a protester who was violently beaten by soldiers in Tahrir Square so that her torn abaya revealed her blue bra. Sometimes only the iconic bra is painted or stencilled on a wall, in other instances the woman is depicted surrounded by attack dogs representing the military.[20]

Many soon realized that change could not happen immediately, and as the protests and violence continued so did the painting. *Harimi* (female) graffiti worked to change attitudes toward women and break social taboos. The piece shown here, located on Mohamed Mahmoud Street in Cairo (an area particularly associated with protest graffiti accompanying the demonstrations), is a portrait of Egyptian activist Samira Ibrahim. The soldiers beneath her bear the face of Ahmed Adel al-Mugi, who forced Ibrahim and seventeen other female protesters held by the military in March 2011 to have 'virginity tests' (which were widely considered to be an act of punishment and humiliation) after their detention. Ahmed Adel al-Mugi was ultimately acquitted when Ibrahim took legal action.[21]

Another mural on the street once showed eighteen portraits of injured men and women, twelve of whom were depicted with eye-patches representing clashes between anti-SCAF (the Supreme Council of the Armed Forces, the military body that took interim control of the state between Presidents Mubarak and Morsi) protesters and riot police in November 2011. During the fighting, forty died and 2,000 were injured – many of them shot in the face. Allegedly more than sixty people lost an eye, giving rise to accusations that the riot police were 'eye hunting'. Visitors to the

1. Street art: the woman with the blue bra. Egypt 2012. Photograph by Mia Gröndahl.

2. Street art: the woman's portrait in red is Samira Ibrahim; the soldiers bear the face of Ahmed Adel al-Mugi who forced her and seventeen other female protesters to suffer the humiliation of a 'virginity test'. Egypt 2012. Photograph by Mia Gröndahl.

3. Street art, Nasr City: 'Egyptian', by the Freedom Painters, a group of twenty-five students dedicated to expressing the spirit of Egypt through street art. Egypt 2012. Photograph by Mia Gröndahl.

4. Street art, Nasr City, by the Freedom Painters. Egypt 2012. Photograph by Mia Gröndahl.

5. Street art: a policeman shoots a protester. Egypt 2012. Photograph by Mia Gröndahl.

1.

2.

3.

4.

5.

mural wrote messages of support on the eye-patches until the authorities had it whitewashed before the anniversary of the revolution on 25 January 2012.[22]

Also on Mohamed Mahmoud Street is a famous mural memorializing the members of the Ultras Ahlawy (fans of the El Ahly football team and one of the groups known to have protected protesters in Tahrir Square from harassment by the regime's thugs) killed on 1 February 2012. The security forces were deemed to have committed the massacre in which seventy-four men were killed (stabbed, beaten or trampled to death) and a further 1,000 were injured on a football field in Port Said. News of the killings prompted the artists Ammar Abu Bakr, Alaa Awad and others to produce a mural of the martyrs on a 30-metre (98-foot) long wall. Brutal clashes followed the massacre and the street filled with violence, but the painting of the mural continued through the tear gas and the fighting. It was completed within several weeks. In a final act of defiance, the artists returned right before the residential elections (May 2012) and painted massive portraits of the martyrs' mothers on top of the mural, along with a bitter, ironic statement in large Arabic script: 'Forget what has passed and focus on the elections'.[23]

6–8. Street art: protesters with an eye missing. The significant number of such injuries led to accusations that riot police were 'eye hunting'. Egypt 2012. Photograph by Mia Gröndahl.

9. (Overleaf) Street art: football martyrs. Egypt 2012. Photograph by Mia Gröndahl.

8.

6.

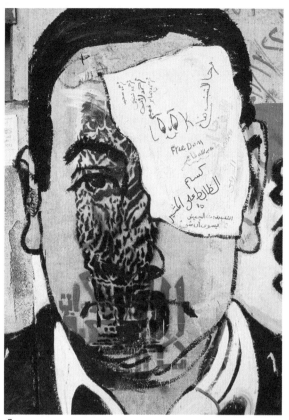

7.

SYRIA: DEPICTIONS
OF ONGOING VIOLENCE

Syria's uprising against the Bashar al-Assad government in early 2011 quickly sank into a complicated mire of violence, confused by bloody sectarian divisions, reports of civil war and gang warfare, and the regime's vicious crackdowns and massacres of its own people. The most common features have been brutality and bloodshed (which still continue, the worst borne by women and children).

Nonetheless, the conflict has also engendered an extraordinary outpouring of art. Posters, illustrations, comics, blogs, performances, photographs, stencilled graffiti and street art, films and animations have excelled at storytelling, recording events and carrying cries of resistance – much of it online created by anonymous collectives documenting the constantly changing political and cultural landscape. (Even hand puppets are used by the anonymous group Masasit Mati to create a series of extremely funny 5-minute videos posted on YouTube, Vimeo and Facebook under the title of *Top Goon: Diaries of a Little Dictator*. The size of the puppets allows them to be easily hidden from police.)[24]

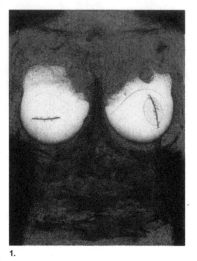

1.

The outpouring of revolutionary graphic material may well be attributed to a reaction against the visual indoctrination that had existed for years, where posters of the 'Great' or 'Immortal Leader' (Assad) and his family had dominated outdoor public spaces as well as public offices and interiors. Such relics and portraits became the first point of attack for the revolution's protesters and new forms of expression were able to emerge.[25]

Artist Khalil Younes has created a series of pen-and-ink drawings entitled *Revolution 2011*, which includes iconic images of the current revolution – of both people and objects – as well as resurrecting key events from Syria's violent past and other struggles. *Hama 30* (2011) refers to the thirtieth anniversary of the 1982 Hama massacre, an event the regime kept hidden for many years and which was only passed on by the accounts of those who witnessed it. *About a Young Man Called Kashoosh* (2011), a portrait of the inspirational singer-songwriter Ibrahim Qashoush who was critical of the regime, represents the many who were brutally murdered in the current uprising.[26]

Yasmeen Fanari posted her drawing *Vomit* (2011) on the 'Art and Freedom' Facebook page (art.liberte.syrie) in December 2011: an act of solidarity with the uprising and, at that point in time, a dangerous thing to do. Artist Youssef Abdelke created the Facebook page to raise awareness of events taking place. Artists were encouraged to sign their real names despite the personal risk, thus adding to the power of their statement.[27]

1. *Hama 30*, drawing commemorating the 30th anniversary of the 1982 Hama massacre, by Syrian artist Khalil Younes. Syria 2011.

2. *About a Young Man Called Kashoosh*, drawing of the murdered singer-songwriter Ibrahim Qashoush, who sang his revolutionary song 'Yalla irhal ya Bashar!' (Come on, Bashar, Get Out!) during mass demonstrations in Hama and other towns and cities. By Syrian artist Khalil Younes. Syria 2012.

3. *Vomit*, poster comment on the situation in Syria by Yasmeen Fanari. Syria/UK 2011.

2.

3.

SYRIA'S REVOLUTIONARY POSTERS

The creation of numerous Syrian revolutionary posters can be credited to the anonymous collective Alshaab Alsori Aref Tarekh (The Syrian People Know Their Way), fifteen activists in Syria and abroad who originally started designing posters for the uprisings in Tunisia and Egypt, then turned their focus to home ground, posting images to Flickr and Facebook for activists to download and use in demonstrations. They came from a wide range of disciplines including philosophy, commerce and fine art, and were united by the desire to obliterate the visual propaganda of Assad's Ba'ath Party. As they are opposed to copyright, it is not unusual for them to appropriate or repurpose other artworks in order to create new designs. Their posters have noted events taking place in Syria, invented phrases or slogans of resistance, and made reference to global influences bearing down on Syria.

Children appear in their posters too – not surprising as so many of them have been injured, tortured or killed in the uprising – and recur as a reminder of one notorious event not to be forgotten. The initial protests of the uprising began in March 2011, when a group of schoolchildren wrote 'Al-shaab yurid isqat al-nizam' (The people want the fall of the regime) on a wall in the south Syrian town of Deraa. They were caught, arrested and tortured, triggering a deep-seated anger that spread throughout the country and rages still. Since then, the depiction of children writing on a wall may be read as a direct reference to the incident in Deraa.[28]

1. Electronic poster by anonymous poster collective Alshaab Alsori Aref Tarekh (The Syrian People Know Their Way). Syria 2012. It reads: 'I'm going to protest'.

1.

صم عَن قتل أخيك

2.

لن تتكرر

3.

يا بابا عمرو

4.

فلسطينية روح في كل ثائر

Electronic posters by anonymous poster collective Alshaab Alsori Aref Tarekh (The Syrian People Know Their Way). Syria 2011–12.

2. 'Fast from Killing Your Brothers', referencing the holy month of Ramadan during which Muslims fast.

3. 'It will not happen again', featuring the waterwheels of Hama, site of a terrible massacre of civilians in 1982. The child writing on the wall references the incident of children tortured in Deraa.

4. Poster released after the Baba Amr massacre

in December 2011. The boy and his slingshot are based on Zaytoun, the Little Refugee, originally designed by Mohamed Tayeb as part of an educational project.

5. 'The spirit of Palestine is in the hearts of all revolutionaries'.

6. 'Enough Mukhabarat', calling for an end to the security services.

7. 'Damascus Rebellion – The sound of victory comes from you, Barada' (Barada is the main river in Damascus).

5.

6.

7.

FLASHBACK:
THE GREEN REVOLUTION, IRAN 2009

Iran's 2009 Green Revolution can be viewed as a portent of things to come. Similar to a number of other Middle Eastern and North African countries, Iran's growing youth population was empowered by the possibilities of emerging technologies. YouTube was founded in 2005 followed by Twitter in 2006 and, perhaps most importantly, internet-enabled camera phones became cheaper and more easily available.[29]

Following Iran's national election on 12 June 2009, hardline President Mahmoud Ahmadinejad was declared to have won a landslide victory against his three opponents, including the conservative reformist Mir-Hossein Mousavi. Many declared the election to have been rigged and when the results were announced, a million people took to the streets of downtown Tehran to protest the fraud (a growling statement on a protester's placard shouted 'I wrote "Mousavi", they read "Ahmadi"'). There followed a bloody popular revolt involving massive street marches, protests, beatings and killings by police that carried on for days. The state even deployed its auxiliary paramilitary group, the Basij, to storm the dormitories of Tehran University.[30]

The colour of the opposition – the Mousavi campaign – was a brilliant green that was readily identified and used by solidarity groups, graphic artists and designers around the world who joined in with their statements of support. However the opposition's greatest weapons were the courage of its people, plus the technology that allowed them to record and spread awareness of the violence and brutality they confronted. Suddenly Iran – the 'closed' country – was open for the entire world to see. Barred Western journalists could access the information, images and documentary footage that were widely reported on social media and then broadcast them on mainstream television.

The Green Revolution only lasted the month. It was unable to achieve its mission of regime change and a heavy price was paid for the insurrection; the authorities continued to round up demonstrators long after and there were allegations of rape and abuse in prisons. Yet the revolt forced a crack in the facade of a country long oppressed by its rulers and gave the rest of the world a glimpse at the hopes of a new generation.[31]

1. *Flight for Democracy*, poster by Iranian designer Parisa Tashakori in solidarity with all people who challenge despotic rulers and 'refuse to be silent'. Iran 2012.

2. *Mighty Mouse*, poster by designer Götz Gramlich in solidarity with Iranians opposing President Mahmoud Ahmadinejad's re-election in 2009, and acknowledging the role of social media in that protest. Germany 2009.

3. *Free All Green Political Prisoners*, poster by ABCNT (Ali Rza) in solidarity with the Iranian student movement as well as other people fighting for democracy and freedom. USA 2011.

1.

2.

3.

SPAIN: LOS INDIGNADOS/15M AND VOCES CON FUTURA

Inspired by the Arab Spring and fuelled by anger over auster-ity measures linked to the 2008 crash, protest camps began to appear in the West, beginning with Spain. Bearing the slogan '*sin casa, sin curro, sin pension, sin miedo*' (no housing, no work, no pension, no fear) and feeling the pain of forty-six per cent youth unemployment, Spanish activists set their sights on jobs and cuts, but even more vehemently at politicians and bankers.

The group Democracia Real Ya or DRY (Real Democracy Now) used the internet to organize a major demonstration for Sunday 15 May, a week before the regional elections. The rally was centred in Madrid's main square, La Puerta del Sol and accompanied by other protests across Spain. Within two days, and despite police brutality, 200 people were camped in the square. In another two days there were 1,000, and by the end of the week, 25,000 – with 35,000 protesting throughout Spain. They became known as Los Indignados (The Outraged) or the '15M' movement (after their 15 May start) and adopted the Twitter hashtag '#spanishrevolution'. By 2 August they had left the Puerta del Sol voluntarily, but their impact was deep and international. They forced public debate into the open, and recruited millions of supporters with the help of social networking. They continued to demonstrate, holding a major march for change on 15 May 2012, and had a strong influ-ence on the international Occupy movement.[32]

Los Indignados/15M also left a continuing visual legacy. The site Voces con Futura (Voices of the Future) was created anonymously in May 2011, at the start of the protests when peo-ple were energetically mobilizing supporters. It was devised as an image-bank for the movement; a place where professional design-ers, illustrators and graphic artists could upload signs, banners and posters for free download by activists and demonstrators. The creator claims not to be an activist, but to have acted out of a sense of moral obligation to the burgeoning movement for change. Much of the artwork adopts the visual theme of black, yellow and red (as in the original protests), and the size of the archive and quality of the work are deeply impressive. It is not surprising to find that within two years of its inception, over 400 people had been involved in its development. Its remit has now moved beyond Los Indignados/15M to include Occupy and other global movements.[33]

1.

1–7. Electronic protest posters for downloading, from the anonymous image bank Voces con Futura in support of Los Indignados, or the Spanish Revolution (15M). Spain 2011. The largest poster shown mixes two symbols of revolution and protest. One is Alberto Korda's iconic 1960 photo of Che Guevara; the other is the modern protester's use of the Guy Fawkes mask. It was originally worn by a masked-rebel fighting a totalitarian government in the comic, graphic novel and film *V for Vendetta* (2005). The mask was then adopted by the hacktivist group Anonymous, became a familiar sight in the Occupy protests of 2011–12 and is still used by protesters around the world.

2.

QUALSEVOL NIT
POT SORTIR EL SOL

CUALQUIER NOCHE
PUEDE SALIR EL SOL

ANY NIGHT
CAN THE SUN RISE

#SPANISH
REVOLUTION
15M

3.

#spanishrevolution

Tienes
voz.

4.

5.

6.

#15M

LA REVOLUCIÓN
ESTÁ DONDE
ESTEMOS

#15M. MÁS ALLÁ DEL SOL

7.

GREECE:
THE LONG ROAD TO RECOVERY

The global economic crash of October 2008 provided the inevitable trigger for the Greek debt crisis or depression. Although the causes of the Greek crisis were highly complex, some of the chief players included a succession of ineffective Greek governments, corrupt state institutions and short-sighted miscalculations by the International Monetary Fund (IMF), the European Commission and the Central European Bank (dubbed the 'Troika' of lenders involved in the much-debated bailouts intended to keep Greece afloat).[34]

1.

Faced with extreme austerity measures, high unemployment and little hope for the future, some form of citizen unrest was probably inevitable. It received further cause on 6 December 2008, when an exchange took place between a group of youths and the police in an Athens suburb that resulted in the fatal shooting by police of fifteen-year-old student Alexis Andreas Grigoropoulos. Demonstrators took to the streets over the incident as anger and frustration grew. There followed nearly six weeks of demonstrations, occupations of schools and universities, as well as outright rioting in Athens and other cities throughout Greece, railing against the 6 December shooting, ongoing police violence, unemployment, corruption and the government.

2.

The deepening crisis brought signs of survival. Collectives and voluntary groups sprung up to encourage communal kitchens, impromptu markets where farmers could trade their products directly with consumers and other methods of skills-sharing and exchange of services, all attempting to deal with vanishing jobs and social welfare systems. However the crisis has also generated a rise in extremism. Greece's neo-Nazi party, the Golden Dawn, has not only achieved an international reputation following vicious attacks on immigrants, but also worryingly secured enough public votes during the 2012 elections to occupy seats in the Greek Parliament.[35]

Posters created by graphic designers during the December 2008 protests, depict the surge of outrage felt by people, much of it aimed at the police. They also twist and dispel proud notions of Greece as the 'cradle of democracy' and home of the 2004 Olympic Games, and instead paint a scenario of violence, rioting and austerity-exhausted people.

This ongoing apocalyptic vision has also been delivered in the Byzantine-style paintings of Stelios Faitakis, in which the rich, the fascists and the riot police mix with the blessed, who are depicted with halos: the protesters, the poor and the generous (who even feed downfallen businessmen).

1. Anti Neo-Nazi Badge ('Never Again Fascism'). UK 2013.

2. Anti Neo-Nazi Badge ('OUT with the Neo Nazis'). UK 2013.

Posters relating to the protests surrounding the debt crisis and austerity measures in Greece, as well as the shooting by police of a young student in December 2008. From the electronic collection (Flickr album) of Nassos Kappa, Greece 2008.

3. *Visit the land of democracy*, by unknown artist.

4. *Shame*, by Ioannis Fetanis.

5. *Athens 2008*, by Dionysis Livanis.

6. *Caution Cleaning in Progress*, by Stavroula Economou.

3.

Ντροπή

σε όλους μας!

061208

4.

ATHENS 2008

5.

CAUT!ON
CLEANING
IN PROGRESS

6.

7.

7. *Untitled*, painting by the Greek artist Stelios Faitakis, of an apocalyptic present (and possible future) where chaos reigns and bankers, businessmen and the rich are reliant on soup kitchens run by the kind-hearted. Greece 2009.

8. Detail from the mural *Imposition Symphony*, by the Greek artist Stelios Faitakis, commissioned for the 54th Venice Biennale as part of a group exhibition on freedom of speech. The large-scale mural has six chapters, each with a story. The story shown here involves a Greek photojournalist who witnessed and captured police drawing guns on protesters during the Athens riots of 2008. The photograph was censored, and so the photojournalist sent the image to foreign news agencies – and was fired by his employer. Greece 2011.

9. *Socrates Drinks the Conium – Left Guard*, from the mural *Destroy Athens* in the 1st Athens Biennial. By artist Stelios Faitakis. Greece 2007.

10. *Socrates Drinks the Conium-Right Guard*, from the mural 'Destroy Athens' in the 1st Athens Biennial. By artist Stelios Faitakis. Greece 2007.

8.

9.

10.

AMERICA:
OCCUPIED AND SATIRIZED

In early June 2011, the radical anti-capitalist magazine *Adbusters* sent an email to its subscribers saying 'America needs its own Tahrir'. The occupywallst.org website quickly followed, and July brought a meeting of activists in New York City keen to set up a protest camp for the movement, under the slogan 'We are the 99%'. When the date of 17 September was set, *Adbusters* published their iconic poster of a ballerina poised on top of the *Charging Bull* statue near Wall Street that represents the New York Stock Exchange and US financial might. Protesters gathered in Zuccotti Park and an encampment was established that vented anger at corruption in politics, the financial institutions responsible for the 2008 crash and the austerity measures that followed. Nearly 300 initially slept in the park. In the next few weeks the camp became more established, and for the next two months hundreds of people were drawn to the movement and the park for discussions and meetings, or free food and medical care.[36]

As of 3 October, the protesters produced their own newspaper – *The Occupied Wall Street Journal*. It began as a four-page broadsheet newspaper, with an initial print run of 50,000. Aimed at the general public, it explained the Occupy movement and their vision of the future. Soon after the Occuprint group began archiving posters relating to the global Occupy movement, as well as encouraging the printing of such posters through the creation of print labs set up to share skills and spread the iconography. Other images came via the internet, such as the 'pepper-spraying cop' – one of the most popular internet memes of the year – which originated from an incident at University of California, Davis, when two police officers pepper-sprayed a line of peaceful, seated protesters directly in the face. Videos from bystanders were uploaded to YouTube, but a snapshot of Lieutenant John Pike caught in the act went viral and he was Photoshopped into myriad situations and contexts.[37]

The police evicted the Zuccotti Park protesters and cleared the park at 1.00 a.m. on 15 November, but that was by no means the end of the story. Attempts were made to return to the park and 'Day of Action' protests (holding sit-ins to block bridges) were staged in New York, Chicago, St Louis, Detroit and other major US cities, sometimes causing major disruption. The Occupy movement spread to many cities around the world and with it the slogan 'We are the 99%'.

1. *Tax the Rich*, poster by US designer and writer John Emerson of Backspace. USA 2011.

2. Pepper-spraying cop (internet meme). USA 2011.

3. *Direct Action!*, poster by Rich Black for the 17 November mass strike as part of the Occupy Wall Street movement. He lends weight and encouragement to the message by using an image of Wang Weilin, the lone protester who bravely confronted a line of tanks during the 1989 Tiananmen Square protests. The crowd also becomes many Wang Weilins; thus the power of collective solidarity can confront the might of the machine. USA 2011.

4. *What is our one demand?*, the evocative Adbusters poster featured in the July 2011 issue of the magazine, announcing the 17 September meeting in Zuccotti Park which kick-started the Occupy Wall Street encampment. Concept: Kalle Lasn; Art Direction: Pedro Inoue and Will Brown. USA 2011.

1.

2.

3.

4.

Other examples form a grim critique of Obama's America and its social problems. Illustrator Ross MacDonald and graphic designer James Victore put their wicked sense of humour into a parody of the *Dick and Jane* reading primers for children, produced from the 1930s to the 1960s. The characters Dick and Jane represented 'everyboy and everygirl',[38] and the world they grew up in was small-town America where life was innocent, trouble-free and secure: the epitome of the American Dream. However MacDonald and Victore have placed Dick and Jane in the modern world, amidst gun-toting families, sinister priests and folk unwilling to help the less fortunate. The nostalgia felt for the Dick and Jane books makes the transfer hurt all the more. It is amusing at first, but on reflection is a reminder of what has grown worse, what has been lost, and, if we value our children, what must be changed. It is a wake-up call for the current generation of Americans.

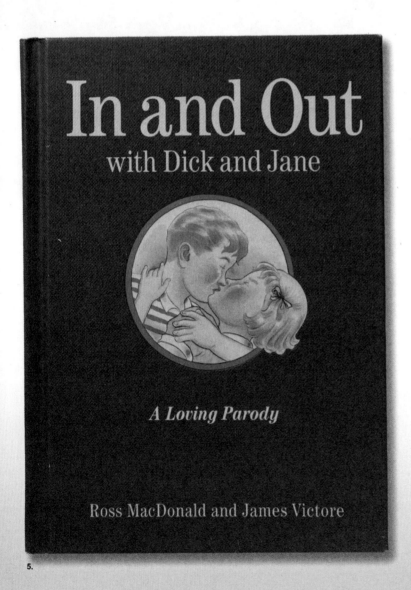

5.

5–6. *In and Out with Dick and Jane*, by illustrator Ross MacDonald and graphic designer James Victore. USA 2011.

This is our neighborhood.
Lots of nice people live here.

There is a lot to do in our town.
We go to church.
We learn about morals and
values and angels.

A Visit to the
Country

Kara Walker also uses humour to shock her viewers out of their comfort zone. Her black paper silhouettes, larger than life and cut out by hand, hark back to America's Deep South of the 1800s – a time when society was thought polite and genteel, but racial violence was commonplace. She hits particularly hard at racial stereotyping: the swooning white women and their suitors and the playful little black girls with their pigtails. All become distorted, exaggerated and somehow threatening. A woman in a ballooning frock leaning in to be kissed suddenly has an extra set of legs under her skirts; a young black woman leaps into the air, back arched in seeming ecstasy, and wildly slits her wrists with a straight razor. Overblown? Distorted? No more so than some of the racial attitudes that still exist in America today, including those directed at President Obama or the issues of discrimination that surfaced in the aftermath of Hurricane Katrina.[39]

7. *Cut*, by Kara Walker, cut paper on wall, 223.5 × 137.2 centimetres (88 × 54 inches). USA 1998.

8. *World's Exposition*, by Kara Walker, cut paper on wall, approximately 3.9 × 1.5 metres (156 × 600 inches). USA 1997.

9. Detail from the mural *Gone, An Historical Romance of a Civil War as it Occurred between the Dusky Thighs of One Young Negress and Her Heart*, by Kara Walker, cut paper on wall, approximately 3 × 4.8 metres (120 × 192 inches). USA 1994.

7.

8.

9.

RUSSIA:
PUTIN VS PUSSY RIOT

The feminist punk collective Pussy Riot was formed in 2011 as a reaction to Vladimir Putin's possible return to the presidency the following year. In January 2012, wearing their trademark coloured balaclavas, they performed a song called 'Putin Got Scared' in Red Square, waving a purple flag bearing a feminist symbol and calling all citizens to revolt.[40]

After a number of other appearances or actions, they planned their most outrageous performance as Putin was about to achieve the Presidency. On 21 February 2012, three members performed *A Punk Prayer* in front of the altar of Moscow's Cathedral of Christ the Saviour (a song laden with profanities, with a chorus of 'Virgin Mary, drive Putin out').[41] Within thirty seconds the performance was stopped by church officials; in the eyes of many, not only had Pussy Riot offended Putin, they had also offended God, right in the heart of the Russian Orthodoxy. Maria Alyokhina, Yekaterina Samutsevich and Nadezhda Tolokonnikova (also known as Masha, Katya and Nadya) were arrested and charged with 'hooliganism motivated by religious hatred'. They received international attention and support throughout their trial and sentencing in July. All were sentenced to two years in prison, although Samutsevich was freed on probation on appeal in October 2012 and Alyokhina and Tolokonnikova were released early under a change in the law in December 2013.[42]

1. *Free Pussy Riot with a Little Help from my Friends*, collage by Jorge Artajo. An appropriation of The Beatles' 1967 Sgt. Pepper's Lonely Hearts Club Band album cover (designed by artist Peter Blake and his wife Jann Haworth) which makes a more colourfully intense statement in solidarity with the imprisoned members of Pussy Riot.

2–4. Three images, from the series *Chronicle of the Resistance* by Victoria Lomasko, which illustrate different perspectives on support (or not) for Pussy Riot. The *March of Millions* refers to a series of mass anti-government rallies held in May, June and September 2012. These images as well as 5 and 6 on page 68, were part of a solidarity project / publication in 2013 entitled *Let's Start a Pussy Riot*, curated by Emely Neu and edited by Jade French in collaboration with Pussy Riot.

2. *Join the Pussy Riot!*, an Orthodox priest quakes with fear at the oncoming march of Pussy Riot supporters. Russia 2012.

3. *Pussy Riot support column*, drawing from the May 6 *March of Millions*. Russia 2012. (The woman's poster reads: 'Women's business is a revolution, not a soup.')

4. *Nationalists' column*, drawing from the '*March of Millions*' 15 September. Russia 2012. (They are chanting 'Pussy Riot – in the trash!'. The flag reads 'Glory to Russia!')

1.

2.

3.

4.

Why does the state in Russia care so much
about every woman?

she is a cheap and
obedient worker

she looks good in hardcore
porn and turns men on

she can give birth and
raise children on her own

Maybe a woman has the right to
change her position?

the campaign against restrictions on the rights of women to use
emergency contraception and the right to legal abortion

If the Patriarch received an unexpected gift of giving birth...

What if some of the gifts given from "above"
can be very unwelcome?

the campaign against restrictions on the rights of women to use
emergency contraception and the right to legal abortion

5.

6.

7.

9.

MUSIC:
VIVIAN GIRLS
KREMLIN HEAD
(MEMBERS OF MIKA MIKO, BLEACHED, AND NO AGE)
PANGEA
RIYP: BRENDAN DONNELLY

DJ'S
ALLISON WOLFE
(BRATMOBILE)
BROOKE CANDY
CULTIST
JIM

MONDAY AUGUST 27 AT THE SMELL
(247 S. MAIN ST) ALL 8PM $10

JOHN 8:32

FACEBOOK.COM/FREEPUSSY

8.

5–6. *Untitled*, by Yekaterina
Samutsevich, one of the
members of Pussy Riot who
performed in the Cathedral
of Christ the Saviour and was
arrested. Both of the images
here relate to a women's
rights campaign demanding
the right to use emergency
contraception and the right to
legal abortion. Russia 2013.

7. Front cover of a special
edition of *POP* magazine
(Issue 30, spring/summer
2014), using the *CA$H 4
PUSSY* fanzine cover by
69 Red Balloons. UK 2014.
According to *POP*, a donation
had been made against

sales to Zone of Justice, the
prisoners' rights organisation
founded by Pussy Riot.

8. *John 8:32*, solidarity
poster by Dominic Pickard
(Cab Studios). UK 2012.

9. Flyer for a Free Pussy Riot
Benefit Show at The Smell
in Los Angeles, illustrated
by artist Brendan Donnelly.
USA 2012.

10. *Pussy Riot Vodka:
Sacred and Profane,* by Gordy
Grundy and Michael Delgado.
Engaging support for the
Pussy Riot cause through
commodification. USA 2012.

10.

RUSSIA: PUTIN VS THE BLUE NOSES AND OTHERS

Pussy Riot were by no means the only artists producing controversial political art and performance in Russia. In 2007 the Andrei Sakharov Museum in Moscow staged an exhibition entitled *Forbidden Art* which contained work by Russian artists that had been banned by the authorities during 2005–06. Most of the artists involved were members of Sots Art (a confrontational satirical/political movement founded in the 1970s) and used to attracting controversy. Following campaigns by nationalist and religious groups the two organizers, Andrei Erofeev and Yuri Samodurov, were put on trial in May 2009 (with their hearing lasting until July 2010) and found guilty of incitement to religious hatred. The pair were fined and barely escaped three years' imprisonment.[43]

Some of the more controversial pieces from that exhibition are included here. Alexander Kosolapov's *This is My Body* and *Icon Caviar* comment on the false icons of consumerism and luxury obsessions of certain sectors of Russian society. The performance art duo, the Blue Noses – founded by Alexander Shaburov and Viacheslav Mizin in 1999 – are known for black or absurdist humour and social critique. Their *Chechen Marilyn* (2005) references the suicide bombings, often carried out by women, which were a prominent feature of the bloody wars driven by the Muslim Republic of Chechnya's repeated (failed) attempts at secession from Russia, starting in 1994. Chechen female suicide bombers, referred to by Russians as 'black widows', tended to be motivated by their nationalist cause and the trauma of family members killed by Russian forces. They were active from 2000 onwards; the year 2004 saw a particularly vicious wave of 'black widow' attacks targeting civilians in Moscow.[44] With their typical irreverence, the Blue Noses dare to depict a female suicide bomber in black burqa, with her skirt flaring up in the style of the famous Marilyn Monroe photograph. While *Era of Mercy* (2005), reminiscent of Banksy's *Kissing Coppers* (2004), shows two Russian policemen kissing passionately in a birch forest. In 2007 the Minister of Culture wouldn't let it leave the country for installation in an exhibition in Paris dedicated to the Sots Art movement, declaring it 'pornographic'; it certainly made a confrontational gesture towards intolerance of homosexuality and LGBT culture in Russia.[45]

The work of Egor Zhgun represents a more designed approach to biting satirical comment in the form of a highly polished poster, along with short humorous animations posted online that often reference contemporary culture such as feature films. Certain visual symbols however still apply: in this parody of the 2012 movie *Ted*, Dmitry Medvedev appears as a little bear ('Medved' is Russian for 'bear'), kicked aside by Putin.

1. *This Is My Body*, by Russian artist Alexander Kosolapov, satirizing the false icon of consumerism in Russian society. Although living in New York since 1975, Kosolapov remains a citizen of Russia and travels back to be involved in the art scene there. This piece, created in the early 2000s, caused fury among Orthodox believers in Russia at the time. Russia/USA 2000.

2. *Icon Caviar*, by Russian artist Alexander Kosolapov, commenting on modern obsessions with luxury in Russia. Russia/USA 1995–2005.

3. *Chechen Marilyn*, photograph by Russian art duo The Blue Noses depicting a female suicide bomber, with skirt flaring a la Marilyn Monroe. Russia 2005.

4. Poster parody of a book cover for the JD Salinger novel, *Catcher in the Rye*. But the word 'Rye' has been replaced with 'Lie'; and 'Salinger' has been replaced with 'Selinger', the location of a summer retreat for Putin's supporters. Finally, the man intently watching his underlings leap to their death has the profile of Putin. A sinister critique of the ruler and his party, by designer Egor Zhgun (Zhgun. ru). Russia 2011.

5. Stills from a short animation by Egor Zhgun which shows Vladimir Putin watching TV on the sofa, while his little teddy bear (former president Dmitry Medvedev) attempts to watch with him – but keeps getting kicked away. Russia 2013. The word 'medved' is Russian for 'bear'.

1.

2.

3.

ДЖ. СЕЛИГЕР

НАД
ПРОПАСТЬЮ
ВО ЛЖИ

4.

5.

6.

8.

9.

7.

6. *Kids from our Block*, a project by Russian performance art group the Blue Noses: Alexander Shaburov and Viacheslav Mizin. It was produced for the Russia 2 exhibition in January 2005 organized by the Marat Gelman Gallery (known for its support of avant-garde and provocative work). The exhibition aimed to show 'another side' of Russia, dealing with subjects such as Putin and Chechnya and confronting established thinking. Russia 2005.

7. The Blue Noses satirize Modernism and its icons, as worshipped by the art and design world. In their installation entitled 'Kitchen Suprematism', pseudo-compositions in the style of the great Russian artist Kazimir Malevich are produced using black bread and sausages. Russia 2006.

8. *An Epoch of Clemency (Kissing Policemen)*, photograph by the Blue Noses. Paying homage to Banksy's 'Kissing Coppers', two men dressed in the uniform of the Russian military kiss passionately in a birch forest. Add *Kissing Airbornemen* (9), *Kissing Ballerinas* (10) and *Kissing Football Players* (11), and it seems that all of Russia's most favoured icons (the military, ballet, sport) are 'at it'. It's a forceful show of humorous irreverence by the Blue Noses, created in a country where the authorities are deeply intolerant of homosexuality. Russia 2005–09.

10.

11.

OCCUPY GEZI

In May–June 2013, when central Istanbul's Gezi Park was due for demolition and development, mass protests to save the park began a power struggle between the will of the people and the authoritarian Prime Minister Recep Tayyip Erdogan. Despite escalating police brutality, protesters seized Istanbul's central Taksim Square and occupied neighbouring Gezi Park, setting up food stalls, a library, a stage and so on, while inviting a wide range of activists from different organizations and causes to join in through social media. Erdogan denounced the protesters as thugs and looters and ordered a heavy police crackdown on 31 May. Anti-government protests exploded throughout the country and central Istanbul became a battleground.[46]

Excessive use of violence, tear gas and water cannon became prevailing themes in the reports and images emerging from the protests. Protesters made innovative use of two-litre plastic water bottles for homemade tear-gas masks (turn the bottle upside down, cut out a large area of the side in which to insert your face, place a vinegar-soaked mouth-cover in the bottom, and tie straps on the sides to attach it to your face). The violence also became pictorialized in imagery: gas masks or facemasks became signs of honour or bravery when worn by protesters in posters, or stencilled on Twitter's bird logo, or on the face of a defiant penguin (when CNN Turk, a mainstream news channel, chose to ignore the most violent protest and instead broadcast a bird documentary, birds and penguins began to be depicted as having joined the protesters). A photo showing a policeman pepper-spraying a woman in a red dress achieved iconic status on social media, as well as being repeatedly stencilled around the city. And a popular image of brazen resistance to the police came in the form of a woman with arms outstretched, defiantly confronting the force of the water cannon.[47]

On 17 June, a quieter variety of protest took place – also requiring unshakeable nerve. A performance artist, Erdem Gunduz, stood still in Taksim Square – mute and serene, staring at the giant portrait of Mustafa Kemal Ataturk (founding father of the Turkish Republic, and deeply admired by the protesters) hanging on the Ataturk Cultural Centre – for over six hours, ignoring any interference by police. He became 'Standing Man' on Twitter, and was joined by more than 300 people in the square, while his image became iconized by a line-sketch on social media. Soon other similar protests in which people stood still were taking place in different cities. The 'Standing Man' inspired the 'Taksim Square Book Club', which involved protesters standing in similar fashion in the square, silently reading appropriate books by authors such as Camus and Orwell.[48]

1. Online 'resistance wall' of graffiti and writing. Turkey 2013.

2 and 3. A whirling dervish performing in a gas-mask is popularized in stencil form, along with the words 'come along' (to the protest). Turkey 2013.

4. Online poster showing key elements of the protest: the gas-mask, the news media and an iconic image of a woman with arms spread, bravely confronting a police water cannon. Turkey 2013.

1.

2.

3.

4.

5.

6.

7.

#occupygezi

8.

5 and 7. Photograph by
Osman Orsal (and stencil) of
a policeman pepper-spraying
a woman in a red dress, which
was circulated on social
media and stencilled widely.
Turkey 2013.

6. Stencil graffiti of a penguin
with a gas-mask, a symbol
of anger at a major news
channel for not broadcasting
an extremely violent protest.
Turkey 2013.

8. Stencil graffiti of the Twitter
bird logo with a gas-mask,
as twitter was crucial to
protesters for information
dissemination. Turkey 2013.

9.

10.

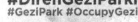

11.

12.

9 and 10. Photograph of 'Standing Man' (Erdem Gunduz), who stood still and mute in Taksim Square for over six hours and became a symbol of passive resistance. Supported by a sketch that circulated on social media, shown here, hundreds of other protesters joined him in his silent, standing protest. Turkey 2013.

11. '#DirenGeziParki' or 'Resist Gezi Park', online poster. Turkey 2013.

12. Jamie Reid's Sex Pistols cover (for *God Save the Queen*) is manipulated to show Prime Minister Erdogan with the words 'God Save the Sultan', a comment on his growing authoritarianism. Turkey 2013.

BRAZIL:
SOCIAL INEQUALITY AND
MEGA-EVENTS

In June 2013, a rise in São Paulo bus fares (the less-advantaged person's preferred mode of transport) sparked off Brazil's largest public demonstrations in thirty years. For at least a decade, global media had enthused about Brazil's economic growth, its burgeoning middle class and its seeming escape from the recession of 2008. Its politicians – anxious to show Brazil as a 'world-class player' rather than a 'developing country' – pushed it forward to grasp the hosting of the 2014 FIFA World Cup and the 2016 Olympics in Rio. Brazil however is a country of vast economic disparities, government services hadn't kept up with the rate of growth, and the cost of running global mega-events had started to take its toll. (Plus its 7.5 per cent economic growth rate had, in the aftermath of the 2008 crash, sunk to 0.9 per cent by 2012.)[49]

Frustrations boiled over in 2013: cries of political corruption, poor medical facilities, overcrowded hospitals, poor education and high rates of illiteracy in its cities clashed with the lavish spending and rolling deadlines for 'FIFA-standard' stadiums. The mass demonstrations of June 2013 collided with the Confederations Cup (an international, status-laden precursor to the World Cup) and protests in every major city pointed towards the publicly funded stadiums. As the games progressed inside the stadiums, demonstrators were met with police beatings, tear gas, stun grenades and rubber bullets outside. Reports of placards carrying slogans such as 'We need FIFA-quality schools' and 'We need FIFA-standard hospitals' persisted. Although global media did not report on the protests at quite the same level in June 2014 when the World Cup actually arrived (accompanied by a strong police presence) the allegations of corruption and levels of criticism aimed at FIFA throughout have not gone away. And there are still the Olympics and the requirements of the International Olympic Committee to contend with.[50]

Within this scenario, some of Brazil's major cities – overbuilt, densely populated and bearing chronic poverty – experience continual attempts to reclaim public spaces for people, rather than for development. One such project is depicted by BijaRi design studio based in São Paulo, a heavily populated city of tall buildings, too many motorways, flyovers and traffic problems, and little space to breathe. Their *Lambe Lambe* posters (one of their personal projects) have accompanied recent popular movements of discontent with statements such as 'What are we fighting for?', 'Body Technology' (pedestrians not cars), and simply 'Public Space' – as if one has to define it and then claim it. (*Lambe Lambe* roughly means 'Lick It, Lick It', in reference to old-style, woodblock-printed posters produced quickly and immediately pasted up in the streets.)[51]

1 and 4 (overleaf). *Public Space*, poster by BijaRi design studio. Brazil 2013.

ESPAÇO PUBLICO

1.

2.

2. *Lambe Lambe* posters, stating 'Body Technology' (with unicycle) and 'What are we fighting for? (with protester), part of a series about reclaiming public space. By BijaRi design studio in São Paulo. Brazil 2010.

3 and 5. Poster placed in situ to protest gentrification. By BijaRi design studio in São Paulo. Brazil 2013. The poster states: (in the circle) 'Gentrified' (and beneath) 'Gentrification: the process of restoring and/or improving deteriorating urban property; carried out by an emergent or middle class; and usually resulting in removing the impoverished population.'

6–9. *Lambe Lambe* posters aimed at reclaiming public space for 'Body Technology' (for use by pedestrians) – highly necessary in an overbuilt city such as São Paulo with too many cars, highways and traffic jams. By BijaRi design studio. Brazil 2010.

3.

4.

5.

6.

7.

8.

9.

BRITAIN: SIGNS OF DISCONTENT

In Britain's general election of 2010 the cracks caused by escalating social and economic inequalities during the Blair years (1997–2007) finally began to show. Much of the aggravation was aimed at wealthy and private-school-educated politicians. The new prime minister, David Cameron, and his cabinet were perceived as a political elite dealing out austerity cuts to the rest of the country. A popular site during the election campaign was mydavidcameron.com, which became a modern-day version of the medieval stocks – download his campaign poster, change the message, and upload it again for millions to see. The premise was also repeated through graffiti in the streets.

Another graphic project – less visible but much closer to reality – was Laura Oldfield Ford's post-Punk zine entitled *Savage Messiah* (2005–09). A combined diary, journal and poetic commentary, Ford's zine chronicles her movements as she drifts through the hidden wastelands of London. She documents deserted landscapes, rundown estates, dilapidated buildings and the people (out of time, out of mind) who have been left behind in the drive for 'regeneration'. All have become part of the urban dispossessed: squatters, young punks, old gents, girlfriends, boyfriends. Conversations are noted, as well as encounters and disappearances. And there is much contemplation and protest about how Blairism and Cool Britannia moved in the yuppies, planners and developers to transform every bit of unoccupied space into a shopping centre or a 'controlled zone'. The future spectre of London 2012 is viewed as one of the worst offenders with regard to this transformation.

The visual rendering of these characters and places is dynamic and richly detailed. A complex collage of photographs, magazine cut-outs, strips of text in typewriter type, and the lettering of timely signs and ads ('CASH 4 GOLD') is held together by a stream of drawings: people, buildings, scribbles and doodling. All are printed and viewed through the textural grittiness of dark photocopying, suited to the anger Ford expresses at the burial of history and a way of life.

1. Conservative Party election poster in London, with graffiti relating to the privately educated politicians who dealt out austerity cuts to the rest of the population.

2. Digitally manipulated Conservative Party election posters uploaded to the mydavidcameron.com website, during the general election campaign of 2010. (David Cameron was head of the Conservative Party at that time.) UK 2010.

3. *Savage Messiah* (overleaf), front cover and inside spreads from a compilation of Laura Oldfield Ford's non-digital cut-and-paste zine, which lasted from 2005 to 2009 and documented the impact of Blairite consumerism and branding on different communities in London's run-down housing estates.

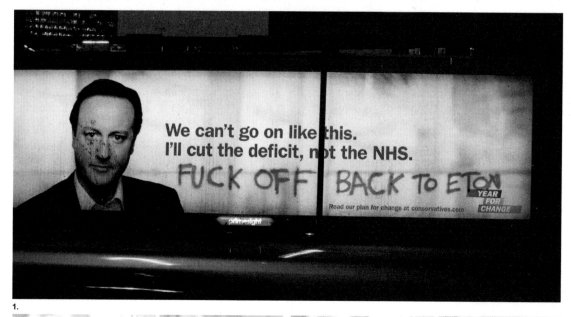

1.

2.

SAVAGE MESSIAH

Introduced by
Mark Fisher

"Be warned: this is
a city you won't find
in any guidebook."
—Independent

LAURA OLDFIELD FORD

The Aylesbury estate. Redevelopment plans were
thwarted after a no vote in 2001. The Heygate are
denied a direct ballot.
    Taplow , my old block. Rows of George crosses
blocking smeared windows.   Old Testament names,
Ezekiel , Ephraim graffed in the lifts. There were
yellow signs outside the block when I came in at 6
in the morning after an ugly night on ketamine in a
New Cross squat. Police tape spanned the stairwells,
the lifts were out of order and the Old Bill were on
the landing.
Door to door.

3.

DEVELOPERS!!HACKNEYCOUNCIL!!YUPPIES!HANDS OFF OUR ESTATES!!!
FUCK OFF TO THE THAMES GATEWAY!!!!!!!!

APARTME...
READY FO..
IMMEDIATE
OCCUPATION!

Constant's nomadic architecture
took the idea of nomadism as
subversive, he thought of itinerant
life as   freedom and that
architecture embodied the potential
for revolution.
Deleuze and Guattari talk about the
nomad who does not desire to have
control or stability.."a warrior
without a strategy" This is a way
of being, using the power of
language, breaking free of
discourse, living in the now. Every
aspect of the environment is of
equal value, no place, time or
setting are privileged. The nomad
is always becoming, with a line of
flight ever open, of "choices and
chances, commission and omission,
opportunities taken and missed" Fox
1999

! VIVA SAVAGE MESSIAH !
SAVAGE MESSIAH DEMANDS THE ABOLITION OF ALL ZONES!!
.... SMASH THE VILLE RADIEUSE, SAVAGE MESSIAH IS CALLING FOR A MASS
RETURN TO THE LABYRINTH!!!

YUPPIES!!! Hands off our houses! There's plenty of space for you in the
THAMES GATEWAY! GET OUT OF HACKNEY!!!

Demand an end to boring, mediocre architecture, build your own social
housing: DESTROY THE MASTERPLAN!

Of course, she knew she'd let him go, not pushed him exactly,
just let him drift away gently, without making the effort to
pull him back in. There wasn't really an exact point when the
malaise had started, when it didn't matter anymore that he saw
her without make up, looking dishevelled in the morning,
bloated and tired and rough with a hangover. She couldn't even
figure out when it was that she'd stopped wanting him to desire
her, when did that start, that feeling of just not being
bothered anymore.? It had gone on a long time , that feeling
of heaviness, the weight under the ribs, of being pushed deep
into a bed kept for sleeping now. It all became futile. Waking.
Living. There was no rhythm, no thrills to shred the tedium. It
was all condensed in a grey dread that made every hour, every
day the same. It surrounded her, no past no future, just
suspension in the fog.

Then the first letter arrived, she could pinpoint that
date ,it rose sharply in her mind.
, a brown envelope stamped first Glasgow then Peterlee, PLEASE
REDIRECT.
    where you been?   been missing you, me especially

haven't been the same since you
disappeared, and so I'm wondering where the hell are
I hope you get this

Love   always,

There was a photo of him outside by a fire with Scottish hills
in the background. She studied his face, unchanged, still the
same thick dark hair, pale skin and dark eyes, Scots-Italian.
He was still handsome, still had that way of smiling that made
you think of kissing him, of hiding away in some cottage for
the winter. What would he think of her now. She couldn't bear
to see his disappointment, he'd recoil at the sight of her.
She nipped her thighs and looked with dismay at the dimpled
flesh, and her face, she peered deep into the mirror and

The London riots of 2011 could therefore be considered as an explosion of pent-up anger that was a long time coming. Although the police shooting of North Londoner Mark Duggan on 6 August was certainly the flashpoint (and the details of what actually happened that day are still hotly contested), the rioting that followed spread with incredible fury and speed to other parts of London and then to at least nine other British cities. The profile and intent of the rioters was confusing; the crowd was composed of teenagers and kids as young as nine to angry adults, opportunistic looters and a lot more people fed up with no job, no prospects and no future. (One of the many statements shouted at police was 'Your job next!')[53]

The riots calmed down after a week, but for months thereafter participants were pursued through images caught via surveillance cameras, mobile phones and the news media – pictures were even published for identification in local newspapers, while forthright mothers dragged their participating kids into police stations to apologize. Yet one chilling image remained the most prevalent: the 'posterboy' of the riots was a masked young man staring straight into camera as flames raged behind him. The figure was a symbol of a society out of control, and which threatens to return at any time.

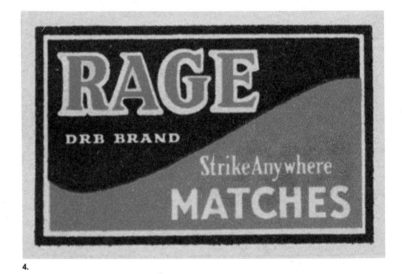

4.

4. A range of *Dirty Rotten Art Works* by British artist DRB (aka DRB Match Industries), inspired by the London Riots of August 2011. UK 2013.

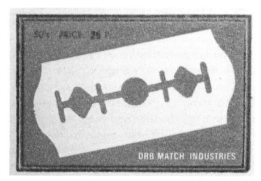

OCCUPY LONDON: THE CAMP AT ST PAUL'S

Less than three months after the London riots, another equally serious statement of discontent began, but in the form of a protest with more consolidated targets in sight and little or no violence. On 15 October the activist group Occupy London walked to the Stock Exchange for the purposes of occupying and demonstrating against the injustices of globalization and its agents – the banks, the inequalities inherent in being 'the 99%', present-day failings of capitalism and other burning issues. Finding it impossible to approach due to police blockades, they walked further and set down to form a camp in the small space of pavement in front of St Paul's Cathedral. Despite confused reactions from the Anglican Church and irritation from the City of London as well as the news media, the protesters' sustained a long-term presence and managed to stave off eviction until 28 February 2012.[53]

1.

During those four months, the camp was extremely organized and attracted visitors off the street as well as university lecturers and politicians to its organized debates (held in a tent or on the cathedral steps). Protesters offered food to visitors, asking only for a donation from those who could afford it, established a book exchange, produced occasional performances and were deeply popular with foreign tourists wanting a 'selfie' with a protester in a Guy Fawkes mask.[54]

Crucially they also never failed to provide a visual presence for the serious issues at hand. Written placards and hand-drawn or cut-and-paste posters appeared everywhere, stuck to tents throughout the camp, on trees or surrounding buildings. In addition, nine days after arriving at St Paul's, a supporting newspaper – *The Occupied Times of London* – was produced on site, starting as a weekly title of twelve A4 pages for the first six weeks, then an A3 broadsheet, and eventually growing in content to become a twenty-four-page monthly. Tzortzis Rallis and Lazaros Kakoulidis designed it, using Jonathan Barnbrook's radical, anti-corporate 'Bastard' typeface for headlines and Panos Vassiliou's 'PF Din Mono' typeface (widely used for corporate branding projects) for the body text. Thus, according to Rallis, the radical typeface 'occupies' the corporate typeface both in design and ideology, therefore 'visualizing the Occupy metaphor'. They considered it important to utilize the 'permanence of print', believing that passers-by and others would be more likely to read a printed newspaper, as opposed to following directions to a website. They were also keen not to leave out the homeless or other groups that may not own or have access to a computer. The newspaper was nominated for the London Design Museum's 'Designs of the Year 2013', an award given in recognition of the most innovative designs from around the world.[55]

1. *Occupy London*, poster by designer Monika Ciapala (merdesign.co.uk) for the activist group Occupy London. UK 2011.

2–4 (opposite and overleaf). Front pages of *The Occupied Times of London*, designed by Tzortzis Rallis and Lazaros Kakoulidis. The second issue (#02) – 'Fears of a Violent Eviction' – was distributed at the St Paul's occupation on 2 November 2011.

The Occupied Times

ᐟ OF LONDON ᐟ

#02 | theoccupiedtimes.com   02NOV2011

FEARS OF A VIOLENT EVICTION

STACEY KNOTT

Relations between OccupyLSX and St Paul's Cathedral took another twist last Monday when the Dean of St Paul's, Graeme Knowles, resigned amid the controversy of St. Paul's handling of the occupation. Last week the cathedral sought legal action to evict occupiers, which has caused three clergy to quit.

In a statement, Knowles said he had resigned to "give the opportunity for a fresh approach to the complex and vital questions facing St Paul's, I have thought it best to stand down as dean, to allow new leadership to be exercised. I do this with great sadness, but I now believe that I am no longer the right person to lead the Chapter of this great cathedral."

With Knowles stepping down, the Cathedral has asked the Bishop of London Dr Richard Chartres to assist in providing an independent voice on the ongoing situation at St Paul's.

Two other St Paul's clergy quit their posts in solidarity with the protesters.

The first was the canon chancellor of St Paul's Cathedral, Dr Giles Fraser. He said he could not support the possibility of "violence in the name of the church", then the Rev Fraser Dyer, who worked as a chaplain at St Paul's, stepped down because he was "left feeling embarrassed" by the cathedrals eviction decision.

Knowles' announcement came one day after he and Chartres met with the occupiers to listen to and speak to them about their concerns.

At the public meeting, they said they did not want the eviction to be violent, and that they were willing to open dialogue over the issues the movement was trying to address.

However, many protesters told the Occupied Times they felt the clerics were evasive of their questions, and did not say anything of real substance.

Many in the movement were concerned about a violent eviction, after it was announced on Friday that St Paul's and the City of London Corporation were planning on getting high court injunctions to remove the protesters.

Chartres told the occupiers "nobody wants to see violence." Musician and occupier Ben Doran felt the men were contradictory with their intentions to evict, but also not wanting violence.

"An eviction would apply violence. As a logical process you can't be against one and for the other," he said.

Occupier Tanya Paton, who was part of a working group responsible for liaising with the cathedral, told the Occupied Times she had been trying to open dialogue with the cathedral for the past two weeks, and was pleased they had finally started talking to occupiers.

However, she was also concerned about a violent eviction and hoped the church would commit to protecting the occupiers from one.

CHURCH & STATE SEEK LEGAL ACTION

RORY MACKINNON

Camp residents voiced anger this week as clergy and councillors alike threatened legal action to force them from a public square.

Between 200-300 campers from Occupy London Stock Exchange have held St Paul's Square for more than a fortnight after police barred them from the privately-owned Paternoster Square directly outside the exchange.

But both St Paul's Cathedral and the City of London confirmed late last week they were seeking an eviction order to break up the camp on grounds of obstructing a public highway.

City of London said in a statement they believed protest was "an essential right" in a democracy – "but camping on the highway is not."

"We believe we will have a strong highways case because an encampment on a busy thoroughfare clearly impacts the rights of others," it read.

Meanwhile the Cathedral said only that legal action had "regrettably become necessary."

"The Chapter only takes this step with the greatest reluctance and remains committed to a peaceful solution," the Cathedral's ruling Chapter said in a statement. >>

2.

The Occupied Times

~ OF LONDON ~

ANOTHER BRICK IN THE WALL
MARK KAURI

A number of emerging occupations cropped up at university campuses last week, with student activists railing against funding cuts, supporting teachers in the face of public sector pension cuts, calling for an end to neoliberal economic policies and backing the global occupy movement. The protests have emerged in light of the government's higher education White Paper, which would permit private providers to offer degrees.

In Bloomsbury, students from various University of London institutions began occupying a property owned by the School of Oriental and African Studies. The previously disused property at 53 Gordon Square was subsequently renamed the Bloomsbury Social Centre by occupiers and a statement was issued outlining plans for the site to be used as a community resource and a material instrument in the build-up to the N30 strike against public sector cuts. Despite the threat of arrests and >>

MARK KAURI

Millions of public sector workers and protesters are today staging a walkout over the government's changes to pensions contributions, in what is being hailed as the largest UK strike for a generation. Fourteen trade unions initially committed to the action during the TUC conference in September, but further support has since been pledged, raising the total number of participating unions to 33.

The unions' strike represents a critical response to the government's plan to increase pensions contributions beyond the agreed rate that came into force in 2008. Unions argue this overhaul should have meant the contribution rate would not need to be re-examined for a generation, but the government is now planning to remodel the rates at a cost to public >>

TIME TO STRIKE!

3.

The Occupied Times

~ OF LONDON ~

#07 | theoccupiedtimes.com | @OccupiedTimes   14DEC2011

MARK KAURI

OCCUPY EVERYWHERE: GOING VIRAL

This week, coinciding with the two-month anniversary of the emergence of Occupy London, calls have been made for a national day of creative, non-violent action to highlight economic and social injustice. Occupy Everywhere (December 15th) is an invitation for concerned citizens and communities across the UK to engage with the global dialogue on the changes and re-imaginings our society desperately requires.

The invitation comes on the heels of concerns of further instability in the markets and the continuing drive by the government to proceed with extensive cuts to public services, the perpetuation of neoliberal economic policies and corporate rule, and a blind eye-turned attitude towards the ecological devastation entailed by this agenda. In short: the same formula to have run amok in the build-up and consequent come-down of the recent global financial crisis is being re-bottled, re-branded – and sold at a higher price (rolling out at coffee shops this festive season: the Neoliberalatte!). Occupy Everywhere may represent the latest batch of antidote attempting to remedy this poison, but this action – together with the wider initiative of the Occupy movement – is also representative of an historic and intertwined domino chain of social reform.

In the seventeenth century, it took a dissolved parliament more than a decade to reform and stand up to the tyrannical reign of King Charles I – and longer still for the ensuing civil war to see the autocratic rule of monarchs ousted from the British Isles altogether. This period of turmoil gave rise to the actions of dissenting groups, including the Levellers and the Diggers, who occupied themselves with efforts towards economic equality.

A century later, against the backdrop of the industrial revolution that would propel our society into the late modern age, the trade union movement saw those outside of the aristocracy take social reform into their own hands. Workers formed unions to stand in solidarity against injustices and exploitation. It was from this front that 'occupy' as terminology can find its origin - with workers' industrial action having included moves to occupy factories to prevent lock-outs by their employers.

With the kindling of reform set down for future generations, the 20th century saw the fire of change stoked like never before: with direct action from feminists leading to the civil right to vote, the post-world war years giving rise to the welfare state and a national health service and the 1960s playing host to a plethora of social reforms, civil rights movements and revolutionary general strikes >>

4.

CHINA: LEAVING THE PAST AND FACING THE PRESENT

1989 was a significant year for progressive Chinese artists, and continues to cast a long shadow to this day. At that point, Western art and political movements had already begun to inform various Chinese cultural and artistic stances against authority and ongoing conformity, and a number of artists influenced by these ideas were to be celebrated in the two-week *China/Avant-Garde* exhibition in Beijing. The exhibition started in style: being shut down within hours of opening because of the use of gunfire in one of the exhibits and again later following bomb threats.[57] Only four months later, the pro-democracy demonstration in Tiananmen Square ended in a massacre of over 2,000 protesters. Although the demonstration failed and brought terrible punishment to the participants, it was clear that from thereon the Chinese leadership would have difficulties keeping its creative culture under control.

In 1993, experimental artist Ai Weiwei returned to China following ten years of studying and soaking up radical influences in New York City. Over the next two decades he would consolidate his status as a conceptual artist, architect, designer, activist and provocateur. In his earlier work he had satirized Chinese cultural and political traditions (in works such as *June 1994* for example) as well as international symbols in the photo-action *A Study of Perspective 1995–2003*, where he gives the finger to locations and objects of cultural authority and power such as the White House, Tiananmen Square, and the Eiffel Tower. However in his more recent work, criticism of the government and issues of social responsibility are very much steeped in recent events. One project in particular represents his persistence in questioning and researching, while drawing public attention to injustice.

On 12 May 2008 an 8.0-magnitude earthquake occurred in Sichuan province, with its epicentre located in Wenchuan County. China's central government acknowledged that the quake caused the collapse of 6,898 school buildings, but soon rumours of 'tofu-dregs engineering' (i.e. shoddy construction) surfaced in the media. Allegations of corruption were made, suggesting that low-standard construction was agreed between the government and contractors in order to pocket surplus funds. Over 5,000 students in primary or secondary schools died and, given China's 'one child policy', many families lost their only child. Grieving parents were silenced, kept away from the ruins and dissuaded from speaking to journalists.[57]

A year later, the Sichuan government still refused to pursue the matter on the basis that if the earthquake-magnitude surpasses the level of the earthquake-proofing standards of the buildings, the deaths must be seen as being of natural causes. And according to Ai Weiwei's blog at the time, over 5,000 children still lacked an identity, with no recorded name or age.

1.

2.

3.

1–3. *Study of Perspective*, Chinese artist Ai Weiwei makes an obscene gesture at cultural icons and the authority they represent. China 1995–2003. From the top: *Study of Perspective – Tiananmen Square; Study of Perspective – Eiffel Tower; Study of Perspective – White House.*

5–6 (overleaf). Artwork and exhibition pieces created by Ai Weiwei, relating to the Citizen's Investigation into the 2008 Sichuan earthquake and memorializing the schoolchildren who lost their lives.

4.

4. Detail of an art installation by Ai Weiwei listing all of the student earthquake victims (including name, date of birth, class and sex) who died in the collapsed school buildings in Sichuan due to poor construction standards. The information was compiled from 2008 to 2011, by the Citizen's Investigation launched by Ai Weiwei's studio. China 2012.

Soon after the earthquake, Ai Weiwei travelled to Sichuan to document the disaster and, with the help of hundreds of volunteers, created a citizen's investigation to research, document and memorialize the students. The volunteers, many of them grieving relatives, played a crucial role in gathering information in difficult circumstances, with some under threat from government surveillance and retribution. A number of works emerged to form a requiem for those who died:[58] *Names of the Student Earthquake Victims Found by the Citizen's Investigation, 2008–11* lists more than 5,000 students (including name, date of birth, school class and gender); *Remembrance, 2010*, is a 3-hour, 41-minute recording reciting the names of all students; the sculpture *Snake Ceiling* (2009) is constructed from backpacks representing those worn by the schoolchildren (photographs from one of the earthquake sites show backpacks scattered in the rubble); and *Straight* (2008–12) is thirty-eight tons of steel in an 'orderly arrangement of rebar recovered from schools that collapsed in the earthquake'. The bars are laid together to create a gentle, rolling surface. Seams form where rows meet, creating lines or indentations in the rolling surface, similar to fissures in the ground.[59]

While Ai Weiwei fights injustice and wrangles with the authorities, other artists present a haunted present constructed of elements from the past. Qiu Jie deals with the historical and 'heroic' visual domination of Mao, and challenges it by replacing it with a cat. The portrait bears the beauty and detail of traditional Chinese painting, but the intricate plant-life is beginning to overtake and conceal the cat (or is the cat hiding?). There is also a hint of wordplay: one of the many meanings of the word 'mao' in Chinese is 'cat'. Again, traditionally, the image of a cat has been used to help bestow a blessing. But this cat is ever watchful, and surely a ghost from the past. As with most cats, it is difficult to be certain of its intentions. Provocative artist Sheng Qi deliberately and forcefully pulls the dark shadows of the past into the present day. He defiantly chopped off the little finger of his left hand in protest at the time of the Tiananmen Square massacre. Then in 1999 he began photographing it, creating an ongoing series of hundreds of images that position his disfigured hand as a frame for postage stamp-sized images of modern China – ordinary citizens, protesters, children, communist leaders – thereby making the political deeply personal. It is a portrait of both personal and collective pain that may stretch far into the future.[60]

Ai Weiwei
According to What?

5.

5. *Snake Ceiling*, a giant snake constructed of backpacks similar to those worn by the children who died. By the artist Ai Weiwei. China 2009.

6. *Straight*, an arrangement of (thirty-eight tons of) steel rebar, i.e. reinforcing bars, recovered from schools that collapsed in the earthquake. By the artist Ai Weiwei. China 2008–12.

6.

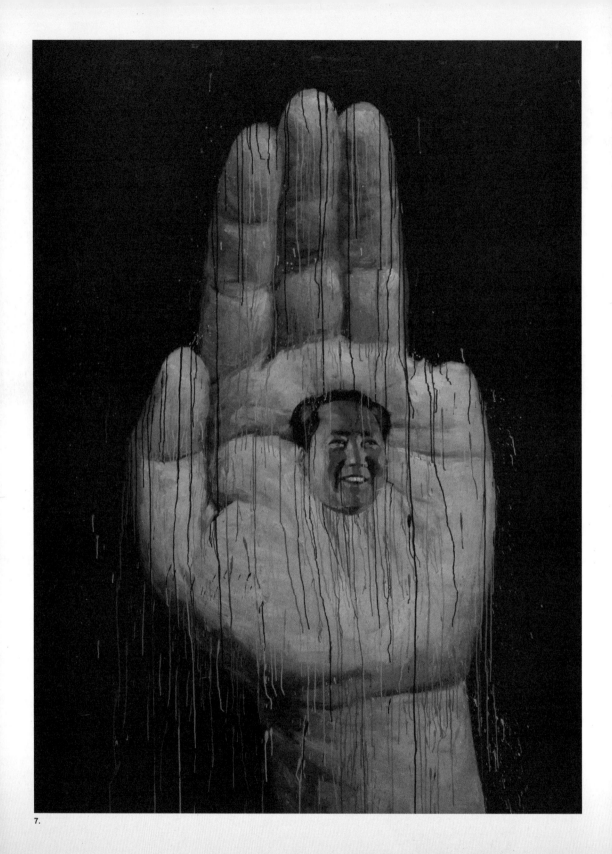

7.

7. *My Left Hand in Black and White*, from a long-standing series of artworks by artist Sheng Qi associated with his violently cutting off his little finger in solidarity with the protesters at the time of the 1989 Tiananmen Square massacre. China 2010.

8. *Portrait of Mao*, by artist Qiu Jie. Irreverent treatment of Mao Zedong's image, and a bit of word-play: one of the many meanings of the word 'mao' in Chinese is 'cat'. China 2007.

8.

HONG KONG AND THE UMBRELLA REVOLUTION: 'WE WILL BE BACK!'

In 1898, during a period of European colonial expansion in China, the majority of Hong Kong was leased to Britain for ninety-nine years. Hong Kong was therefore under British governance for most of the twentieth century, while mainland China underwent massive transitions including a Nationalist government, a Japanese takeover in the 1930s, the creation of the People's Republic of China and Mao Zedong's Cultural Revolution, followed by the hardline leadership of Deng Xiaoping from 1977 to 1998. It was Deng's government that ordered the crackdown at the 1989 pro-democracy protests in Tiananmen Square. Hong Kong responded by holding an annual large-scale commemoration of the 1989 massacre, and, when Britain returned Hong Kong to China in 1997, it became the only place on Chinese soil to hold such an event every year.[61]

Therefore it is no surprise that the spirit of protest and activism lives on in Hong Kong today. Activists from a pro-democracy movement are currently demanding open elections for the Hong Kong Chief Executive in 2017 (official rulings insist that any vote can only involve three pre-screened candidates). Public demonstrations began in late September 2014 and the movement became known as the 'Umbrella Revolution' because protesters carried umbrellas to protect themselves from tear gas and pepper-spray. Yellow, representing universal suffrage, became the dominant colour of the protests and many wore ribbons of support. The wearing of blue ribbons, however, signalled pro-Beijing sympathies.[62]

The first week of the protest began with class boycotts by hundreds of university students, followed by the launch of the 'Occupy Central with Love and Peace' campaign and days of street theatre and speeches. However in rapidly escalating scenes, the police stepped in at the end of the week and shot tear gas into the peaceful protest. By the following Monday 150,000 people were blocking the main commercial districts, their thoroughfares and commuter hubs. Barricades were built at key intersections and entrances to the subway. Finding themselves outnumbered, the police withdrew and the protesters formed encampments within one of the world's most important financial centres.[63]

The peaceful protests were coordinated through social media. Activists equipped themselves with surgical masks and diving goggles, or covered their faces and arms with plastic wrap as protection from pepper-spray. Yet the umbrellas proved most useful when pushing their way past barricades or as protection against riot police, rain or the fierce midday sun.[64]

As months passed, the occupying camps and demonstrations became known worldwide for the paintings, graffiti, sculptures, crowd-sourced installations and exhibitions that had sprung up

1. *Umbrella Man*, a 3.6 metre (12 foot) tall sculpture made of wood set up by students outside city government headquarters, and one of the many impromptu art pieces produced in the occupying demonstrations during the Umbrella Revolution in Hong Kong, September – December 2014. Photograph by Vincent Yu, AP.

2. *Lennon Wall*, a growing mass of Post-its on the wall of a staircase: a popular art piece, carrying messages of support from the public. Hong Kong 2014. Photograph by Victor S. H. Wong.

1.

2.

in the streets. For example, a sculpture called *Umbrella Man* – a 3.6 metre (12 foot) figure made of wood and holding a yellow umbrella – was erected near to the Hong Kong government headquarters, while a staircase outside the headquarters carried a collage of thousands of coloured Post-it notes, all bearing messages of support for the protesters from the public. In a city normally known for heavily restricting graffiti, the occupied areas provided unique spaces for street art to flourish. However the work was under constant threat of being dismantled or destroyed by the police. Groups such as 'Umbrella Movement Art Preservation' made attempts to save the art with a 'rescue team' network able to mobilize and perform critical preservation at short notice. The art made during the protests is not only seen as documentation of the demands of the protesters, but also as a portrayal of the city's identity and the zeitgeist of the time.[65]

Sadly, although the protests initially had a great deal of backing from the general public, support began to erode over time. By December, the public were keen to have their roads unblocked and to get back to work, particularly as Hong Kong officials and Beijing leaders had not given an inch in response to the protesters' demands. In mid-December, hundreds of police bearing chainsaws and bolt-cutters destroyed the barricades and shut down the central protest site. More than 200 were arrested for unlawful assembly and obstructing the police. Many protesters listened to police warnings and left to avoid arrest, but some remained in the street and were eventually hauled away, chanting: 'We will be back!'[66]

3. *YOU are the Heroes!*, impromptu art piece consisting of a mirror bearing goggles and a mask. Look at the mirror and find yourself reflected as a hero and protester! Photograph by Kevin Martin Peterson.

4. Electronic poster for the Umbrella Revolution, by designer Raven H. Ma, showing two symbols crucial to the movement. Umbrellas were used as defence against police brutality, tear-gas and pepper-spray attacks. Ribbons in the adopted colour yellow, symbolizing universal suffrage, acted as visual identifiers of the movement and its sympathizers.

5. *Resilience and Endurance*, illustration in support of the Umbrella Revolution by Japanese artist and illustrator Yuko Shimizu, based in New York City.

6. *Umbrella Movement – One Month*, electronic poster by designer Raven H. Ma.

3.

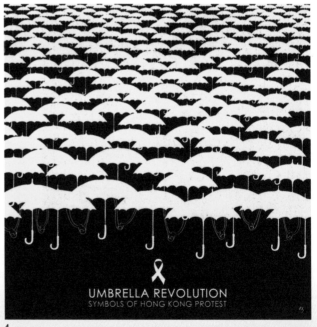

4.

5.

6.

7.

7. *When the police used tear gas, I cough for 10 minutes*, electronic poster by Siutaam.

8. *Occupy 1989 to 2014*, by Chinese artist Badiucao, a poster/graphic that makes a distinct connection between the Tiananmen Square protest of 1989 and the Hong Kong protest of 2014.

8.

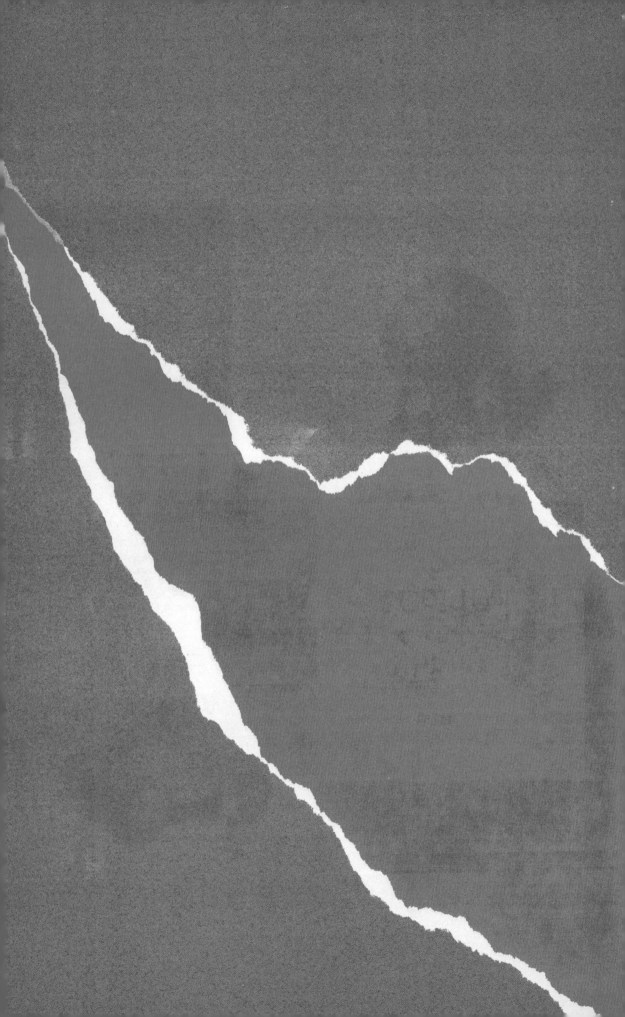

THE 360°
FRONTIER:
WARS IN
AFGHANISTAN
AND IRAQ

After the start of the US-led invasion of Iraq and the fall of Baghdad in April 2003, US Secretary of Defense Donald Rumsfeld responded to reporters' enquiries about the looting of the Baghdad palaces and ministry buildings with the infamous remark 'stuff happens'.[1] This passive, irresponsible phrase could be seen as a euphemism for events surrounding both of the wars that are the focus of this chapter. Words often used in hindsight to describe those wars – such as 'misguided' or 'mistaken' – never quite live up to the fog of disillusionment, or confusion of purpose, that allowed both wars to drag on for a decade while the public reeled over the human and material costs.

As time moved on, the wars in Iraq and Afghanistan would open up many frontiers of action: political deceit, misuse of the military, cultural destruction, religious divisions, internal power struggles, and last but not least, the mounting disapproval of US and UK citizens.[2] All would contribute to the notion of war as a crazed form of 'theatre in the round': no clearly defined battlefields, opposing sides or objectives, but myriad confusions from a 360-degree perspective. The nightmarish tapestry *Vote Alan Measles for God* (2008) by British artist Grayson Perry, crowded with military hardware, 9/11 references, video terrorists, oil wells, suicide bombings and many, many coffins illustrates appropriately the long-term sense of chaos.

The tragic events of 11 September 2001 shocked the world and set the USA on the road to retaliation as US President George W. Bush initiated the 'Global War on Terrorism', otherwise known as the 'War on Terror'.[3] In acknowledgement of the historic US/UK 'special relationship', British Prime Minister Tony Blair quickly joined Bush in the campaign, despite growing irritation and satirizing from the British press and public. The US fixed its sights on Afghanistan and initiated Operation Enduring Freedom, its military response to terrorist network Al-Qaida for the 9/11 attacks, with the help of a small coalition of countries including the UK. The aim was to capture the Al-Qaida leader, Osama bin Laden, rid Afghanistan of the Taliban regime and, more broadly, strike a blow against terrorism and the drugs trade (especially Afghan opium).[4]

Meanwhile, the US naval base in Guantanamo Bay in eastern Cuba became the most prominent site for detention of Al-Qaida or terror-related suspects. Since it is not located in a US territory, Guantanamo is not subject to US law nor obliged to uphold any of the rights normally allowed to US

prisoners. Guantanamo consequently became as well known for alleged torture, abuse and injury of prisoners, as it was for the bright orange overalls worn by the detainees. The treatment and incarceration of prisoners at Guantanamo has been a long-standing hot topic for anti-war and human rights protesters, particularly as suspects have, over the years, been detained without trial.[5]

In January 2002, Bush declared the existence of an 'axis of evil', naming Iraq, Iran and North Korea as countries who sponsored terrorism and armed themselves with 'Weapons of Mass Destruction' (WMDs) in order to threaten world peace.[6] There followed a number of attempts to send UN weapons inspectors to Iraq to search for WMDs, but all were inconclusive and the oppressive Iraqi leader Saddam Hussein did all he could to hinder the process.

'Patchy' information from an unreliable contact was fed into US intelligence dossiers concerning alleged WMDs and Iraqi ties with Al-Qaida; while in Britain the dossier that presented the government's case for war (later known as the 'dodgy dossier') not only claimed that Iraq possessed WMDs, but also that they could be deployed within forty-five minutes (a detail later proved to be unfounded).[7] The massive front-page headline '45 minutes from attack' carried by London's *Evening Standard* newspaper raised tension levels of both politicians and the public considerably.[8] Arguments continue to rage today as to whether either government knew there were flaws and false information in their intelligence. Nevertheless, in 2003 the leaders of both countries felt they had sufficient reasons for 'regime change' and justification for the invasion of Iraq. Once again, a coalition of countries agreed to invade, but there was no UN resolution to do so. (And to this day no weapons of mass destruction have ever been found.)

There was significant objection to the planned invasion and anti-war demonstrations were held worldwide. On 15 February 2003, over one million people marched through London in protest. It was a highly visual affair, parading placards from many trade unions and peace organizations, makeshift banners carried by young and old, and more than a few iconic posters. Some employed humour, such as advertizing and design agency Karmarama's 'Make tea not war' poster sporting a stern-looking Tony Blair, wearing a teacup on his head and holding an assault rifle. Others, such as David Gentleman's 'NO' poster, were angry, bold and – when repeated in a crowd – built up to a powerful crescendo (see page 110). Gentleman's highly effective 'splashes of blood' motif would reappear in many more protests for years to come, a haunting reminder of mounting casualties. Near simultaneous protests were held in over sixty countries worldwide with many millions of demonstrators in attendance – yet all their voices were ignored.

'Shock and Awe' was the phrase used to describe the overwhelming US airstrike of precision-guided missiles that pounded Baghdad, starting the War in Iraq (also known as the second Gulf War) on 19 March 2003. Saddam Hussein fled and on 9 April the central statue of the Iraqi dictator in downtown Baghdad was toppled, providing the myth-making news footage that marked the fall of the city.[9] Photographs of US soldiers lounging, joking and smoking in Saddam's palace also appeared in the global news media. On 1 May 2003, against the backdrop of a banner declaring 'Mission Accomplished' and wearing an airman's flight suit, Bush delivered his victory speech aboard aircraft carrier USS *Abraham Lincoln*. It was a heavily staged publicity coup, considered by many to be worryingly premature and a distasteful show of triumphalism.[10]

Later, in December that same year, US forces captured Saddam Hussein in northern Iraq with the help of Kurdish Special Forces. (He was tried by an Iraqi court and hanged in December 2006.) With Saddam captured, many thought this was the end of the conflict, to be followed by damage

repair and the rebuilding of the new Iraq. They were wrong.

IRAQ – FROM A DIFFERENT PERSPECTIVE

Iraqi citizens had already been suffering from ten years of sanctions. When Saddam Hussein invaded Kuwait in 1990, the UN imposed trade sanctions on Iraq. These stayed in place throughout the first Gulf War of 1991, including a blockade by coalition warships. Iraq's economy collapsed and ordinary Iraqis lacked jobs, food and medical supplies. The UN offered to let Iraq export oil in return for credits for food, medicine and other basics – but Saddam wouldn't agree until 1995. Beyond that, with WMD inspections taking place, the sanctions remained until the US invasion of 2003. Saddam lived royally throughout the period, building new palaces and asserting his power while countless numbers of civilians starved to death or died because of the shortages, many of them children.[11]

The impact of the economic sanctions therefore also fed into the ongoing story of the 2003 invasion and its post-war chaos, as told by Iraqi bloggers such as Riverbend (female) and Salam Pax (male).[12] Both resident in Baghdad, their blogs presented a wider, human perspective of the war than was possible to grasp via corporate and traditional news media.

In addition, emergent mobile technology at this time saw the rise of 'citizen journalism'. International news media began to use photographs and videos shot on phones by ordinary people, often at great personal risk. Again, this offered a broader perspective to news coverage and war reporting than ever achieved before. New technology also enabled 'whistle-blowing' and uncovered actions that might have previously remained hidden.

In May 2004 photographs of tortured Iraqis, made by civilians, soldiers and mercenaries at Abu Ghraib prison (a prison complex outside Baghdad used initially by Saddam Hussein's regime and then by US forces) were revealed on US television and disseminated globally. Not only did the photographs show US soldiers acting in an inhuman and abusive manner (and clearly enjoying it), they also projected an image of the 'occupiers' that was just as low as the tyrant that had been deposed. One of the most powerful images, a hooded Iraqi made to stand on a c-ration box in a 'stress position' (placing the body so that a great amount of weight is placed on just a few muscles causing intense pain) with arms open wide and wires apparently dangling from his body, was put to heavy use by the anti-war movement in coalition countries. It became representative of the way the conflict had moved beyond the notion of 'good vs evil' (as quoted by the politicians) to become a war that was out of control.[13]

The coalition occupiers never managed to get a grip on the power struggles (tribal, religious or Al-Qaida related) unleashed by the deposition of Saddam Hussein. The fighting carried on, as did the coalition and civilian casualties. Al-Qaida forces and other factions kept up terror attacks (employing numerous improvised explosive devices or IEDs), which saw a steady stream of dead, injured, disabled and traumatized coalition soldiers returning to their home countries.[14]

Years passed and there was still no solid plan for reconstruction: Iraqi civil society was destroyed; religious fundamentalism and Al-Qaida were on the rise; and a number of confusing exit plans for coalition troops were proposed. George Bush left the White House; Barack Obama entered in 2009 and withdrew US troops from Iraq in 2011. Nevertheless, in 2014 the US State Department still had the responsibility of training Iraqi police and operating drones. UK troops were also withdrawn in 2011, as national newspapers bitterly observed that still no weapons of mass destruction had been found.[15]

Since 2001, our experience and understanding of the Wars in Afghanistan and Iraq have included over ten years of questioning and debating many issues: some through news media, some through activism in the street, some through creative practice. Over that period of time, blame or regret over the illegitimacy or illegality of the wars never left our newspapers, magazines or computer screens. This chapter explores how artists and designers have tackled some of the issues relating to those wars. The motives behind the wars have been interrogated by projects such as the elabo-

BUT WHAT OF AFGHANISTAN?

The conflict in Afghanistan remained unresolved. By 2005 much of the US and UK military resources had been directed to the war in Iraq. As time passed and the world's attention was diverted, there was a Taliban resurgence. Troops became disillusioned and Afghanistan slowly moved out of focus of the media as Osama bin Laden was still nowhere in sight.

However, after withdrawing US troops from Iraq in 2011, Obama increased US military presence in Afghanistan. He ramped up the controversial use of drones (remotely piloted, unmanned aircraft) to search for Al-Qaida and their associates.[16] Drones had been used for surveillance and occasional targeting since the early 2000s, but the notion of fighting a sanitized war from the air, that seemed to inflict substantial collateral damage, didn't sit well with many US-friendly nations, including Britain. Drones are however big business in the US and aren't going to go away.[17]

Osama bin Laden was finally killed in a covert US Special Forces operation in Pakistan in 2011, and October 2014 saw the withdrawal of both UK and US troops and advisors from Afghanistan. However a new threat has presented itself in Iraq, the jihadist group known as Islamic State, and the US has once again ordered airstrikes to help the Iraqi and Kurdish troops fighting on the ground but (to date) refuses to send in US ground troops.

rate *War on Terror: The Boardgame*. The nature of modern conflict has been confronted by anti-drone activists in many forms of direct action. While the nature of heroism has been contemplated through the manipulation of toy soldiers in both David Levinthal's thoughtful soft-focus photographs and the Dorothy art collective's customized figurines. It is little wonder that towards the end of this chapter and over a period of ten years, artists and designers turned to the act of documenting. It is a manner of reflecting, of looking for lessons to be learned and of avoiding repetition. Yet, although the conflict in Afghanistan is apparently over, Iraq is hotting up again, and an interview with a doctor operating in a secret hospital in Syria (see page 142) points to a very unpredictable future.

YOU HAVE
A DREAM,
I HAVE
A DRONE

UnitedUnknown.com/i-have-a-drone

Page 104. *Vote Alan Measles for God*, by Grayson Perry. Handmade wool tapestry with War on Terror imagery, and his childhood toy appearing as an incarnation of war. Also influenced by the designs and drawings used in Afghan war rugs, and other popular imagery of the time. UK 2007.

Page 105. Afghan war rug, produced after 2001. War rugs have a long, complex history but are usually assumed to be products of Afghanistan and the surrounding areas. They take their imagery from 'modern', popular subjects and scenarios, hence more recently from wars.

Page 106. Left: Front page of the *Daily Mirror* newspaper, 14 February 2003, right before the start of the Iraq invasion.

Although it openly makes fun of the 'special relationship' between Britain and the US, the message was deadly serious: don't go to war. Top right: Photograph of 15 February 2003 London march against the War in Iraq, by Peter Macdiarmid/Reuters. Below right: Photograph by David Levinthal from his *I.E.D.* project about war. USA 2008. IED's – improvised explosive devices – were bombs planted in roads and buildings by resistance fighters, and a major source of death or maiming for the US and other occupying forces, as well as civilians, in Iraq and Afghanistan.

Page 107. Artist David Gentleman's 'splashes of blood' motif for the Stop the War Coalition featured

in the installation, *100,000 Drops of Blood*. It was staged in Parliament Square in February 2006 with each drop representing an Iraqi, American or British death in Iraq due to the war. Photograph by Jess Hurd.

Page 108. Left: Artist David Gentleman's 'splashes of blood' motif for the Stop the War Coalition, shown here on march placards used to protest against the invasion of Iraq and particularly aimed at Prime Minister Tony Blair and other politicians. UK 2003 onwards. Right: US anti-drone protesters with a mock drone, carrying messages aimed at Obama, the government and the public. One protester dons orange overalls, which were heavily associated with Guantanamo ('Gitmo') prison-

wear. Photograph by Kevin Lamarque/Reuters.

Page 109. Electronic poster that manipulates the famous quote from Martin Luther King – 'I have a dream' – to protest Obama's use of drones. By the anonymous group of online activists, The United Unknown. USA 2013.

2003:
'DON'T ATTACK IRAQ!'

With the 'War on Terror' declared and the War in Afghanistan already engaged, it soon became clear in early 2003 that the US/UK 'special relationship' was headed towards an invasion of Iraq with the intention of 'regime change' through the ousting of Saddam Hussein. Doubts over WMD claims and suspicions as to governmental motivations circulated and protests reverberated around the world.

On 15 February 2003 over one million people marched through London in what was 'the biggest political protest in British history'. The streets were filled with hardcore activists as well as people who had never marched before; all ages were present and families came with babies and buggies in tow. It was a visual extravaganza with a sea of posters, placards and banners shouting slogans: 'Make tea not war', 'Not in my name', 'Regime change starts at home', 'Don't attack Iraq!' or simply 'NO'. Millions more marched around the world in over 300 cities and sixty countries. Much of the blame for the impending conflict was aimed at the US and UK leaders George Bush and Tony Blair, politicians and the oil industry.

Other important visual agitation markers of that time included projects initiated by, or in collaboration with, Britain's Stop the War Coalition. Founded in September 2001, the group was dedicated to stopping the wars in Afghanistan and Iraq as well as making their voices heard on other issues such as supporting Palestinian rights.[18] Believing in the power of visual messages, they also engaged heavily with the art and design community. In 2003 Stop the War commissioned a series of eight anti-Iraq war posters from a number of Britain's best-known graphic artists and cartoonists. David Gentleman's NO poster with its splashes of blood motif was one of the most dominant images of the 15 February march, while Jamie Reid's poster of John Wayne wearing lipstick and sporting a badge saying 'Peace is tough' is highly distinctive, suggesting that the heroic notion of testosterone-fuelled wars has failed and that peace is the real challenge.

Recognition cards, whether aimed at troops or civilians, have been present in a number of recent conflicts. A reproduction pack of playing cards issued by the US military to their troops depicted the fifty-two 'most wanted' Iraqi figures in the war in Iraq. UK designer Noel Douglas appropriated the concept for the British anti-war movement in a pack entitled *Regime Change Begins At Home* (2003). The cards show the 'most un-wanted individuals and organizations – the warmongers and profiteers within our own countries' who pose a threat to global peace and security.

1.

1. *NO* (War in Iraq), poster by David Gentleman for the Stop the War Coalition, which was carried in the 15 February march in London against the War in Iraq. UK 2003.

2. *Make Tea Not War*, poster by ad agency Karmarama, carried in the 15 February march in London against the War in Iraq. UK 2003.

3. *Regime Change Begins At Home*, a selection from a set of playing cards designed by Noel Douglas, showing 'our most un-wanted individuals and organisations – the warmongers and profiteers within our own countries'. They were created in response to the *Iraqi Most Wanted* playing cards issued by the US military to their troops as a means of recognizing 'the enemy' (selected cards from a reproduction pack created by The USA Playing Card Company are shown at the bottom). UK 2003 / USA 2003.

KARMARAMA

2.

A ♠	A ♣	A ♦	K ♥	Q ♠	9 ♠
GEORGE W BUSH aka "Dubya" **President of the United States** "This is still a dangerous world. It's a world of madmen and uncertainty, and potential mental losses."	**TONY BLAIR** aka "Bomber Blair" **British prime minister** "It's worse than you think, I really do believe in it" —on the neo-liberal project of New Labour.	**JAMES D WOLFENSOHN President of the World Bank** 20 million people are not going to get out of poverty"—explaining why the bank should focus on other issues.	**ROBERT MALLETT Senior VP Pfizer** "We are pricing by market. Generic AIDS drugs—30 cents. Pfizer equivalent—$1.70.	**DONALD RUMSFELD US Secretary of Defense** It has nothing to do with oil, literally nothing to do with oil." But then again... "In wartime, truth is so precious that she should always be attended by a bodyguard of lies." (quoting Churchill).	**CONDOLEEZZA RICE US National Security Advisor** "The idea that you have to wait to be attacked to deal with a threat seems to us simply to fly in the face of common sense." A former Chevron Oil executive so popular with the industry she had a supertanker named after her!

3.

A ♠	A ♣	A ♥	K ♠	Q ♥	Q ♦
SADDAM HUSAYN AL-TIKRITI President	**QUSAY SADDAM HUSAYN AL-TIKRITI** Special Security Organization (SSO) Supervisor/Ba'th Party Military Bureau Deputy Chairman	**UDAY SADDAM HUSAYN AL-TIKRITI** National Assembly Member/ Olympic Chairman/ Saddam Feyadeen Chief	**ALI HASAN AL-MAJID AL-TIKRITI** Presidential Advisor/ RCC Member	**BARZAN ABD AL-GHAFUR SULAYMAN MAJID AL-TIKRITI** Special Republican Guard Commander	**MUZAHIM SA'B HASAN AL-TIKRITI** Air Defense Forces Commander

Also operating in the run-up to the Iraq war was the French artist Blek le Rat, one of the most revered figures in stencilling and street art (and apparently a large influence on the UK street artist Banksy). He laid the foundations for street art in 1980s Paris, creating stencils of humans and rats that he sprayed all over Paris. He then moved on to stencilled posters and cut outs, pasted onto walls. In the following decades his work dealt with overtly political themes. In early 2003, demonstrating his disapproval of invading Iraq, he took part in the anti-war demonstrations in Paris and pasted-up posters of a US soldier (shown here) as he went along – often with the word 'NO' stencilled on the soldier's chest.[19]

In the US, where there was substantial visual protest to the war, Steven Lyons' *No Blood For Oil* poster stands out for its colourful artwork and popular slogan as well as its use for both Gulf Wars (1991 and reprinted for 2003). It evidences the belief held by many in the anti-war movement that the possession of Iraqi oil may be the root cause behind the invasion. US cartoonist and writer Peter Kuper pointed an incriminating finger at George W. Bush for choosing to ignore many of his nation's ills, preferring to invade and wreak devastation in another country instead. Both posters represent main themes – the slippery oil industry and even more slippery politicians – still present in the US anti-war movement.

4.

5.

6.

4. *No Blood For Oil* poster by Steven Lyons, originally created in 1990 for the first Gulf War, then reprinted in 2003 for the second Gulf War (the War in Iraq). USA.

5. *Ceci n'est pas une comic* (This is not a comic), poster by New York illustrator and writer Peter Kuper, pointing towards political deceit and counting out reasons not to start a war. USA 2003.

6. *Peace is Tough* (John Wayne with lipstick), poster created by Jamie Reid in 1992 and used again by the Stop the War Coalition to protest the War in Iraq. UK 2003.

7 and 8. Stencilled posters of US soldier with 'NO', created by French artist Blek le Rat. (Above) A stencilled soldier appears at Checkpoint Charlie in Berlin. (Below) Blek le Rat pasted up stencilled soldiers along the routes of anti-war marches in Paris, as shown here on a bus shelter. France 2003.

7.

8.

VISUALIZING THE SHAME OF ABU GHRAIB

Although Bush declared 'Mission Accomplished' on 1 May 2003, the invasion of Iraq became 'the occupation' of Iraq and, with violence escalating, there seemed no possible cut-off point. An insurgency ensued, and in an attempt to identify the enemy, thousands of (possibly innocent) Iraqi men were captured by the US military for questioning. They were thrown into a prison complex at Abu Ghraib, west of Baghdad, which had formerly been used by Saddam Hussein for imprisonment and torture, and so had particularly fearsome associations in the minds of Iraqis.[20]

On 4 May 2004 the CBS News programme *60 Minutes II* broadcast a series of shocking photographs of abused and tortured Iraqis at Abu Ghraib prison.[21] The whistle-blower Joe Darby, a US Army reservist serving in the military police at Abu Ghraib, had been casually handed the pictures, and finding them deeply upsetting he passed them to the US Army's criminal investigator on site. The army began criminal enquiries but the images were also leaked to the media. As news spread, it became clear that such abuse and torture were commonplace and the military police involved had taken the digital pictures 'just for fun'.[22]

Once leaked, the brutal and sadistic images were everywhere: a female guard holds a type of leash that is collared to a naked Iraqi man lying on the floor; a hooded prisoner in a poncho is made to stand on a box with arms outstretched and wires dangling from his body; a male and female guard grin broadly behind a pyramid of naked Iraqi prisoners; military dogs are used to terrify naked Iraqi prisoners; and many more images showing nudity and activities specifically designed to humiliate Muslim sensibilities and offend the Islamic religion.[23]

The visual evidence of Americans committing such atrocities hit hard and artists and activists seized the opportunity to use the images in anti-war statements that were equally memorable. The hooded prisoner standing on a box with wires dangling from him became a symbolic representation of everything that had gone wrong with the war. Its power as a Christ-like image, particularly when thrown into silhouette, was substantial. Two design collectives, Copper Green (New York) and Forkscrew Graphics (Los Angeles) used stylistic elements from Apple's iPod advertizing campaign to create a series of anti-war posters that were available for download by activists. The entire poster series is colourful and eye-catching, but it was the application of the familiar Apple styling to the hooded prisoner image that created one of the most iconic and damning anti-war posters of the era. The graphic treatment is stark and simple; the idea behind the image unbearable.

1.

1. *Liberty*, two views of a 3D postcard which, when tilted, changes from the Statue of Liberty to the hooded Abu Ghraib prisoner. Design/ photomontage by Leon Kuhn. UK 2004.

2. *iRaq*, iconic anti-war poster utilizing the silhouette of a hooded prisoner being tortured, taken from one of the photographs in the Abu Ghraib scandal. By Forkscrew Graphics, Los Angeles and Copper Green, New York. USA 2004.

2.

At the same time art activist Leon Kuhn made a similar bold play on the Abu Ghraib imagery by associating the hooded prisoner with the Statue of Liberty. Whether slowly morphing from one image to another on a holographic postcard, or simply substituting the hooded prisoner for Liberty on a t-shirt or poster, the result is a brutal comment targeting Bush's so-called war of 'good vs evil' and American notions of decency.

Although the art world was initially slow to react to the Iraq War, in 2005–06 art criticizing the invasion began to be exhibited in major museums around the world, including Washington, DC. One of the most visible works was the cycle of paintings produced by Colombian artist Fernando Botero. Living in Paris and New York, Botero was so shocked by reports of the Abu Ghraib scandal that he spent eleven months working obsessively on sketches and paintings that would bear testimony to the events. (Interestingly his inspiration came from reading feverishly about the incidents, rather than viewing the photos.) The result is a series of over fifty works that focus on the vulnerability of the prisoners: naked men are blindfolded, beaten, dressed in women's underwear, forced into humiliating positions, dangling from ropes, harassed by vicious dogs and more – creating a shaming 'permanent accusation' of wrongful actions.[24]

The scandal of Abu Ghraib did irreparable damage to America's image throughout the world, and within its own borders. All the military police involved were punished and the prison commander demoted – but the photographs and the protest images remain.[25]

3. *Like Apple Fucking Pie*, by artist Clinton Fein, showing an image of the American flag – but the stars are formed from the repeated silhouette of the hooded Abu Ghraib prisoner, and the stripes are text relating to the investigation of the abuses committed. USA 2004–05.

4 and 5. Paintings by the Colombian painter, Fernando Botero, from a series relating to the Abu Ghraib scandal, exhibited widely in the USA. (4: *Abu Ghraib 45, 2005*, and 5. triptych: *Abu Ghraib 44, 2005*) France / USA 2005.

3.

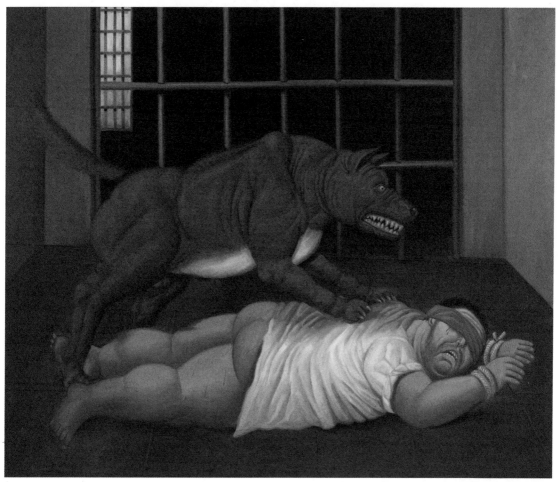

4.

5.

COUNTING THE DEAD

From 2005 onwards, the War in Afghanistan moved into the background while the War in Iraq stayed in focus. Yet it became clear that both wars had entered a period of the unknown with no clear strategies, no pause in the escalating violence and no end in sight. A process of counting began that would continue throughout both wars: the counting of material losses to Iraqi and Afghan economies, infrastructure, hospitals, schools, power supplies, security, food and medicine. And the counting of material costs to the coalition for airpower, soldiers on the ground, equipment and weaponry, hospitals, energy and power, security, food and medicine. Plus the human costs to both sides: the dead, the injured (physically and mentally), the funerals, the bereavements, the shattered lives. For US and UK citizens, counting took the place of political or military strategies, direction or reasoning.

For the coalition this process of counting rarely encouraged notions of 'winning' or feelings of security, as in the first Gulf War when media and press briefings brought endless maps, charts and displays of military hardware and precision-guided weapons, alongside promises of sanitized warfare and a 'quick fix' (see page 21). Instead the counting revealed the imbalances in numbers killed on both sides, told through elaborate info-graphics that brilliantly communicated complex statistics and made the depressing information all the more accessible. Images of coffins draped with US or UK flags remained a potent symbol of those who fought and died, and their appearance inevitably initiated a silent tally of death and loss. The power of the symbol can be seen in the mock advertisement shown here, depicting cars as soldiers' coffins in order to make the connection between oil addiction and the wars in the Middle East.

The costs were counted almost anytime and anywhere – shown in a flyer handed out at a Foo Fighters concert in Tampa, Florida, in 2005, entitled *Mission Accomplished*. Dick Cheney, Vice President to the Bush Administration for two terms and a leading advocate of the US wars in the Middle East, is depicted as a flasher hiding a woeful string of statistics about the Iraq War beneath his raincoat. The list amounts to a passionate anti-war message, and is a clear indication of the growing sense of disillusionment and anger.

1. *31 days in Iraq, 2007,* an infographic illustrating Iraqi civilian deaths in January 2007; it ran in the *New York Times* in February 2007. Designed by Adriana Lins de Albuquerque and Alicia Cheng. USA 2007.

2. *The ultimate price of oil addiction.* Mock advertisement in the US political magazine *Mother Jones,* December 2004. Cars rolling off the production line are made to resemble soldiers' coffins. USA 2004.

3. Front and back of a flyer handed out at a Foo Fighters rock concert in Florida entitled *Mission Accomplished.* The flasher is Dick Cheney, George W. Bush's Vice President and a heavy advocate of Bush's wars. USA 2005.

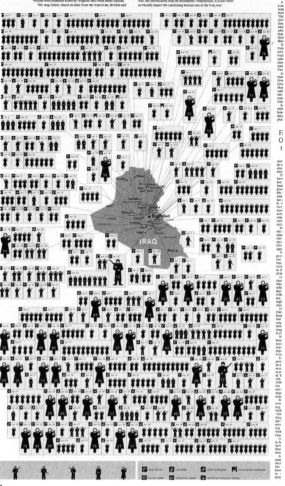

1.

The ultimate price of oil addiction.

Gas guzzling is a dangerous addiction, and Ford Motor Company doesn't know when to say when.

The facts don't lie. Ford is on an oil binge. According to the EPA, Ford cars and trucks have ranked the worst in overall fuel efficiency of all major automakers for 20 out of the last 30 years including every year since 2000. Ford's fleet today gets fewer miles per gallon on average that the Model-T did 80 years ago.

Americans are paying the ultimate price for oil addiction. The United States consumes more oil and emits more greenhouse gases than any other nation on Earth, and the auto industry is the single largest cause of our oil addiction. More than 50 percent of our

oil comes from conflict regions like the Middle East, and here at home, more than 100 million Americans live in cities that exceed federal health guidelines for air quality.

Declare independence from oil and demand zero emissions cars today at JumpStartFord.com. Jumpstart Ford is an international grassroots campaign to compel America's flagship automaker to chart a new course to a zero emissions future. Join the movement calling on Ford to improve its fleet-wide fuel efficiency to 50 mpg by 2010 and eliminate tailpipe emissions by 2020.

JUMPSTART Ford
JumpStartFord.com

2.

MISSION ACCOMPLISHED.

What is he hiding?

Mission accomplished? Only if that mission was fighting a mis-guided war, stretching our Army to the breaking point, and throw-ing more fuel onto the already raging fire of global terrorism.

Even the Bush Administration admits that the number of global terrorist attacks has tripled since the war began, topping 650 in 2004. The conflict in Iraq has created a training ground for the next generation of terrorists as foreign fighters pour into the country to wage war against U.S. and Iraqi forces.

Meanwhile, after more than two years of intense fighting, our military is close to broken. The Army can't meet its recruitment goals. Our soldiers are still being sent to fight with faulty equip-ment and insufficient armor. Fully 72% of soldiers first deployed to Iraq report "low" or "very low" unit morale. We have almost 2,000 young Americans, another 14,000 have been wounded, and we have spent over $200 billion on the war. **We can do better.**

Find out more at **campusprogress.org/Iraq.**

{ •PROGRESS }
Center for American Progress

Not afraid to expose the truth.

3.

PROTEST AND SATIRE IN POPULAR CULTURE

1.

As the years passed, the actions and images of the global War on Terror were subsumed into popular culture in interesting ways. Frustrated by the start of the Iraq War despite mass marches and protests, Cambridge-based web designers Andrew Sheerin and Andy Tompkins devised 'War on Terror: The Boardgame' (2006), which satirized the Bush Administration and the build-up that pre-empted the UK's entry into the War in Iraq. The game requires two to six players: each player builds an empire on the world map, acquiring land, oil and cities. An empire can decide of its own accord to become a 'terror state' or it can be randomly chosen to be one through use of an 'Axis of Evil spinner' (in which case that player has to don an enclosed balaclava with 'EVIL' stitched across it). An empire can also train terrorists to attack other empires, although there's always the risk that the terrorists might turn against their creator. The terrorists can use cards such as 'Suicide Bomber' or 'Plane Hijack' to get ahead. Overall, the empires compete and wage war against each other, using such tactics as espionage, 'regime change' or forcing their competitors to sign-up to the Kyoto protocol in order to bring on bankruptcy or ruination.[26]

High-street stores in the UK claimed they couldn't sell the game because of lack of interest. Within two years 12,000 copies were sold online and through independent stockists, where it obviously connected with its audience. It achieved further status when one game was seized from protesters and confiscated by police during a raid on a much-publicized climate change camp near Kingsnorth power station. The game was allegedly taken because the balaclava could be used to conceal identity in the course of committing a criminal act![27]

1 and 2. 'War on Terror: The Boardgame', a satirical view of the Global War on Terror. Also shown are the 'Terrorist Attack' card, the 'Suicide Bomber' card, and the 'Weapons Inspector' card included. The game was created by web designers Andrew Sheerin and Andy Tompkins. UK 2006.

TERRORIST ATTACK

Lock up your civil liberties, the terrorists are here.

Incite any terrorist unit to attack the development in the country they occupy or incite terrorist infighting.

Roll to attack the following sized units

				6	7	8	9	10	11
				6	7	8	9	10	
				6	7	8	9		

■ Strike ☐ Partial Strike

2.

WEAPONS INSPECTOR

You need to make sure they haven't got anything that might trouble your liberating forces.

Inspect another player's cards. Confiscate and keep any *Nuclear Weapons* or *WMDs* that you find.

SUICIDE BOMBER

Like a boomerang, but more dangerous. And he doesn't come back.

Requires at least a Terrorist Vanguard ◯ in target country.

2	3	4	5	6	7	8	9	10	11	12

■ Terrorists destroy themselves and target.
■ Terrorists blow themselves up but little else.

'Make love not war' was a popular anti-war slogan used during the Vietnam War in the 1960s and early 1970s. It originated within hippie culture but had proliferated through a wide range of protest cultures by the end of the war and has kept surfacing ever since.

Artist and activist Favianna Rodriguez provided a modern update to the well-worn slogan with 'Make out not war', while also reviving the ageing peace symbol, in a poster that sizzled with heat and the power of protest. This approach was appropriate for the people behind the poster, CODEPINK – a highly active, women-led peace group founded by Medea Benjamin and Jodie Evans. Their name satirizes the Bush Administration's Homeland Security colour-coded alert system (yellow, orange, red) warning of a potential terrorist threat. CODEPINK believed that the 9/11 attackers should be brought to justice, but not by taking the nation to war. They argued for a re-examination of US military presence around the world (suggesting that there were too many bases causing anti-American resentment) and a review of US support for the Israeli government. They fought hard – organizing mass rallies and even staging hunger strikes – in an attempt to get US troops withdrawn from Iraq. CODEPINK backed Barack Obama in the 2008 elections and his removal of troops from Iraq in 2011. However they were horrified when he then increased troops in Afghanistan. He also engaged in drone warfare soon after his inauguration and has continued to favour high-tech weaponry. Appalled by the civilian casualties involved, CODEPINK continues to campaign against drone warfare to this day.[28]

Another, barely recognizable version of 'Make love not war' was offered in absurdist form by Seattle-based design company Modern Dog. Known globally for their off-the-wall humour, Modern Dog's chewing gum packaging stating *More Bill Less Kill* (2006) is a modern update of the same anti-war message. 'More Bill' alludes to President Bill Clinton's affair with intern Monica Lewinsky in 1998–09, while 'less kill' rather speaks for itself.

3.

www.CODEPINKALERT.org

4.

3. *More Bill Less Kill*, chewing gum packaging by graphics studio Modern Dog. USA 2006.

4–5. *Make Out Not War*, and *Make Bridges Not Enemies*, posters by artist and activist Favianna Rodriguez for the women-led, anti-war, and later, anti-drone organisation CODEPINK. USA 2008.

5.

The Dorothy art collective, based in Manchester in the UK, is known for mixing satire with provocation. Deeply serious, often political subjects – torture, war, and environmental pollution – have been tackled head-on and communicated with a brutally subversive sense of humour.

The *Guantanamo Bay Collection* is a mock fashion shoot produced for the 'Corruption Issue' of *Ctrl.Alt.Shift* magazine. The adventurous magazine ran from 2008 to 2010 as a project by UK charity Christian Aid, aiming to introduce young people to issues of social injustice and activism. Through its magazine and associated website, the *Ctrl.Alt.Shift* project initiated demonstrations and marches as well as exhibitions and events dealing with topics of the time – war, global conflicts, gender issues, poverty, HIV/AIDS – and attracted significant media attention.[30]

In the *Guantanamo Bay Collection*, Adrian Nettleship's slick photography simulates the high quality and professionalism of a fashion shoot. Yet the collection comprises symbolic representations of the torture and abuse thought to be common in Guantanamo Bay and Abu Ghraib, as well as in other secret detention centres believed to be operating outside of the terms of the Geneva Convention (see page 114). One image references the hooded prisoner from Abu Ghraib, representing the use of hooding, 'stress positions' and electroshock. A picture of a bound man, lying face down on the floor suggests the use of nudity and humiliation techniques, as well as binding, beating and sensory deprivation. Another image recreates a form of torture known as 'waterboarding' or simulated drowning, where a prisoner is strapped down with their face covered with a cloth then doused with water to produce the feeling of drowning.[30] The grimly satirical images point to serious debates about secret detention centres, the practice of torture and US treatment of 'unlawful combatants' (captured individuals who were not considered 'prisoners' and therefore fell outside the legal frameworks normally protecting prisoners).[31]

6–9. *The Guantanamo Bay Collection*, mock fashion shoot produced for The Corruption Issue of *Ctrl. Alt.Shift* magazine (Volume 2, Issue 1) and a satire on the use of torture in the War on Terror. By Dorothy art collective. UK 2009–10. Photography by Adrian Nettleship.

6.

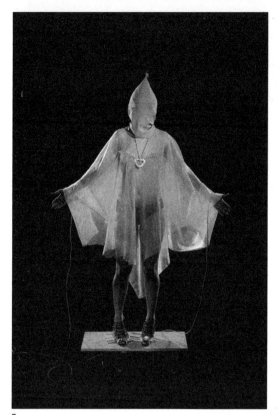

7.

8.

9.

REFLECTIONS ON WAR

Fiona Banner investigates war by reinterpreting objects associated with it and collating the images and language surrounding them. Her project *All the World's Fighter Planes* (1999–2009) is a collection of newspaper images of every fighter plane in service during that time period. The cuttings were bound together in book form in 2004 and 2006; the nicknames of the enclosed aircraft are listed on the front and back cover. The news images demonstrate our everyday perception of these planes as tiny objects more often than not looking like mechanical toys or alien bugs. They are rarely seen up close at actual size. They seem very detached from human experience, yet the listed names on the cover often take on the names of birds or animals and resonate with nature.[32]

Then in 2010–11 Banner took her examination to the next level. In Tate Britain's spacious Duveen Galleries, she installed two decommissioned fighter planes in a work entitled *Harrier and Jaguar* (both models still in active service at that time). In the South Gallery, a Sea Harrier was suspended vertically from the ceiling, nose cone almost brushing the ground. The inversion turned the machine into a serene, bird-like form, overwhelming and beautiful as a piece of sculpture devoid of its ferocity or predatory nature – yet still a killing machine. In the North Gallery, a Sepecat Jaguar, stripped of paint and highly polished, was laid belly-up on the floor. Again, its positioning produced a sculptural object of beauty, like a big cat waiting to be stroked. In both cases, the human-machine relationship changed dramatically. And the contention between the beautiful form and the deadly function was deeply unsettling.[33]

1. *Harrier*, installation using a BAe Sea Harrier aircraft, (7.6 × 14.2 × 3.71 metres (24 × 46 × 12 feet) by the artist Fiona Banner, Tate Britain Duveens Commission. UK 2010.

1.

Kennardphillipps' masterful photomontage entitled *Photo Op* (2005) transposes an image of UK Prime Minister Tony Blair grabbing a 'selfie' against a background of burning oilfields. The piece echoed the rising tide of public opinion that blamed Blair for leading the UK into wars in Afghanistan, and then Iraq despite overwhelming protest. He stepped down as Prime Minister in 2007 but was pursued for 'crimes against peace' by the anti-war movement for years after.

During the time of the Vietnam War, US artist Martha Rosler produced a powerful photomontage series entitled *Bringing the War Home: House Beautiful* (c.1967–72). She used advertisements of ideal American home interiors carried within *Life* magazine and combined them with photos of Vietnamese civilians and soldiers, often selected from within that same magazine. The critique of the morality of the Vietnam War was explicit; so was the critique of wars waged in distant places, that can only be seen or experienced via the television (and may therefore seem unreal or be easily forgotten).

Decades later, Rosler responded to the US involvement in Afghanistan and Iraq – which she saw as a similar military adventure – in a comparable way, using photomontage to juxtapose the model US home with scenes from modern distant wars, thereby ensuring once again that viewers must not be allowed to simply ignore or disengage from such conflicts.

2. *Photo Op*, photomontage by UK artists kennardphillipps, showing Prime Minister Tony Blair doing a 'selfie' against a background of burning oilfields. UK 2005.

3. *Gladiators* photomontage by US artist Martha Rosler, relating to US involvement in Iraq and Afghanistan. USA 2004.

4. *The Gray Drape*, photomontage by US artist Martha Rosler in response to US involvement in Afghanistan and Iraq. US 2004. Both images 3 and 4 combine the notion of modern home living in the West with the carnage created in foreign wars; from the series *Bringing the War Home: House Beautiful* (Iraq).

2.

3.

4.

HEROES, CASUALTIES AND MEMORIALS

US photographer David Levinthal's projects about war, brought together in his 2013 exhibition and book entitled *War Games*, consist of defocused photographs of constructed battle scenarios peopled by collectible figures or toy soldiers and their paraphernalia. The powerful, dream-like quality of the photographs evokes childhood imaginings of playtime battles and romanticized heroics. And despite the frequent use of soft focus, the viewer never loses their ability to read a shape. Instead there is a constant interplay between dream and reality.

In Levinthal's project, *I.E.D.* (2008), his blurred soldiers seem to be scouting, moving in slow motion, caught in suspended animation or lost in their own absence of thought. They are identifiable only by occasional glimpses of blood and the beige uniforms of desert campaigns. The weight of tension or presence of the unknown lurking in the shadows is unbearable. This is not a childlike war of heroic stances and gestures; it is an adult war full of fear and horror.

The project title is particularly apropos; IEDs – or improvised explosive devices – were bombs, often planted in roads or buildings, deployed by resistance fighters in both Iraq and Afghanistan and were a major source of death and injury for the US and other occupying forces.[34]

The *Casualties of War* action figures, a starkly serious project created by the subversive UK art collective Dorothy, were inspired by two articles about soldiers returning home. A two-part series published in July 2009 by the *Colorado Springs Gazette* (entitled 'Casualties of War') focused on a battalion based in Colorado Springs who, after returning from duty in Iraq, had been involved in beatings, rape, suicide and other violent acts. Returning soldiers were committing murder at a much higher rate than other young US males. Another investigation into suicide among veterans (published in the *New York Times*) in October 2010 disclosed that three times as many Californian veterans and active-service members died soon after returning home than those killed in Iraq and Afghanistan combined.[35]

Moved by the plight of real soldiers returning home from duty, Dorothy chose plastic toy soldiers (and the childhood imaginings of the heroics of war) as tools for presenting a different kind of comment. They created a box set of four 7-centimetre (2¾-inch) high resin-moulded figurines fashioned like familiar plastic toy soldiers, but showing cruel realities: one is committing suicide, one berates a cowering woman, one is begging in the street and the last is in a wheelchair with an amputated leg.

1.

1. Photographs by David Levinthal from the project *I.E.D.*, relating to the wars in Afghanistan and Iraq and consisting of defocused, dream-like images of battle scenarios using collectible figures and toy soldiers. USA 2008.

2. *Casualties of War*, action figures created by Manchester-based Dorothy art collective, showing the realities of soldiers returning home from the war. UK 2012.

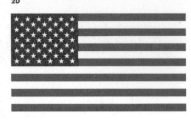

Whether acting as an anti-war statement or a call for support for veteran's associations, their impact is substantial – and might earn Dorothy a few accusations of bad taste. However they reveal the brutal nature of the after effects of war – and the problems that often return home with the veterans.

Some soldiers don't return home at all. German poster artist Lex Drewinski's stark image of a 2D American flag transitioning to a 3D flag-draped coffin is extremely powerful. Its simplicity allows for multiple anti-war interpretations: fighting America's wars brings death; misguided patriotism and where US interests go, death follows.

3.

One of the most sensitive memorials to the British soldiers killed in Iraq is *Queen and Country* (2007) produced by the Turner Prize-winner Steve McQueen. The artist was sent to Iraq in 2003 as an official war artist by the Imperial War Museum, but on arriving at his destination in Basra, he found his movements so restricted that he only stayed for six days. He returned home with nothing more than the conversations he had had with the soldiers there.[36]

Inspired by the people he had met, however, McQueen had the idea of putting faces on a postage stamp as a way of commemorating those killed in action. Eager to contact the families, McQueen found that the Ministry of Defence wasn't keen and a request to the Director of Royal Mail to produce real commemorative stamps was rejected. McQueen carried on independently and out of 115 families contacted, 98 offered portraits of their child or relative for use in the project. The pictures were made into 98 sheets of facsimile stamps. Each sheet contains 168 stamps (12 across, 14 down) bearing the face of a lost member of the armed forces, as well as their name and when they died. The sheets of stamps weren't perforated, but small dots were printed instead.[37]

The 98 sheets were arranged chronologically, according to date of death, and each sheet was presented in a sliding vertical drawer housed in a standing wood cabinet. Moving slowly between the sheets of stamps, in close contact with the sea of faces, was a very intimate experience and underlined the tragedy of lost life. McQueen himself considers the project unfinished until the portraits are formally issued as stamps by the Royal Mail, allowing the smiling faces to flow through the postal system in a sea of letters up and down the country – visiting many homes as a reminder of the importance of remembering sacrifice.

Both McQueen and Britain's leading art charity, the Art Fund, led a campaign for an official set of postage stamps to be issued, with a supporting petition – but to no avail. The Art Fund gifted the cabinet of facsimile stamps to the Imperial War Museum in 2007 and toured the work to museums and galleries nationally from 2007 to 2010.[38]

3. A 2D American flag shifts to a 3D flag-draped military coffin, a simple but effective graphic statement from poster artist Lex Drewinski. Germany 2006.

4. *Queen and Country*, artist and filmmaker Steve McQueen's attempt to commemorate soldiers who lost their lives in Iraq by placing photographs of their faces on postage stamps. It succeeded as an art installation of facsimile stamps, but an official set of stamps was never produced by Royal Mail. UK 2006–10.

LANCE CORPORAL BENJAMIN HYDE ADJUTANT GENERAL'S CORPS (ROYAL MILITARY POLICE) DIED 24 JUNE 2003 AGED 23

LANCE CORPORAL BENJAMIN HYDE ADJUTANT GENERAL'S CORPS (ROYAL MILITARY POLICE) DIED 24 JUNE 2003 AGED 23

4.

MAKING WAR INVISIBLE: DRONE WARFARE

Shepard Fairey's *Hope* portrait poster of Barack Obama was ubiquitous throughout the 2008 campaign for the US Presidency, and has been credited as having a substantial influence on Obama's victory. It was also heavily appropriated: the style was copied, sometimes the face changed, but often Obama or symbols of his administration remained with the word 'Hope' morphed into 'Dope', 'Joke' and other similar titles.

Obama ran as the peace candidate and many expected that he might change the direction set by the Bush Administration by, for example, bringing the troops home from Iraq and Afghanistan or closing Guantanamo. Obama signed an official order for the closure of Guantanamo upon taking office, but the issues and practicalities of either returning detainees to their home countries or bringing them to the US for trial proved to be highly contentious. And although Obama began to wind down combat involvement in Iraq in 2010, formally ending American occupation in December 2011, in an attempt to round off the mission in Afghanistan he ordered a surge of troops from 2010 to 2012. That same strategy also saw the employment of covert drone attacks, targeting insurgent hideouts inside Pakistan.[39]

A drone is an unmanned aircraft that is piloted remotely and can therefore kill by remote control. Killer drones tend to have extremely accurate sensors and can hone in on a human body in the street from 3,000 metres (10,000 feet) or follow a truck on its route from several miles in the air. Its pilot may be controlling it from a room thousands of miles away in the US (journalists have interviewed drone operatives working 12,800 kilometres (8,000 miles) away in Nevada). As if that isn't frightening enough, the so-called 'precision strikes' often cause civilian casualties – a point that has produced an outcry by peace activists and organizations around the world, such as CODEPINK (see page 122) with their 'Ground the drones' campaign as well as the UK's Drone Campaign Network, a coalition of organizations and individuals working to share information and stop the use of drones.[40]

Artists and graphic designers have presented eloquent protests relating to this issue. For example, The United Unknown (an online group of activists keen to preserve their anonymity) has produced beautiful graphics with a vicious bite. They describe themselves as 'united by the use of art as a weapon of mass subversion' and, although their targets are wide-ranging, they reserve a special surge of anger for drone warfare both graphically and in street protests. The photographs of their protests are particularly chilling since the faces of the protesters are blocked out to mask their identity.

1.

1. Poster illustrated by Shepard Fairey that was considered to be highly influential in Barack Obama's victorious US Presidential campaign of 2008.

2. Electronic poster (for downloading by protesters) that simulates Obama's *Hope* poster but instead becomes a sharp critique of his use of drones. By the anonymous group of online activists, the United Unknown. USA c.2013.

2.

DOCUMENTING THE WARS

As the wars progressed, individual artists and activists as well as organizations documented the conflicts from a range of perspectives. With little clarity provided by politicians or military strategies, this documentation provided a focal point for the mounting sense of hurt and anger felt by many over both the human and cultural loss, as well as providing graphic or reimagined evidence for a collective viewpoint against the horrors of war.

US artist Janet Hamlin produced court sketches for the military tribunals at Guantanamo Bay, involving pre-trial hearings of detainees suspected of being 'enemy combatants' or associated with the 9/11 attacks. A selection of this work from 2006 to 2013 has now been published under the title *Sketching Guantanamo*. The admission of journalists and sketch artists was initially used by the Bush Administration to show that justice was being achieved for America and that the proceedings were transparent. However, any visual information from Guantanamo, whether in the form of photographs or drawings, has been minimal and heavily controlled. These court sketches, although greatly restricted in themselves, provide what little visual history exists.[41]

1.

Hamlin normally performed her job in heavily restricted situations, using limited methods: certain faces were off-limits to her or features might have to be smudged; juries could seldom if ever be drawn (even in silhouette); she had to agree to 24-hour military custody in order to do her job; and a Pentagon security officer had to add an 'approved' sticker to each drawing before it could leave the courtroom – sometimes requesting that details be erased before approval was granted.[42]

Her working methods are equally interesting and often geared to working at speed. Brown paper is used for its ability to disguise empty or unfinished areas drawn in haste and pastels allow for quick changes or alterations. She focuses on what is important, editing out the rest. Her view is often obstructed – poles, desks or even people may be between her and her subject – and requests to move to seating offering a better view were often refused. There were even instances when she wasn't allowed inside the court so drew from images on monitors. Despite this, all of her sketches present a 'human' face; she aims for accuracy and thus avoids stereotypical characteristics of good and evil.[43]

The detainees she drew range from so-called foot soldiers – an Al-Qaida cook and Osama bin Laden's driver – to five accused 9/11 co-conspirators including alleged terrorist mastermind Khalid Sheikh Mohammed. Every detainee's story is explained in a text accompanying Hamlin's sketches, and together they form a

Selected court sketches by US artist Janet Hamlin for the Military Tribunals at Guantanamo Bay 2006–13, involving pre-trial hearings of detainees associated with the 9/11 attacks. USA 2006–13.

1. Osama bin Laden's cook and sometime driver.

2. One of the youngest captives to be held at Guantanamo Bay (on the monitor, he can be seen in earlier years making a bomb). In 2010 he received a forty-year sentence but would only serve eight years at most.

3. Three detainees sit with their defence teams while the man at the witness stand answers questions from a civilian Pentagon defence lawyer.

2.

3.

long parade of complicated motivations and explanations, along with the emotions of families, lawyers, journalists and others involved. It is fortunate that Hamlin has such an obvious gift for working at speed, as well as diplomacy and patience. For it may well be that Hamlin's swift sketches are the only visual catalogue the public may ever see of the lengthy process of attempting a judicial response to the 9/11 terrorist attacks.[44]

Within days of Saddam Hussein's statue being pulled down, marking the fall of Baghdad, looters attacked public buildings and ministries, including Baghdad's National Museum and Library. Between 10 and 12 April 2003, 15,000 ancient artefacts were stolen from the museum (although fortunately archivists had time to hide some of the most famous exhibits).[45]

Soon after the looting, the Oriental Institute of the University of Chicago launched a database entitled 'Lost Treasures of Iraq' which attempted to document the known content of the museum and library collections, with the help of scholars and archives around the world contributing photographs and object descriptions as well as relying on information/material from their own collections. This information could then be used to help locate and recover missing items.[46]

The Invisible Enemy Should Not Exist was created in 2007 by Michael Rakowitz (a US artist of Iraqi descent). It is an ongoing project aiming to recreate some of the stolen artefacts, using the packaging of Middle Eastern food and local Arabic newspapers found in US cities. He thereby makes use of material that is culturally visible in order to recreate what is now lost or invisible. The objects are produced using the 'Lost Treasures of Iraq' database as a resource, as well as information from Interpol's website. When displayed as an exhibition, the reconstructed objects are accompanied by a label listing details about the lost piece, its original museum number and provenance as well as quotes from Iraqi archaeologists, US military commanders and others reacting to the looting. The reconstructed objects thereby become modern-day surrogates for what has been lost, as well as symbolizing the commitment to locate and recuperate the objects that remain missing.[47]

The Iraq Book Project (2008–10) by US artist Rachel Khedoori was created as an ongoing documentary piece that collated online news articles, dating from the start of the Iraq War in March 2003 and intending to continue until the war ended. The articles were sourced from around the world, using the search terms 'Iraq', 'Iraqi' or 'Baghdad' in the title, then translated into English. They were then chronologically compiled, designed in a flat, uniform manner – so that each article visually flowed into the next, interrupted only by the bold lettering of the title, date and source at the start of each article – and printed as a series of large books. By 2010, seventy-two books were exhibited in London (presented on tables with stools for readers to sit on) as a never-ending sea of words. Articles were still being compiled, printed and added to the books throughout the exhibition.[48]

The project shows the glut of information about the war accumulated over the years, or acts as an opportunity to explore different attitudes to the war since the information came from sources as disparate as *Kenyan Daily Nation*, Iraqi satellite channels, the *New York Times* and Kurdish television. However, it also represents a symbolic attempt to capture the vast amount

4.

4–7. Items from Michael Rakowitz's on-going project, *The Invisible Enemy Should Not Exist* which involves the recreation of looted and stolen artefacts from the Iraq Museum in Baghdad (in the aftermath of the US invasion) using Arabic food packaging and newspapers found in US cities. The recreated artefacts are displayed on a long table; its shape derives from the measurements and layout of the Processional Way, a brick-paved corridor which runs through the Ishtar Gate in Babylon. The project name, *The Invisible Enemy Should Not Exist*, is derived from a translation of Aj-ibur-shapu (the Processional Way). USA 2007 to present.

8. (overleaf) *The Iraq Book Project*, a documentary piece of online news articles (printed and bound into books), dating from the start of the Iraq War, March 2003, and lasting, theoretically, until its end. By US artist Rachel Khedoori.

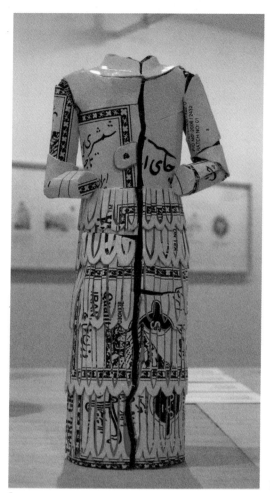

5.

6.

7.

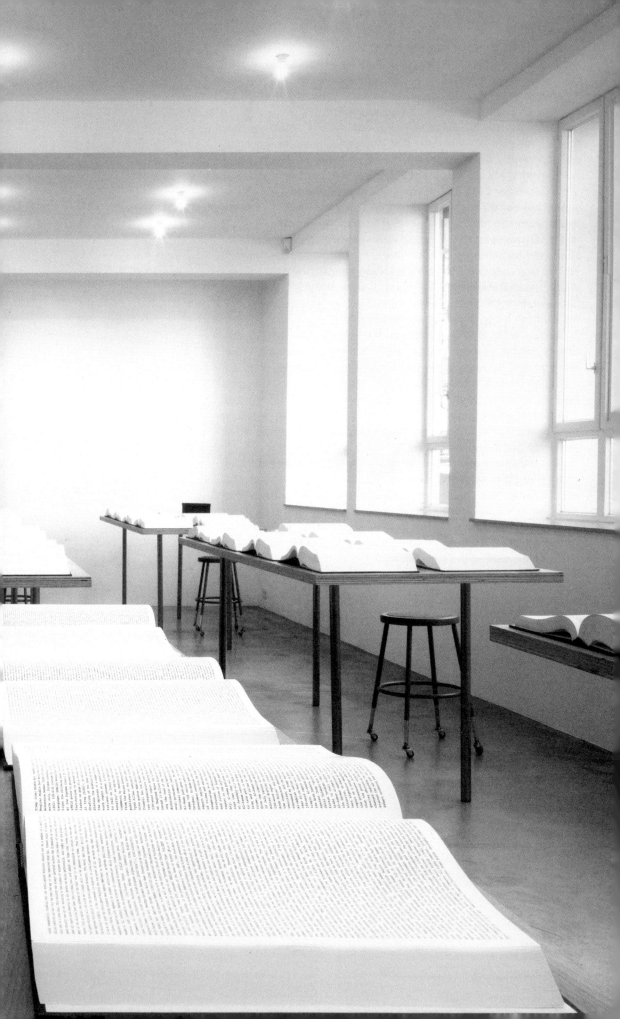

of war information and reporting that exists in the digital realm – forgotten and disappearing into thin air – and forces it into physicality. In its massive form it becomes an embodiment of the never-ending events, the tragedies and the mistakes that for so long seemed self-generating and without end.[49]

The last piece of documentation relates to a relatively new conflict and acts as a reminder that although Afghanistan and Iraq are supposedly seeing the withdrawal of coalition troops, other political intrigues and conflicts continue to defy notions of stability.

In December 2013 BBC Radio 4 *PM* presenter Eddie Mair interviewed consultant and trauma surgeon David Nott shortly after his return from volunteering in a secret hospital in war-torn Syria. It was a harrowing interview during which David Nott spoke candidly about his experiences: the constant flow of casualties (largely women and children), the life-threatening injuries, the blood everywhere, the excruciatingly long hours of work, the basic equipment, his despair at the sniper-targeting of civilians and his anger that more wasn't being done to stop the violence.[50]

British artist Bob and Roberta Smith (aka Patrick Brill) was deeply moved by the interview and determined it shouldn't fade away as with so many other radio interviews. He transcribed the entire interview and hand-lettered the text, using black paint, on a number of canvases which, when assembled in order, produced a huge text painting almost 5 × 4 metres (16 × 13 feet) in size. It took nearly five months to paint and was exhibited in the Royal Academy Summer Exhibition in 2014.[51]

The size and experience of the painting is monumental; it cannot be read quickly – it takes time and effort – and is also mesmerizing. Horrors abound, one after the other. By the end of the interview it becomes clear that there is no 'right' side to the fighting, just endless slaughter with no end in sight. And the slow, deliberate hand lettering (inexact, varying in size and thickness) conveys the pain of the storytelling.

10.

10 and 11. *Interview with David Nott by Eddie Mair,* by Bob and Roberta Smith, transcription of a radio interview by broadcaster Eddie Mair with trauma surgeon Dr David Nott relating to his recent work in a secret hospital in war-torn Syria. The painting measures approximately 5 metres (16 feet) high by 4 metres (13 feet) wide; the text is black paint on white canvas. It was exhibited at the Royal Academy of Arts Summer Exhibition 2014. UK 2014.

INTERVIEW WITH DAVID NOTT BY EDDIE MAIR 1.1.2014

I WAS ABIT THICK AT SCHOOL AND I HAD TO RESIT MY A LEVELS I WAS DETERMINED I WAS GOING TO BE A DOCTOR. I THINK THE REASON WHY I WAS SO DETERMINED WAS BECAUSE NOBODY THOUGHT I COULD DO IT AND I WAS ABSOLUTLEY 100% DETERMINED. MY PARENTS WERE WELL BEHIND ME. SECOND TIME ROUND I GOT INTO ST ANDREWS UNIVERSITY. FROM THAT MOMENT I JUST FLEW EDDIE. THAT REALLY INTERESTS ME. I WONDER WHY YOU CONSIDERED YOURSELF THICK OR WHY THE FIRST SET OF EXAMS WAS SO PROBLEMATIC? DAVID. I THINK THEY WERE PROBLEMATIC BECAUSE I DID NOT KNOW HOW TO STUDY NOBODY SAT DOWN WITH ME. HOW DO YOU STUDY SO HARD TO GET YOUR CORRECT A LEVELS? EDDIE. HOW DID YOU LEARN THAT THEN? DAVID. WELL BECAUSE I FAILED AND I FAILED SO MISERABLY

I WENT HOME AND TOLD MY DAD AND HE SAID NEVERMIND JUST GIVE THEM ANOTHER GO. AND SO I DID AND THIS TIME I WAS DETERMINED. I WENT TO THE TEACHERS AND I SAID YOU NEED TO TEACH ME HOW TO PASS THESE EXAMS, THAT'S WHAT I REALLY NEED TO GET TAUGHT. IF YOU DONT I AM NOT GOING TO BECOME A DOCTOR AND ONE OF THE BIOLOGY TEACHERS HAD THIS PACT WITH MY PARENTS AND HE SAID 'HE IS NOT GOING TO GET IN BUT I WILL JUST GO ALONG WITH IT' AND I STILL LIE IN BED PINCHING MYSELF, DID I REALLY GO TO MEDICAL SCHOOL? AND IT MEANT THAT MUCH TO ME. EDDIE. WAS THAT AN AMBITION YOU HAD FROM A VERY YOUNG AGE BECOMING A DOCTOR? DAVID. I WANTED TO BE A PILOT WHEN I WAS. WHEN I WAS A YOUNG BOY MY FATHER WAS AN ORTHOPEDIC SURGEON HE WAS IN INDIA AND TRAINED IN INDIA HE WAS ONE OF THOSE TYPICAL INDIAN FATHERS. HE SAID TO ME YOU ARE NOT GOING TO BE A PILOT YOU ARE GOING TO BE A DOCTOR, INFACT I DID BOTH I GOT A PILOTS LICENCE AT UNIVERSITY, I GOT A COMMERCIAL PILOTS LICENCE. EDDIE SOMETHING TO FALL BACK ON IF THE MEDICINE FALLS THROUGH? WHICH IS MORE EXCITING?

DAVID. LEARNING TO BECOME A PILOT WAS VERY INTERSTING AND GOING THROUGH ALL THE EMERGENCIES - BUT WHEN YOU ARE ACTUALLY FLYING, TO BE HONEST WITH YOU IT'S NOT THAT INTERESTING. BEING A SURGEON IS WHOLLY INTERESTING. EVERY SINGLE TIME YOU OPERATE ON A PATIENT YOU CAN GET YOURSELF INTO TERRIBLE TROUBLE AND REALLY HELP SOME BODY AND EVEN NOW MY HEART IS IN MY MOUTH, MY HEART IS BEATING FAST, THIS PERSON REALLY REQUIRES MY ULTIMATE CONCENTRATION TO GET THROUGH. I THINK MEDICINE, I THINK SURGERY IS A WONDERFUL ART. EDDIE WHAT DO YOU DO NOW FOR YOUR MAIN DAY JOB? DAVID FOR MOST OF THE YEAR I WORK AT 3 VARIOUS HOSPITALS IN LONDON. I WORK AT ST. MARY'S WHERE I DO VASCULAR SURGERY AND TRAUMA SURGERY, I WORK AT THE ROYAL MARSDEN WHERE I WORK WITH THE SARCOMA SPECIALISTS. I HELP THEM TAKE OUT MASSIVE TUMOURS AND HELP THEM DO THE RECONSTRUCTION OF ALL THE BLOOD VESSELS, MY WORK AT CHELSEA & WESTMINSTER WHERE I MAINTAIN MY GENERAL SURGICAL PRACTICE

I DO LAPARSCOPIC AND UPPER INTESTINAL SURGERY. YOU MIGHT LOOK AT ME AND SAY, WHY DO YOU DO SO MUCH? BUT THE REASON IS BECAUSE I WANTED TO KEEP ALL THE PLATES SPINNING. I WANT A GENERAL SURGION A VASCULAR SURGEON AND A TRAUMA SURGEON. KEEP ALL MY SKILLS UP. EDDIE THAT WOULD BE ENOUGH FOR MOST PEOPLE BUT FOR A FEW WEEKS A YEAR YOU TAKE A BREAK FROM THE PLATE SPINNING TO DO SOME THING ELSE WHICH SEEMS TO ME EVEN MORE DIFFICULT, CERTAINLY MORE DANGEROUS. HOW DID THAT START? DAVID THAT STARTED WITH ME WATCHING A PROGRAMME 1993 CHRISTMAS TIME ABOUT SARAJEVO AND I SAW THE DEVISTATION THAT WAS HAPPENING THERE. I REALLY FELT I WANTED TO GO OUT AND HELP SO I CONTACTED AN AID AGENCY AND WITHIN 3 OR 4 DAYS I WAS OUT IN SARAJEVO. I HAD LEFT MY FLAT IN HAMMERSMITH AND I WAS WORKING UNDER GROUND IN A HOSPITAL IN THE MIDDLE OF SARAJEVO FOR A PERIOD OF SIX WEEKS AND I LOVED EVERY SINGLE MINUTE OF IT. I LOVED IT BECAUSE

A LIGHT WENT ON IN MY HEAD. MY ALTRUISTIC GENE GOT TURNED ON AND I THOUGHT THIS IS WHAT I WANT TO DO FOR THE REST OF MY LIFE. EDDIE WHAT INSPIRED THAT DO YOU THINK IN YOU? I CANNOT STAND TO SEE PEOPLE SUFFERING ANYWHERE AND WHEN PEOPLE SUFFER AND THEY HAVE NOBODY TO HELP THEM... THAT'S THE REASON WHY I DO IT THAT'S PURELY THE ONLY REASON WHY I DO IT. EDDIE HAVE YOU BEEN IN THAT POSITION YOURSELF? DAVID I THINK SO I MEAN I HAVE BEEN IN POSITIONS IN THESE ENVIRONMENTS WHEN I HAVE FELT MY LIFE MIGHT BE TERMINATED. I HAVE BEEN IN THOSE SITUATIONS WHERE I HAVE WANTED HELP. BEFORE THAT I HAD LIVED THIS EUROPEAN LIFE STYLE WHERE I HAD EVERYTHING I EVER NEEDED. I HAD NEVER SEEN POVERTY, I HAD NEVER SEEN SUFFERING AND I GO THERE THE FIRST TIME TO SEE PEOPLE REALLY SUFFERING. WITHOUT ANY HELP THEY WOULD HAVE DIED. THAT WAS THE THING THAT TURNED THE LIGHT ON. EDDIE I HAVE NOT SEEN WHAT YOU HAVE SEEN BUT FOR ME ARRIVIING IN SARAJEVO I WOULD HAVE BEEN QUITE FRIGHTENED

DAVID YES I KNOW BUT I WAS NOT FRIGHTENED I DONT QUITE KNOW WHY? I'VE BEEN IN TERRIBLE SITUATIONS BOMBED AND FIRED AT AND I HAD NEVER BEEN FRIGHTEND ALTHOUGH I HAD PRAYED 'PLEASE DON'T LET THIS COME TO AN END'. BUT I HAVE NOT BEEN SCARED NOT TO GO INTO AN ENVIRONMENT EVER. EDDIE THAT'S UNUSUAL I WOULD SUGGEST. DAVID I THINK YOU ARE RIGHT, THAT IS UNUSUAL EDDIE DO PEOPLE EXPRESS THE KIND OF SURPRISE I AM EXPRESSING TO YOU? DAVID WELL THERE IS A CORE GROUP OF PEOPLE WHO HAVE BEEN DOING THIS FOR MANY YEARS AND I AM PART OF THIS CORE GROUP OF PEOPLE THAT YOU SEE, VARIOUS MISSIONS AND THEY ARE A HARD CORE GROUP AND ITS JUST THAT WE ARE ONE END OF THE BELL CURVE, THE NORMALITY BELL CURVE AND IF YOU ARE AT THAT END YOU DO THAT KIND OF WORK EDDIE THAT'S MEDECINS SANS FRONTIERES AND THE INTERNATIONAL RED CROSS DAVID YES MOST OF IT IS MEDECINS SANS FRONTIERES ALOT OF IT IS I.C.R.C. THIS TIME I WENT TO WORK WITH SYRIA RELIEF WHICH WAS A SYRIAN/BRITISH CHARITY EDDIE THIS WAS JUST A FEW WEEKS/MONTHS AGO AND YOU WOULD HAVE SEEN SYRIA REPORTED. YOU'LL HAVE SOME IDEA WHAT TO EXPECT. TELL ME WHAT IT WAS LIKE WHEN YOU GOT THERE? DAVID WELL IT WAS VERY DIFFICULT TO GET ACROSS THE BORDER. THERE WAS A LOT OF ISLAMIC FUNDEMENTALISTS ON ROUTE AND THAT SCARED ME SLIGHTLY. I WORKED IN ONE OF THE MAJOR CITIES IN THE NORTH AND I DON'T WANT TO SAY WHERE I WORKED IN BECAUSE SECURITY IS SUCH THAT EVERYONE WHO WORKS IN THESE HOSPITALS, IN FIELD HOSPITALS BECAUSE THEY WILL BE TARGETED BY WHO IS TARGETING THE HOSPITALS AND THE DOCTORS WILL ALSO BE TARGETED SO THE DOCTORS ALSO HAVE FALSE NAMES AND I HAD A FALSE NAME AS WELL AND WE USED TO CHANGE OUR NAMES EVERY 3 MONTHS, OR, SO THAT NOBODY KNOWS WHO IS WHO EXCEPT THOSE WHO ARE WORKING IN THE HOSPITALS AND SO NONE OF THE HOSPITALS ARE HIGHLIGHTED WITH BANNERS OR RED CROSSES LIKE THIS THEY ARE ALL HIDDEN FROM VIEW. EDDIE THEY ARE SECRET HOSPITALS? DAVID THEY ARE SECRET

HOSPITALS. THEY ARE SECRET BECAUSE IF THE GOVERNMENT KNEW THEY WERE THERE THEY WOULD PROBABLY TARGET THEM. EDDIE YOU HAVE BEEN IN FAR MANY MORE WAR ZONES THAN I HAVE. WHAT HAPPENED TO THE NOTION THAT MEDICAL PROFESSIONALS CAN GET ON WITH THEIR JOB AND GO ABOUT THEIR BUSINESS? DAVID WELL THAT SHOULD BE, AND INTERNATIONAL LAW PROTECTS MEDICAL WORKERS BUT ACROSS THE BOARD, GO TO SOMALIA, SUDAN, SYRIA HEALTHCARE WORKERS ARE USED AS A TARGET REALLY AS A WEAPON OF WAR, AND IF YOU CAN TAKE OUT A HEALTHCARE WORKER THAT HAS A KNOCK ON EFFECT BECAUSE THE HEALTH CARE WORKER CANNOT HELP THE NEXT 2 OR 2000 PEOPLE AND CERTAINLY I WAS TOLD TO BE A DOCTER IN SYRIA AT THE MOMENT IS PROBABLY THE MOST DANGEROUS DANGEROUS JOB IN THE WORLD BECAUSE DOCTORS ARE DEFINATLEY TARGETED NO DOUBT ABOUT IT. IN THE HOSPITAL WHERE I WORKED THERE WAS A GROUP OF SAY 60 PEOPLE SOME OF THEM WERE DOCTORS SOME OF THEM WERE PEOPLE WHO JUST WANTED TO HELP SHOPKEEPERS I.T. CONSULTANTS PEOPLE LIKE THAT DOING MEDICAL JOBS BECAUSE ALOT OF THE DOCTORS HAD LEFT AND NURSES HAD LEFT AND SO THEY WERE HELPING BUT ALL OF THEM HAVE A STORY TO TELL, THEIR PARENTS ARE IN PRISON LOTS OF THEIR RELATIVES HAVE BEEN KILLED. THEY ALL HAVE A STORY TO TELL. THEY HAVE GOT TOGETHER AND THEY ARE ALL LIVING AND WORKING IN THIS HOSPITAL. ANY DAY ANY MOMENT IT COULD HAVE BEEN TARGETED. EDDIE YOU PROBABLY DIDN'T HAVE A TYPICAL DAY FROM THE SOUNDS OF IT BUT CAN YOU TELL ME WHAT WOULD HAPPEN WHEN YOU GOT INTO WORK? DAVID I LIVED IN THE HOSPITAL, SO WE LIVED... DOWNSTAIRS. UNDERGROUND WAS THE OPERATING THEATRE ANOTHER FLOOR ON TOP OF THAT WERE THE WARDS AND WE LIVED ON TOP OF THERE AND ON THE TOP OF THAT WAS A PLACE SO WE COULD HAVE SOME FOOD AND RELAX AND EVERYDAY I WOULD TURN TO MY COLLEGUE WHO WAS A

SURGION. A YOUNG BRILLIANT SYRIAN, A BRITISH DOCTOR WHO CAME TO LOOK AFTER ME THROUGHOUT THE DAY, LOOK AT HIM IN THE MORNING AT SIX THIRTY? AND WOULD BOTH ROLL OUR EYES AND THINK WHAT, WHAT WOULD TODAY BRING BECAUSE EVERYDAY WAS A DAY FULL OF UPSET OF PRESSURE OF A SIGNIFICANT AMOUNT OF CASUALTIES, BLOOD EVERWHERE AND I WOULD SAY 'WELL I WONDER WHAT TODAY IS GOING TO BRING?' EDDIE BUT IT WAS ALWAYS THE SAME? DAVID IT WAS ALWAYS THE SAME. IT WOULD START AT ABOUT 7-30, QUARTER TO 8 WITH THE FIRST GUN SHOT ROUND AND THAT PATIENT WOULD BE BROUGHT IN THEN WE WOULD MAKE THE DECISION TO OPERATE. IF THE PATIENT IS SHOT IN THE CHEST YOU CAN GET AWAY WITH PUTTING A CHEST DRAIN IN. A LOT OF THE WOUNDS WERE HIGH VELOCITY SO SIGNIFICANT BLEEDING. THEY NEEDED TO HAVE THEIR CHEST OPENED THAT WOULD BE THE FIRST CASE. DURRING THAT WE WOULD HEAR THERE WERE 4 OR 5 MORE COMING IN

AND IT WOULD GO ON AND ON AND ON AND WE WOULD SOMETIMES WORK TO 2 OR 3 O'CLOCK IN THE MORNING AND I WOULD CRAWL UPSTAIRS TO BED AND I HAD THIS FUNNY BED WHERE I WOULD SLIDE ALL OVER THE PLACE. IT WAS LIKE ON A PLASTIC MAT AND I WOULD BE SLIDING OFF THIS BED IN THIS FUNNY STATE OF STUPOR AND DREAM AND THEN 3 HOURS LATER I WAS BACK DOWN IN THE OPERATING THEATRE EDDIE HOW DID YOU COPE WITH THAT? DAVID YOU JUST DO, YOU JUST. YOU ARE ON ADRENALINE AND EVERYONE ELSE IS TOO AND WE ARE ALL WORKING BUT OBVIOUSLY YOU CAN'T WORK CONTINUOUSLY LIKE THAT SO SOME OF THE TIME ANOTHER YOUNG SURGEON WOULD TAKE OVER AND I WOULD GO BACK TO BED FOR A BIT THEN I WOULD GET OUT OF BED WHEN. EDDIE SLIDE ABOUT FOR A FEW HOURS? DAVID SLIDE ABOUT YES THAT'S EXACTLY WHAT IT WAS LIKE. EVERYDAY I WOULD LOOK AT THE OPERATING THEATRE. IT WAS LIKE A BLOOD BATH. THERE WAS BLOOD EVERYWHERE.

BLOOD ON THE... EDDIE CAN YOU DESCRIBE THAT IN GREATER DETAIL? I CAN'T IMAGINE DAVID SO YOU WOULD GO INTO THE OPERATING THEATRE AND YOU WOULD HAVE NOTICED A HUGE AMOUNT OF BLOOD BUT YOU WOULD HAVE 3 OR 4 UNITS OF BLOOD SAY 12 LITRES OF BLOOD TO GIVE TO THE PATIENT BECAUSE HE WAS BLEEDING TO DEATH THEN YOU WOULD QUICKLY OPERATE ON THE PATIENT, WITH THE DRAPES THAT WE HAD THAT WERE NOT LIKE THE DRAPES YOU HAVE IN THE UNITED KINGDOM. THE BLOOD WOULD FALL ONTO THE FLOOR AND YOU WOULD BE BASICALLY SQUELCHING AROUND, BLOOD ON THE FLOOR AND AFTER EVERY TIME THERE WOULD BE A MAN COMING IN WITH A BIG BRUSH LIKE AN ABATTOIR. IT WAS LIKE THAT...

EDDIE EVERYDAY?
DAVID EVERYDAY, EVERY SINGLE DAY WAS THE SAME

EDDIE AND ADRENALINE GOT YOU THROUGH? DAVID I WOULD SAY SO IT WAS JUST TO TRY TO SAVE ALL THESE PEOPLE AND I WANT TO TELL YOU SOMETHING ELSE, APART FROM DOING THE OPERATING MYSELF. I DIDN'T DO ALL THE OPERATING MYSELF. I TAUGHT. MY ROLE NOW IS WHEN I GO TO THESE VARIOUS ENVIRONMENTS, IS TO TEACH THE SURGEONS OPERATING. DURING THE DAY AT TEATIME ABOUT 6 WE WOULD HAVE SUPPER TILL 7PM THEN I WOULD GIVE A LECTURE ON MY COMPUTER BETWEEN 7 OCLOCK IN THE EVENING UNTILL 8'OCLOCK EVERYDAY THEN I WOULD GIVE A DEBRIEFING ON WHAT WE COULD DO BETTER NEXT TIME AND TRY AND DO IT GENTLY SO THAT WE COULD IMPROVE OUR MORTALITY RATE AND I AM VERY PROUD TO SAY THAT FOR THREE WEEKS DURING THE TIME THERE WHEN WE HAD BETWEEN 12 AND 14 INJURIES A DAY GUN SHOT WOUNDS WE DIDN'T LOSE A SINGLE PATIENT IN 3 WEEKS EDDIE CONGRATULATIONS DAVID THANK YOU EDDIE YOU MUST AND SHOULD BE VERY PROUD. DAVID I AM, I AM NOT ONLY PROUD TO SAY THAT BUT I AM PROUD OF THE DOCTORS WHO WERE THERE, THEY WERE IN A TERRIBLE SITUATION AND THEY ARE STILL IN THAT TERRIBLE SITUATION BUT I WANTED TO IMPROVE THEIR MOOD I WANTED TO SAY THAT I AM HERE TO HELP THEM I AM HERE TO TEACH THEM. I DIDNT WANT TO BE THE BIG GUY THAT COMES IN AND DOES THE OPPERATING I WAS ON THE OPPOSITE SIDE OF THE OPERATING TABLE GUIDING THEM THROUGH IT THIS IS HOW

YOU DO IT. THIS IS HOW YOU SEW IT. THIS IS HOW YOU STOP THAT BLEEDING THIS IS WHAT YOU DO AND BEFORE I GOT THERE THEY HAD NEVER OPENED A CHEST BEFORE AND BY THE END OF IT THEY WERE DOING IT BY THEIR OWN. I WAS HORRIFIED, THE DEVASTATION ALL THE FACTORIES, THINGS HAD BEEN BLOWN UP ALL AROUND THE CITY ITSELF A LOT OF THE HOUSES HAD BEEN BLOWN UP, VARIOUS BOMB HOLES BULLET HOLES AND LOTS OF THE BUILDINGS WERE LEVEL DOWN TO THE GROUND THERE WAS A ROUND ABOUT NOT FAR AWAY FROM THE HOSPITAL AND THE WHOLE OF THAT AREA IS COMPLETELY FLATTEND BUT PEOPLE ARE GOING TRYING TO GET ALONG IN THEIR WAY AND THEY ARE BUYING FOOD AND SELLING FOOD. THERE ARE LOTS OF PEOPLE AROUND BUT IT WAS A VERY VERY DANGEROUS ENVIRONMENT TO WORK IN BECAUSE THERE WAS SNIPERS LOTS OF SNIPERS AIRSTRIKES

CONTINUING ALL THE SIX WEEKS I WAS THERE EDDIE WHAT SORT OF EQUIPMENT WAS THERE? DAVID YOU DON'T HAVE A CT SCANNER OR MRI SCANNERS YOU HAVE A VERY COARSE X-RAY MACHINE WHICH IS USED OCCAISIONALLY IT'S NOT USED ALL THE TIME BUT THE EQUIPMENT THAT YOU HAVE IS VERY BASIC SO YOU HAVE A BASIC SURGICAL SET. SISSORS, A KNIFE, SOME CLAMPS, CLIPS, ARTERIAL CLAMPS, YOU HAVE, SMALL SIZED SUTURES TO SEW UP ARTERIES AND VEINS AND BIG SUTURES TO SEW UP BOWELS. YOU CAN GET AWAY REALLY BY USING A LOT OF CLINICAL ACUMEN. YOU CAN SAVE LOTS OF PEOPLES LIVES WITH NOT THAT MUCH EQUIPMENT TO BE HONEST. WE HAD PATIENTS WHO WERE SANGUINATED BLEEDING TO DEATH AND WE HAD A LOT OF BLOOD BECAUSE WE HAD PEOPLE OF THE CITY, WOULD DONATE BLOOD. WE DID HAVE A PROBLEM WITH CROSS MATCHING TO INSURE THE BLOOD

WAS TYPED. ONE OF THE WORST THINGS THAT HAPPENED WAS THAT I OPERATED ON A 14 YEAR OLD BOY WHO WAS SHOT IN THE LEG AND HE HAD A CRONIC PROBLEM WITH HIS ARTERY THAT HAD BLOWN UP HUGELY, IT'S CALLED ANEURYSMAL. IT'S A MASSIVE BLOOD VESSEL AND IT HAD POPPED WE ELECTED TO OPERATE. THERE WERE NOT MANY ELECTED OPERATIONS. I OPERATED ON THIS YOUNG BOY AND 4 HOURS LATER SOME THING SERIOUS HAD HAPPENED TO HIM. HE BECAME WORSE AND WORSE AND DIED THE FOLLOWING DAY, AND HE HAD BEEN GIVEN THE WRONG CROSS MATCHED BLOOD AND THIS WAS ONE OF THE BIGGEST UPSETS I HAD. EDDIE AND LOTS OF THE INJURIES WERE FROM THE SNIPERS YET THEY WERE CIVILIAN WOUNDS. THEY WEREN'T FIGHTERS? DAVID I HARDLY OPERATED ON ANY FIGHTERS, THE INJURIES I SAW WERE WOMEN WANDERING ABOUT THEIR JOBS HARDLY ANY FIGHTERS IN MY TIME THERE MAYBE I OPERATED ON ONE OR TWO FIGHTERS A DAY BUT TEN WERE CIVILIAN

EDDIE THEY WERE HIT BECAUSE THEY WERE IN THE WRONG PLACE AT THE WRONG TIME? WERE THEY DELIBERATELY TARGETED, WERE THE FIGHTERS LOOKING AT A WOMAN OR A CHILD THINKING I AM GOING TO INJURE YOU DAVID NO WHAT IT WAS, ONE HALF OF THE CITY IS ON THE REGIMES, AND ONE HALF IS ON THE FREE SYRIAN ARMY SIDE, THE SYRIAN ARMY HAVE MUCH MORE FOOD AND PROVISIONS THAN THE REGIEME SIDE SO EVERYDAY THERE WOULD BE ABOUT 10000 PEOPLE FROM ONE SIDE TO THE OTHER SIDE TO GET FOOD AND RESOURCES. THEY WERE THE ONES WHO WOULD BE TARGETED. THERE WAS A GAP OR ROAD THAT THESE PEOPLE WOULD GO DOWN AND SNIPERS WOULD TARGET THOSE PEOPLE. ITS THE AREA THEY ARE COMING FROM WHICH IS ABOUT A KILOMETER FROM WHERE OUR HOSPITAL WAS EDDIE IN THOSE CIRCUMSTANCES I AM ASSUMING MORE PEOPLE WERE KILLED OUT RIGHT THAN INJURED OR IS THAT NOT THE CASE? DAVID ITS NOT THE CASE MOST OF THE PEOPLE THAT WERE SHOT WERE BROUGHT TO OUR HOSPITAL BECAUSE IT WAS A FRONT LINE HOSPITAL AND SOME OF THEM WERE SHOT IN THE HEAD SO THEY DIED IMEADIATELY SOME OF THEM WERE SHOT DIRECTLY IN THE HEART SO THEY DIED IMEADIATLY PEOPLE WERE SHOT IN VARIOUS AREAS, ARM LEG NECK CHEST AND I THINK IF A SNIPER WITH A TELESCOPIC SITE WOULD SHOOT PEOPLE HE WOULD SHOOT THEM ALL IN THE HEAD.

BUT THEY WEREN'T SHOT IN VARIOUS PARTS OF THEIR ANATOMY EDDIE SIMPLY PUT THEY WERE TRYING TO INJURE THEM, DAVID I THINK SO, I THINK SO SURE EDDIE I AM SHOCKED BY THAT. DAVID WELL I AM TOO, I WAS VERY SHOCKED AT THE AMOUNT OF WOMEN AND CHILDREN THAT WERE SHOT, REALLY SHOCKED THAT IT ONLY REALLY HIT ME WHEN I CAME BACK THAT PEOPLE COULD BE REALLY SO INHUMANE TO OTHER PEOPLE AND WHY ON EARTH WOULD A SNIPER WANT TO SHOOT A WOMAN OR A CHILD? AND THEY WERE.. WERE AWFUL INJURIES REALLY, REALLY AWFUL INJURIES THEY WERE.... IF WE WERE NOT THERE THEY WOULD HAVE ALL DIED EDDIE TELL ME SOME OF THE OTHER PLACES YOU HAVE BEEN? YOU STARTED WITH SARAJEVO WHAT ARE THE PLACES IN BETWEEN? DAVID THOUGH I HAVE DONE THIS JOB FOR ABOUT 20 YEARS I STARTED OFF IN SARAJEVO, IN KABUL AFGANISTAN THEN I WENT TO KANDAHAR IVORY COAST, LIBERIA, SIERA LEONE, CHAD, CONGO TWICE, I HAVE BEEN TO THE YEMEN I HAVE BEEN TO THE NORTH WEST FRONTIER PAKISTAN, HAITI FOR THE EARTH QUAKE IN HAITI. I WAS IN LIBYA WHEN GADDAFI'S FORCES WERE FIGHTING I MISSED A COUPLE OF PLACES OUT. EDDIE YOU HAVE BEEN TO A LOT OF PLACES A LOT OF PEOPLE WOULD TRY TO AVOID. DAVID I HAVE BUT IF YOU DON'T GO THERE, IF YOU DONT GO PEOPLE SUFFER EVEN MORE EDDIE HOW DOES SYRIA COMPARE? DAVID SYRIA WAS FAR WORSE BECAUSE PEOPLE WERE ALWAYS CAUGHT IN CROSS FIRE WHERE EVER I HAVE BEEN ITS NEVER DELIBERATLEY TARGETING CIVILIANS BUT THIS TIME IT IS COMPLETELY TARGETING CIVILIANS AND I DONT UNDERSTAND WHY THE CIVILIANS ARE BEING TARGETED? BUT IN ALL THE SYRIAN WAR, ITS REALLY THE CIVILIANS WHO ARE SUFFERING, ITS NOT REALLY THE FREE SYRIAN FIGHTERS OR THE REGIEME FIGHTERS. THE CIVILIANS ARE HAVING A TERRIBLE TIME WITH THE COLD WE CAN SEE ON THE TELEVISION. I GOT SENT A PHOTO YESTERDAY WITH A CHILD WITH ITS LEGS BLOWN OFF FROM AN AIRSTRIKE THAT HAPPENED YESTERDAY. WHY IS THIS HAPPENING? THATS WHAT REALLY GETS TO ME, AND I THINK THE THING THAT GETS TO ME WAS THAT IT WAS SO FULL ON. I HAD NEVER WORKED THAT HARD AND WHEN I CAME BACK I HAD THINGS FLYING AROUND MY HEAD BOUNCING AROUND INSIDE MY HEAD AND I THINK I HAD SUFFERED ALOT THIS TIME WITH POST TRAUMATIC STRESS MORE THAN I HAD EVER SUFFERED BEFORE BECAUSE WE WERE WORKING SO HARD SO FLAT OUT TRYING TO SAVE AS MANY PEOPLE AS WE COULD POSSIBLY THEY WERE ALL CIVILIANS AND THAT'S WHAT I DONT REALLY UNDERSTAND EDDIE HOW DO YOU COPE WITH SOME THING LIKE THAT DAVID WELL ITS DIFFICULT.

THERE WAS ONE PARTICULAR INCIDENT THERE WAS A BOY, I REMEMBER SO VIVIDLY, HALFWAY THROUGH THIS MISSION THERE WAS A BOY WHO HAD BEEN SHOT IN THE CHEST IN OUR EMERGENCY DEPARTMENT AND HE HAD LOST HIS LIFE BUT HE HAD A SMILE ON HIS FACE AS I WAS DEALING WITH THE OTHER CASUALTIES I KEPT TURNING AND LOOKING AT THIS BOY WHO WAS NAKED FROM THE WAIST UP AND HE HAD THIS GRIN THIS BIG SMILE ON HIS FACE AND EVERY TWO OR THREE MINUTES, I WOULD TURN AND LOOK AT HIM. I COULD NOT UNDERSTAND WHY HE WAS SMILING AND THAT, AND THAT HAS STAYED WITH ME. STAYED WITH ME EVERY SINGLE DAY AND EVEN THIS MORNING I WAKE UP TO THE SAME, THE SAME PICTURE IN MY MIND. EDDIE HOW DO YOU STOP IT HAUNTING YOU? DO YOU SPEAK TO SOME ONE? DAVID I COULD DO. I KNOW MYSELF IT'S GETTING BETTER. IT USUALLY TAKES THREE MONTHS TO GET OVER SOME THING LIKE THIS. EDDIE BUT THIS IS WORSE THAN EVER BEFORE? DAVID I CAME BACK IT IS MUCH WORSE THERE IS SOMETHING I THOUGHT COULD POSSIBLY CHANGE THIS. I HAD A PHOTOGRAPH OF A BABY WHO WAS SUPPOSED TO BE DELIVERED BY BREACH ABOUT TO BE DELIVERED A WEEK LATER WHOSE MOTHER WAS SHOT IN THE UTERUS AND WE HAD THIS PICTURE OF THE BABY WITH A BULLET IN ITS HEAD. WHEN I CAME BACK I SAID TO 'SYRIA RELIEF' SURELY THIS IS GOING TO DO SOMETHING. SURELY THIS WILL CHANGE THE WAY THIS WAR IS VIEWED. I SAID SHOULD WE PUBLISH IT OR NOT PUBLISH IT? BECAUSE HOPEFULLY IT WILL CHANGE SOMETHING. LET'S GO FOR IT. LET'S SEE IF WE CAN CHANGE SOME THING AND WAKE UP THE WORLD TO THE HORRORS OF WHATS GOING ON BUT I AM REALLY DISAPPOINTED THAT, THAT PHOTOGRAPH HAS BEEN PUBLISHED AND NOTHING HAS CHANGED AND I HAVE KNOCKED ON THE DOORS OF VARIOUS PEOPLE IN GOVERNMENT, I HAVE GONE TO SEE VARIOUS PEOPLE AND I HAVE SHOUTED AT VARIOUS MEETINGS ABOUT HOW THE UNITED NATIONS SHOULD DO SOMETHING, PUT BOOTS ON THE GROUND PROTECT PEOPLE, PROTECT WORKERS GET HUMANITARIAN AID IN. I AM VERY DISSAPOINTED THAT NOTHING HAS REALLY HAPPENED EDDIE YOU KNOW THE ARGUMENTS THAT ARE PUT FORWARD, WHAT DO YOU SAY TO THEM DAVID I THINK THAT NOBODY IS TAKING ANY CONTROL OF THIS, NO LEADERSHIP, YOU KNOW WHEN I WAS, WHEN WE WERE GOING I REMEMBER DAVID CAMERON SAYING WE WERE NOT GOING TO USE MILITARY AIRSTRIKES. WE WERE GOING TO KILL THEM WITH KINDNESS. WE WERE GOING TO HAVE HUMANITARIAN AID WELL HE HASN'T. THERE HAS BEEN NO HUMANITARIAN CORRIDOR CREATED BY THE UNITED NATIONS. IN BOSNIA I REMEMBER THE UNHCR. TRUCKS GOING IN THATS WHAT SHOULD HAPPEN AGAIN SOMEBODY SHOULD HAVE A BIT OF LEADERSHIP AND SAY THIS IS WHAT WE ARE GOING TO DO BECAUSE THE SITUATION IS GETTING WORSE AND WORSE AND WORSE AND THEY HAVE LEFT IT SO LONG NOW THAT EVERYONE IS WASHING THEIR HANDS AND HOPING SOMETHING WILL HAPPEN BUT ON THE OTHER HAND IF YOU ARE PART OF THE BRITISH GOVERNMENT AND YOU KNOW CIVILIANS ARE BEING KILLED EVERY SINGLE DAY AND YOU KNOW ABOUT THAT YOU HAVE BLOOD ON YOUR HANDS AS WELL. EDDIE HOW WELL DO YOU SLEEP? DAVID NOT BRILLIANTLY AT THE MOMENT. I THINK ABOUT THIS CONSTANTLY ALL THE TIME. I TRY TO HAVE A GOOD NIGHTS SLEEP BUT I AM STRESSED WITH ALL THIS AT THE MOMENT. DO YOU MIND IF I ASK YOU, AND THIS IS PERSONAL, TELL ME TO GET LOST? YOU MENTIONED PRAYING WHEN YOU SAID YOUR LIFE WAS UNDER THREAT. ARE YOU A RELIGIOUS PERSON? DAVID I AM NOT RELIGIOUS BUT SOME TIMES WHEN YOU ARE UNDER SUCH DURESS YOU SUDDENLY PUT YOUR WAVE BAND ONTO A DIFFERENT FREQUENCY AND EVERY NOW AND AGAIN I HAVE TO PRAY AND I DO PRAY TO GOD AND I ASK HIM TO HELP ME BECAUSE SOMETIMES I AM SUFFERING BADLY AND ITS ONLY NOW AND AGAIN THAT I AM ABLE TO TURN TO THE RIGHT FREQUENCY TO TALK TO HIM AND THERE IS NOT A DOUBT IN MY MIND THERE IS A GOD. I DON'T NEED HIM EVERYDAY, I NEED HIM EVERY NOW AND AGAIN BUT WHEN I DO NEED HIM HE IS CERTAINLY THERE.

11.

DIVIDED COUNTRIES AND CULTURES: SIGNS OF TENSION AND RESOLVE

DIVIDED COUNTRIES AND CULTURES: SIGNS OF TENSION AND RESOLVE

The Israeli-Palestinian conflict dates back to the creation in 1948 of Israel itself: a Jewish state within Palestine. Palestinians either fled to other countries or resided in the administered territories of West Bank and Gaza. Both, including East Jerusalem, came under the control of Israel after the Six-Day War of 1967. The Palestinian nationalist movement initiated the first *intifada* (uprising) in 1987, forever remembered through the visual symbols of young men throwing stones or firing slingshots. The second *intifada* launched in 2000 brought years of suicide attacks against Israel. Israel responded to both revolts with well-equipped military force.

A peace treaty was reached in 1993 that planned for the disputed West Bank territory to become a self-governed, Palestinian area, but talks failed and Israel reoccupied much of the land in 2001–02, continuing to maintain existing settlements and building new ones. Mistrust and violence continued on both sides. Attempts at negotiating peace settlements kept failing and the valiant efforts of peace organizations could not stop the continued violence. In April 2002, Israel began construction of the West Bank Barrier or Separation Wall – a concrete divide, topped with 'razor wire, sniper towers and electric fences', rising in parts to a height of 8 metres (26 feet). The Wall does not follow a straight line separating Israel from the West Bank, but cuts deeply into the West Bank, circumnavigating Israeli settlements and cutting off access to some Palestinian towns and farmland, forcing thousands of Palestinian inhabitants to pass through Israeli checkpoints in order to go about their daily business.[1]

Over the years an entire culture of art, graphics, film and activism has developed relating to these events and tensions, and the desire for an end to conflict. For example, the film *5 Broken Cameras* (2011) by Emad Burnat and Guy Davidi, explored the Palestinian hatred of the Wall (it is seen by many as representative of the occupation and encroaching Israeli settlements) through the story of the West Bank village of Bil'in. Samuel Maoz's film *Lebanon: The Soldier's Journey* (2009;

released in the US as *Lebanon*) is set during the 1982 Lebanon War and told from the perspective of a crew of four young Israelis inside their tank who reassess what they are doing and who they are doing it to. Poster artists David Tartakover and Yossi Lemel have both consistently provided images of great humanity, calling for a stop to violence and pointing towards the need for reconciliation on both sides. There has been tireless campaigning for decades by organizations such as Peace Now. All have ensured that a dissenting voice, calling for a stop to violence, has remained in the public sphere.

From its very beginning, the Wall and its much-contested route became a cause for activists and eventually for politicized graffiti and street artists from all over the world. Thousands of people have travelled to the Wall and produced written or drawn statements of protest on it, creating a massive visual petition observed by a global audience. In December 2007, the British street artist Banksy and London-based organization Pictures on Walls took their annual 'squat art concept store', *Santa's Ghetto*, to Bethlehem, inviting fourteen other international street artists along. Auctioned artwork raised over US $1 million for local charities. The artists also produced political messages and artwork on the Wall and on other walls throughout Bethlehem, bringing world attention to the life-limiting realities of the Wall as well as its oppressive presence (see pages 152–155). Palestinian reactions to the artwork were mixed; some welcomed the show of solidarity, others challenged the beautification of something they viewed with hatred.[2]

Having arrived at a deadlock derived of constant battling and attacks between the Israeli and Palestinian (Hamas) governments over the past decade, the 'two-state' solution – where Israelis and Palestinians live in harmony together – seems as far away as ever. However artists and designers continue to keep energies and dreams alive through inventive storytelling and narratives that connect past, present and future. Palestinian photographer and filmmaker Larissa Sansour's satirical, imaginative view of the future places the entire Palestinian state and population within a skyscraper, where cities are assigned to different floors. A filmed journey through the building, or *Nation Estate*, is underpinned by cynical humour; but feelings of claustrophobia and sadness creep in as the journey wears on. Israeli designer and poster artist Yossi Lemel, on the other hand, reaches back into the past to tell the story of his father, a survivor of the Nazi death camps. He does so by retracing his father's steps, visiting the places involved, and taking on the clothing and actions of his father. The result is a photographic exhibition that offers a surreal rendering of how the past continues to haunt the present.

NORTH KOREA: A VIEW FROM OUTSIDE AND INSIDE

Since the 1950s, the West has viewed North Korea as a feared communist aggressor. Global media has had little access to the country and over the decades any North Korean propaganda that has reached the West has put forward an image of a militarized, war-ready country cast in the mould

of communist China and the old Soviet Union. Matters have only become worse in the twenty-first century. In 2002 George W. Bush named North Korea, Iraq and Iran an 'axis of evil' aiming to arm themselves with 'weapons of mass destruction' and determined to undermine world peace. North Korea's leaders continued to remain remote and unfriendly and have occasionally provoked a response from the West to a potential nuclear threat by testing missiles with the capacity to carry

a nuclear warhead, or by releasing photographs or film of their huge military parades displaying an array of long-range missile transporters. The result has been the creation of a political chasm between North Korea and the West.

The propaganda posters shown here and on page 166, created for use within twenty-first century North Korea itself, are therefore extremely important as they provide a rare insight into the controlling philosophy under which North Koreans live. It is also crucial to acknowledge events leading to the division of Korea, the Korean War itself and developments thereafter, as they are reflected in the attitudes and messages that emanate from some of the posters and artwork featured.

In 1945, at the end of World War II, Korea was liberated from Japanese colonial rule by its allies, mainly the Soviet Union and the USA. The allies agreed to a demarcation line – the 38th parallel – that divided the Soviet and US occupation zones. The division was both geographic and ideological, separating communist North from capitalist South. Led by former guerrilla fighter Kim Il Sung, the North invaded the South in 1950, initiating the Korean War (1950–53). UN forces, led by the US and assisted by British Commonwealth forces, drove back the North Koreans (assisted by the communist Chinese).[3] After a bloody war of constantly shifting advance and retreat movements – including the South advancing into North Korea, then being driven back – an armistice was finally signed in July 1953. The war was never brought to a formal end, and therefore technically could pick up again at any time. (A point worth considering when viewing the North Korean obsession with self-defence and its constant need to prepare for war or nuclear attack.)[4] In addition, a significant US military presence still remains in South Korea to this day.

After the war, Kim Il Sung rebuilt North Korea as a socialist economy and state – the Democratic People's Republic of Korea – and adopted the *Juche* ideology that valued self-reliance above all and demanded selfless surrender to the common good from the populace. Thus dedication was to the nation, the Korean Worker's Party and, most of all, to the Leader. The national values, shining through propaganda, exuded autonomy, self-reliance and self-defence.[5]

However at the death of Kim Il Sung in 1994, North Korea was facing economic ruin. His son, Kim Jong Il, took his place and faced the crisis by developing the 'Army First' policy. This placed the Korean People's Army as the keeper of the revolution and national unity, drawing its members from throughout the population. Numerous artists were employed to communicate the ideology.

Propaganda posters borrowed stylistically from the Soviet Union's 'socialist realism' but were also guided by Kim Jong II's insistence on qualities of 'clarity, compactness and delicacy' derived from traditional Korean ink painting. The propaganda posters were seen as distinctly Korean, and as tools for mobilization and rousing people into action.[6]

Although North Korea was viewed by the West as a secret society for many years, it is less so now. However, glimpses of North Korean cities, the landscape or the people and their way of life have been few and far between. German architectural photographer Dieter Leistner travelled to Pyongyang, North Korea, in 2006, with permission to photograph public spaces. He later visited Seoul in South Korea in 2012 to photograph similar scenes and spaces. The comparison of the Pyongyang/Seoul photographs shows expected ideological and cultural differences, as well as a few unexpected emotional similarities (see pages 168–169). While French Canadian cartoonist Guy Delisle's graphic-novel memoir of a visit to Pyongyang becomes heavily involved in everyday differences and beliefs, thereby providing an up-close and personal view of ordinary people, while still trying to fathom their ideological constraints.

Kim Jong II died in December 2011, and his son and successor Kim Jong Un has not given the impression of desiring a more open conversation with the West. A number of adventurous tour operators now offer organized and strictly supervised tours of the country, but only time will tell as to how soon film or photography will be able to present a fuller view to the outside world.

THE VEIL AND ITS MANY INTERPRETATIONS

The 9/11 terrorist attacks not only led to the 2001 'War on Terror' and War in Afghanistan, but also produced a lethal by-product in the form of 'Islamophobia' (a deep suspicion of Islam and Muslim culture, which in its extreme assumes that all Muslims are terrorists and somehow associated with violence or oppression).[7] This in turn produced negative portrayals as well as visual stereotypes. One of the most obvious involved women and the veil in its many forms (the hijab, chador, niqab, burqa and so on). Combined with reports of the strictness of the Taliban – as the War in Afghanistan brought news of Afghan women forced to wear the chador or burqa, and forbidden to work or educate themselves – one dominant representation took hold: the veil equalled oppression.

Muslim women themselves particularly in the West often rejected this image, and discussions developed around wearing the veil as a matter of

choice: an expression of faith for example, or for political reasons such as a rejection of Western values, or both. Debates tended to flare up when governments or politicians interfered. France and Britain provide an important example of difference in approach to this issue. In 2004 the French government passed a law banning headscarves and all conspicuous religious symbols from state schools.[8] Taking matters even further, in 2011 President Sarkozy's government passed a law that made it illegal for full-face Muslim veils, the niqab or burqa, to be worn in public: otherwise known as the 'burqa ban'. In this case 'public' meant anywhere – in the street, in supermarkets, on public transport, in offices and so on – despite outcries over the infringement of women's rights and civil liberties.[9]

Attempts at prohibiting the veil have been contemplated in Britain, but they have never followed the path of France. This is perhaps because there is a fundamental political and cultural difference between the two countries in their views on the relationship between religion and the state. In France, the written constitution separates church and state (the 2004 ban only applies to state-run schools, but these are by far the majority). Britain has no such written constitution, which allows room for individual choice and differentiated cultures within educational practice. Both countries have their problems with racial, religious or cultural prejudice; but only one is able to force any kind of religious symbolism out of institutions of the state (and inevitably, this ethos can permeate the larger public domain).

As the new century moved on, the presence of the veil in the West appeared to increase. This was partly in actuality, as second- and third-generation Muslim families grew, consolidating already present communities, but also in our collective consciousness, highlighted by news reports as the wars in Iraq and Afghanistan continued. The debates and mixed cultural influences are now everywhere and pervade art, politics and education. The breadth of the spectrum can be seen in the few examples shown here. The double-page spread from the article 'Why I Love My Little Black Dress' in Middle-Eastern culture magazine *Bidoun* is undoubtedly presenting confident women showing off their identity. Taking matters even further, British artist Sarah Maple – who is Muslim herself, and often engenders debate through humorously shocking images or text – portrays a woman in a burqa wearing a badge saying 'I Love Orgasms' (2008, see page 183). The portrait overtly produces a visual clash of religion vs sexuality; suddenly religious dress no longer hides the sexuality of Muslim women. At the same time she plays with society's lazy tendency to view the world through stereotypes: cover up the badge, and the viewer may perceive a 'threatening' image of a woman in a burqa; uncover the badge and the pair of eyes is asking the viewer to question their assumptions about her beliefs and preferences or attitudes to sex.

The visual debates, and the range of attitudes, continue on pages 170–176. These include the 'hijabizing' of guerrilla artist Princess Hijab, who in 2005 began applying dripping black paint (or black felt-tip pen) suggesting Muslim veils on fashion adverts in the Paris Metro.[10] Then there is the visual transformation that occurs through the progressively increasing covering with the veil (and subsequent disappearance of the person beneath) in a photographic portrait-sequence by Yemeni photographer Boushra Yahya Almutawakel, which cannot help but hint at notions of identity and power. Visual contradictions are at their most powerful in Iranian artist Parastou Forouhar's work, where stark, powerful images of the veil create uneasy feelings of constraint and submission, and printed fabrics with beautiful, intricate patterning carry implications of subjugation and torture.[11]

ONE STEP FORWARD, TWO STEPS BACK: HUMAN RIGHTS AND TERRIFYING WRONGS

In 2013, long-awaited – and in the case of France, controversial – legislation legalizing same-sex marriage was finally passed in France as well as Britain amid much celebration. The Netherlands was the first country to give full rights of marriage to same-sex couples in 2001. By 2014, nearly twenty countries had legalized gay marriage, although the US was only a partial member of the club as some states still lagged behind.[12]

France particularly had much to celebrate, as the legislation of same-sex marriage didn't come easily. Thousands of riot police were deployed in central Paris as the National Assembly gave their final approval, ready to deal with possible outcries from right-wing and fundamentalist Catholic groups. Trouble eventually arrived in the form of 200 hard-right youths trying to force their way

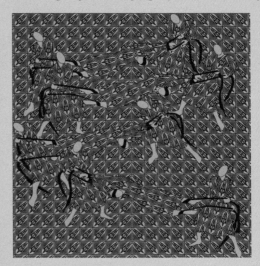

into ministry buildings. Other actions included attacks on gay people and bars, while members of the government were sent threatening mail.[13] However celebrations in the street were joyful, and the front page of centre-left newspaper *Libération* carried artwork by Pierre et Gilles, superstars of unique hand-painted, photographic art-portraits of fashion, film, pop and gay icons since the late 1980s (see page 179).

Sadly, at the same time, enthusiasm for the upcoming 2013 Winter Olympics was dampened by reports of violent actions against gay men and women in the host country, Russia. Prejudice (and violence) against homosexuality was openly condoned in Russia, where new anti-gay laws made it illegal to provide information about homosexuality to anyone under the age of eighteen. Foreign nationals doing so would be jailed and Russians would be fined. Politicians felt free to refer to gay people, in public and in the media, as 'perverse' or 'sick' and there were reports of routine discrimination and abuse. Discussions ensued about such injustices in the British media, and numerous celebrities and politicians added their voices. Rumours circled about the possibility of boycotting the Winter Olympics, but the prevailing view was to challenge prejudice by attending and making a big noise.[14]

In the realm of advancing women's rights: Sarah Maple engenders debate about feminism, culture and religion through her works of art, employing a caustic sense of humour (see pages

182–183). Eca Eps produces visions of beauty, stillness and strength in her photo-series *Naked in Africa* (2013), projecting typographic messages or thoughts onto a black woman's body that is posed in positions of calm or resolve. The messages relate to some of the challenging issues still facing women of today – machismo, religion, abortion, and particularly for women of certain cultures, FGM (female genital mutilation). It is a show of strength, and of resolution.

Yet, the proverbial 'two steps back' comes in the form of hideous acts of violence committed against women in recent years. A few extreme cases acted as representation for the many, providing a shocking reminder that whatever advances are made, violence against women has not been left behind and continues to transfer down through the generations. A news story that received global attention was the Taliban-ordered shooting in October 2012 of the fifteen-year-old Pakistani schoolgirl, Malala Yousafzai, an outspoken advocate of education for girls. She recovered and became an inspiration for many.[15] In December 2012, a twenty-three-year-old student boarded a bus in Delhi where she was beaten and gang raped; she died of her injuries two weeks later. The incident sparked international headlines and unprecedented national debate in India. Major protests for better safety for women took place in cities throughout the country, resulting in the enactment of a stringent new anti-rape law.[16] Then on 14 April, 2014 in the town of Chibok in northeastern Nigeria, 276 schoolgirls

were kidnapped from their school dormitories by Boko Haram, an Islamic terrorist group. Online campaigns were launched immediately in defiance and went viral. #bringbackourgirls and various Facebook pages counted the days and posted photos of the faces, but such international efforts had little effect. Although some of the girls managed to escape, over 230 are still missing.[17] Eca Eps' installation *Chibok 100* showing simply dark-coloured hijabs – the clothing the missing girl's were last seen in – is heartbreaking. All of these cases are grim reminders that even in the twenty-first century, women still live in peril in many parts of the world.

And there was still more terror to come. The brutal killings on 7 January 2015 of twelve staff members of French satirical magazine *Charlie Hebdo* stunned Paris and the rest of the world. Two radical Islamist gunmen committed the massacre out of anger at the journal's repeated use of insulting caricatures of the prophet Muhammad, published under the banner of freedom of speech and the right to criticize or offend. Solidarity followed with the popular chant 'Je suis Charlie', as did fierce debates about sources of social division and radicalization.

The French visual artist known as JR, however, manages to make the world a more engaging place. A filmmaker, photographer, environmental and street artist, JR works at a very large scale, and thrives on the involvement of people in his projects. All of his art is participatory and his installations span the globe, many of them aimed at making 'invisible' people, visible.

Page 146–7. Left: 'Hijabizing', intervention in the Paris Metro, by artist Princess Hijab. France 2006-11. Right: *Have a Year of Peace and Love 2006*, poster by Yossi Lemel. Israel 2006. Lemel appropriates Magritte's 1928 Surrealist painting *Les Amants* (The Lovers) to create a metaphor for two communities, bound together by a greater force but unable to complete the union.

Page 148. Poster from North Korea promoting the turn of the century (2000) as a year for great advances. From the David Heather Collection.

Page 149. 'Why I Love My Little Black Dress', by Farhad Moshiri and Shirin Aliabadi, double-page spread from *Bidoun* magazine of Middle East culture, 2004.

Page 150. *Red is my Name, Green is my Name I*, by Iranian artist Parastou Forouhar. One of a series of 8 digital drawings, alternating in red and green, showing torture devices and actions embedded in an ornamental print. Germany 2007.

Page 151. *Chibok 100*, installation by artist/ photographer Eca Eps to mark 100 days (14 April to 23 July 2014) since the abduction of more than 200 schoolgirls from the town of Chibok in northern Nigeria by the terrorist group, Boko Haram. Created in association with Rosebud Centre for Girls in London. UK 2014.

THE SEPARATION WALL
AND ITS ART

In December 2007, British street artist Banksy and the London-based organization Pictures on Walls relocated their annual 'squat art concept store' called Santa's Ghetto to Bethlehem. They invited fourteen other artists – Ron English, Swoon, Blu, Antony Micallef, kennardphillipps and others – to work alongside Palestinian artists and auction off artwork to art buyers, collectors and the public (who would have to travel to Bethlehem and experience the difficulties of the occupation to bid in person).[18]

The result was over US $1 million raised for local charities, plus the visiting artists produced political artwork and messages on the Separation Wall, as well as on other walls and surfaces throughout Bethlehem and the suburbs of Jerusalem. The project aimed to bring global attention to the illegality of the Wall and its contested route – which doesn't follow the internationally recognized Israel-Palestine border (established in 1949 and often called the 'Green Line') but instead cuts into agreed Palestinian land – as well as to the oppressive conditions of life under the occupation.[19]

Earlier that year, French artist JR and his colleague Marco had created *Face2Face*, a display of monumental photographs of Israeli and Palestinian faces pasted on the Separation Wall and in eight different cities. Beginning in 2005, they travelled to Israel and Palestine in an attempt to find out why the two cultures were in constant conflict. After speaking with local people they were amazed to see many similarities in appearance and language rather than differences. So they created a project that involved talking to people on both sides – an essential working method for JR – and photographing them up close using a 28-millimetre lens. They then posted portraits of people in the same jobs together in a line 'face2face' (or, rather, side by side) on both sides of the wall, and in additional 'unavoidable places' so that each side must confront the other.[20]

Occasionally clothing or uniforms distinguish Israeli and Palestinian people, but most of the time, exhibited side by side, they look extremely similar, thereby defying stereotypes that exist in the minds on either side. And the politics of the project are utterly neutral, desiring a solution where both sides can live in peace, building trust and friendship by seeing similarities rather than divisions.

1. *Protester throwing flowers*, by UK artist Banksy, Santa's Ghetto project, Bethlehem 2007.

1.

2. *Peace dove with flak jacket and crosshairs*, by UK artist Banksy, Santa's Ghetto project, Bethlehem 2007.

3. *Giant baby blowing away soldiers made of money*, by Italian artist Blu, Santa's Ghetto project, Bethlehem 2007.

4. *Grade School Guernica*, by US artist Ron English, Santa's Ghetto project, Bethlehem 2007.

2.

5. Artwork on sentry tower by Italian artist Blu, Santa's Ghetto project, Bethlehem 2007.

6. (Left) Artwork on sentry tower by Blu, (middle) *Who's paying for this?* by kennardphillipps, and (right) *With Love and Kisses* by the New York collective, Faile. Santa's Ghetto project, Bethlehem 2007.

3.

4.

5.

6.

7.

7. *Pardon Our Oppression*, by US artist Ron English, Santa's Ghetto project, Bethlehem 2007.

8. *28 Millimétres: Face2Face*, Separation Wall, Palestinian Side in Bethlehem, by the French artist JR (with Marco). Bethlehem and Israel 2007.

9. The line of words on the Wall are part of a 2,000-word letter by Farid Esack, South African religious scholar and former anti-apartheid activist, urging Palestinians to show nonviolent resistance to Israel. The letter was commissioned by a group of Dutch and Palestinian activists and produced by the group as a line of 60 centimetre (2 foot) high stencilled lettering that continues along a 2.6-kilometre (8,500-foot) stretch of wall on the Palestinian side, near Ramallah. Ramallah 2009.

9.

DIVIDED COUNTRIES AND CULTURES: SIGNS OF TENSION AND RESOLVE

8.

ers and brothers forgotten their humiliation?" But yet in mo

down
in small!

Shame/Vergonya
Josep Anton Catani

ESCALADORES POR LA PAZ.
WWW.ARTROSISCLIMBING.COM

ta Mariona
We hope that you can see
a free Palestina and Catalonia
Carles & Núria

PALESTINE AND ISRAEL: FICTIONALIZING THE FUTURE, RELIVING THE PAST

Palestinian photographer and filmmaker Larissa Sansour locates her work in the politics of the ongoing Israel-Palestine conflict. Questioning the possibility (or impossibility) of Palestinian statehood, she looks to science fiction for inspiration. In her film and exhibition *Nation Estate: Living the High Life* (2012), she envisages a satirical future where the entire Palestinian state and population is housed within a colossal, hi-tech skyscraper. Each city occupies a different floor: Jerusalem on the fourth; Bethlehem on the twelfth. Known landmarks and squares are placed in the lobby of each floor. And floors are connected by elevator; no need for checkpoints. Even a live-water replica of the dead sea has its own floor.[21]

A nine-minute film follows the female protagonist on a journey through the floors of the building (shown in the exhibition as polished large-scale photographs), but as she proceeds into her apartment the glitter disappears and the more insular and sad the experience becomes. For example, an olive tree appears as an artefact in her apartment, to be watered and displayed like a household plant. The end of the film shows that outside the tower the Separation Wall and the watchtowers haven't gone away – thereby increasing the sense of isolation and claustrophobia.[22]

The *Nation Estate* poster is a meaningful appropriation of a travel poster by Franz Kraus (1936) in which the image has been altered and the text originally read 'Visit Palestine'. The travel poster was popularized by the Zionist movement, keen to establish a 'national home' for Jews in Palestine. However by the 1930s the resident Arabs and Jews of Palestine were already deep in hostilities.[23] Thus the sunny travel poster can now be seen as symbolic of a turbulent past, present and future.

1. *Nation Estate: Living the High Life*, satirical promotional poster for an imagined future Palestinian state contained within a skyscraper, and depicted in a photo series and video. By Palestinian artist Larissa Sansour. UK/Denmark 2012.

2–7 (overleaf). Large-scale photo series showing the female lead (Sansour) returning home from a trip and making her way in the elevator to the Bethlehem floor, where she finally arrives in her apartment. There she waters her olive tree, eats sci-fi pre-packaged tabouleh, gazes out the window and later walks by the sea. From top left: Main Lobby, Jerusalem (viewed from the lift), and Manger Square/Bethlehem on the 12th Floor, which is the floor of her apartment.

2.

3.

4.

5.

6.

7.

In 2005, Israeli designer and poster artist Yossi Lemel under-
took a personal project, entitled *Memories of the Holocaust*,
which reached back to a terrible episode in the past. He aimed
to tell the story of his father, Bernard Dov Lemel (born in Bedzin,
in Upper Silesia, Poland). At the age of thirteen he was trans-
ported to the Nazi death camp, Auschwitz-Birkenau. Later, he
was transferred to the concentration camp at Sachsenhausen
where he was subjected to invasive medical experiments,
mainly involving Hepatitis B, which continued until 1945. Despite
being then taken on a long death march to the German city of
Schwerin, he survived, lived in France for three years and later
emigrated to Israel.[24]

In 2005, sixty years later, Yossi shaved his head, dressed in
the striped uniform of camp inmates, and retraced his father's
steps, visiting the same places and playing the role of his father.
Yossi then documented his journey through a series of emotional,
surreal posters, forming an exhibition that was posted on the
walls of the concentration camp at Sachsenhausen.[25]

In 2008, he constructed a similar project relating to his mother,
Batia Lemel. Yossi, his mother and his nine-year-old daughter
Noa travelled to his mother's hometown, Bedzin, and recreated
his mother's childhood seventy years before (with Noa acting
in the role of his mother, laughing and playing). The aim was to
capture a key point in time, barely a moment before the Holocaust
when 'all happiness disappeared'.[26]

The projects were beautifully constructed and haunting
in their indication of the heavy weight of memory. And it is not
surprising that Yossi Lemel would confront the past, as well as
look hopefully to the future. For decades he has produced poster
work outspokenly calling for a two-state solution to the Israeli-
Palestinian conflict, and a peaceful future between the two sides.

1–5. *Memories of the
Holocaust*, by Israeli designer
Yossi Lemel. A photo-
exhibition of Lemel's efforts
in 2005 to retrace his father's
steps as an inmate in a
concentration camp, and
tell his father's story.

6. In 2008, Yossi Lemel
also recreated his mother's
childhood before the
Holocaust. Israel 2005–08.

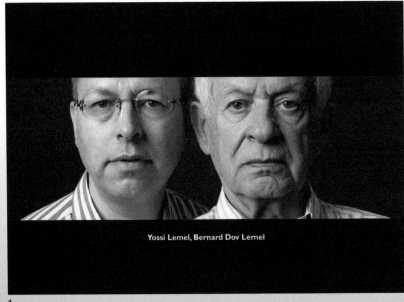

Yossi Lemel, Bernard Dov Lemel

1.

2.

Auschwitz 1, General View, January 27

3.

Auschwitz I Electric Fence

4.

Block 19, Krankenbau Auschwitz I

Appelplatz Sachsenhausen

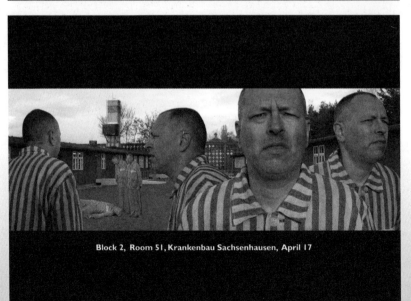

Block 2, Room 51, Krankenbau Sachsenhausen, April 17

5.

Noa Lemel, Batia Lemel, 2008

Modrzejowska street 42 Będzin

Modrzejowska 42, playing in the backyard

The Zamek walls

The Zamek arches

Friday Supper in Jerusalem

In the memory of Haya, Yentl, Sarah, Fella, Rachel and Pearl Garfinkel

Yossi Lemel, Noa Lemel, Batia Lemel, 2008

6.

PERSPECTIVES ON NORTH KOREA

North Korea's historical background is core to its propaganda posters and their visual and textual communication. The division of Korea, the Korean War (including an invasion of North Korea) and the continuing, significant US military presence in South Korea underpin the military hyper-readiness and permanent state of mobilization projected by their propaganda posters.[27]

The hand-painted posters are created by professional artists employed in art studios, and derive from a fine-art tradition. The posters receive recognition and critique in North Korea through exhibitions and journals, as well as being reproduced on a variety of formats, from magazines and postcards to stamps and large billboards. Importantly, the posters play a critical role in projecting North Korea's values and duties. Expecting ultimate sacrifice from its people, the posters speak of submission, determination and resolve – and the need for vigilance.[28]

It is impossible to get a sense of a country and its people solely through its propaganda posters. And although North Korea's doors are slowly opening to cultural visits and other economic opportunities, at present an inside view can only be gleaned through the productions of heavily escorted visitors.

In 2006, German architectural photographer Dieter Leistner travelled to Pyongyang, North Korea with permission to photograph public spaces, and then six years later made a trip to Seoul, South Korea, to photograph similar spaces and scenes. Both visits produced photographs used in the *Korea Power: Design and Identity* exhibition held in 2013 at the Museum Angewandte Kunst, Frankfurt am Main.[29] The comparisons constructed by pairing the photographs – North scenes matched to those in the South – produced a portrait of different worlds but curiously similar people.

Globalization is even opening up North Korea in interesting ways, albeit with limitations. Cartoonist Guy Delisle, working for a French animation studio, was sent on a work visa to oversee production at various Pacific Rim studios. His visit to Pyongyang in 2001, resulted in the creation of a highly personal comic-style travelogue, full of his descriptions of, and reactions to, people, places, food, conversations and everyday dress and behaviour. It also reflects his deep frustration in confronting human rights injustices and the ordinary person's ideological submission, while also trying hard to educate the reader to the historical or political occurrences that may have instigated both.

1.

2.

1 and 2. Posters carrying harsh, anti-US imagery, following US President George W. Bush's State of the Union address in 2002, when he introduced the idea of Iraq, Iran and North Korea as an 'Axis of Evil'.

3. A page of illustrations and text from the graphic novel *Pyongyang: A Journey in North Korea*, by French Canadian cartoonist Guy Delisle. English language version. France 2006.

SINCE THEN, FOOD AID HAS POURED IN, FEEDING UP TO A THIRD OF THE COUNTRY'S POPULATION.

IN THIS HIGHLY STRATIFIED SOCIETY, THE REGIME USES RATIONING TO CONSOLIDATE POWER.

A NATIONAL PUBLIC DISTRIBUTION SYSTEM GIVES CITIZENS PORTIONS BASED ON THEIR LOYALTY AND USEFULNESS TO THE REGIME.

USEFUL POPULATION		USELESS POPULATION	
THE CORE	THE "LUKEWARM"	THE "HOSTILE"	
RICE		250 grams / DAY *	
- PARTY CADRES - ARMY OFFICERS	- SKILLED WORKERS - SOLDIERS, DIPLOMATS (PYONGYANG RESIDENTS)	- CHILDREN OF DISSIDENT PARENTS - POLITICAL PRISONERS (APPROX. 200,000) - LABORERS	AN ADDITIONAL 5 TO 6 MILLION INDIVIDUALS, IGNORED BY THE REGIME, ARE LEFT TO FEND FOR THEMSELVES.

* EQUIVALENT TO HALF THE PORTION DISTRIBUTED BY THE UN IN REFUGEE CAMPS ELSEWHERE IN THE WORLD

AS A RESULT, SEVERAL NGOs – LIKE OXFAM, DOCTORS OF THE WORLD AND DOCTORS WITHOUT BORDERS – LEFT AFTER A FEW YEARS, CONCLUDING THAT AID WAS BEING DIVERTED AWAY FROM THE PEOPLE.

... LEAVING BEHIND HUMANITARIAN INITIATIVES THAT ESSENTIALLY PROP UP THE EXISTING REGIME.

IN ANY CASE, THE DEAR LEADER'S INTENTIONS HAVE BEEN PUBLIC KNOWLEDGE SINCE 96.

ONLY 30% OF THE POPULATION WOULD NEED TO SURVIVE TO RECONSTRUCT A VICTORIOUS SOCIETY.

3.

4.

5.

4–7. Photographs by Dieter
Leistner, and thoughtful
comparisons, from (above left
and right) his travels to Seoul,
South Korea in 2012 and (below
left and right) to Pyongyang,
North Korea in 2006.

6.

7.

THE UBIQUITOUS VEIL: VISUAL DEBATES

Street artist Princess Hijab began her work in 2005, making a dramatic impact by applying dripping, black paint (or black felt-tip pen) suggesting Muslim veils on the half-nude models that she found in fashion advertisements in the Paris Metro. Operating only at night and disguising her identity, 'she' called her guerrilla art 'hijabizing'. Her work usually only stayed up for about forty-five minutes to an hour before Metro officials obliterated it.[30]

An extraordinary series of photographs is shown here by Yemeni photographer Boushra Yahya Almutawakel. Entitled *Mother, Daughter, Doll* (2010) it initially shows a photo-portrait of a mother, young daughter and her baby doll, all dressed in Western attire (only the mother wears a hijab). However in each of the following seven pictures another layer of the veil is applied, until finally the whole scene is draped in black. It is a disorienting journey through pictorial identity. The viewer often struggles to ascertain if the subjects are exactly the same people from one photo to the next, as hiding certain parts of the face – for example, the forehead – can change the sitter's appearance dramatically. A possible interpretation might also suggest the gradual burial of a person or personality by religion or other cultural or political power structures.

Iranian artist Parastou Forouhar was raised in Tehran. She was seventeen when the revolution against the Shah took place in 1979 and, while attending university in Tehran, she experienced the restrictions inherent in living under the new government. She moved to Germany in 1991, but her parents – intellectuals, activists and opposers of the theocratic regime – were brutally murdered in their Tehran home in 1998. This and the revolution itself have influenced her work in many ways.[31]

1. 'Hijabizing', interventions in the Paris Metro, by artist Princess Hijab. France 2006–11. Photographs by A. Breant.

2. (overleaf) *Mother, Daughter, Doll*, a sequence of eight photographs showing a portrait progression from a hijab to full-face veil (niqab) and finally, complete coverage in black. By Yemeni photographer Boushra Yahya Almutawakel. Yemen 2010.

1.

2.

DIVIDED COUNTRIES AND CULTURES: SIGNS OF TENSION AND RESOLVE

Forouhar's explorations of the veil present an uneasy, suffocating or faceless presence: an existence limited or cut-off by a totalitarian regime or brutal home life. A work entitled *Signs* is obvious in intention, depicting women forced into smaller spaces than men. Since the images are designed in the manner of public information or instructional signs, they project a message of misogyny, either institutional or part of agreed cultural behaviour and control.

Her parents' deaths pervade much of her work, particularly in her delicate patterns constructed from implements of torture, or bodies being hurt and pulled apart. Symbolically, she has created a subtle and intricate visual language based on the rhythmic repetition of pain, or the idea or possibility of pain. In her *Eslimi* series (meaning 'ornaments', see page 177), traditional geometric Islamic patterning has become embedded with potential pain and violence, quietly waiting to be unlocked by the institution or persons wishing to make use of it.[32]

3–4. *Signs*, series of laminated digital drawings on aluminium, by Iranian artist Parastou Forouhar. Germany 2004–10.

3.

3–4. *Signs*, series of laminated

4.

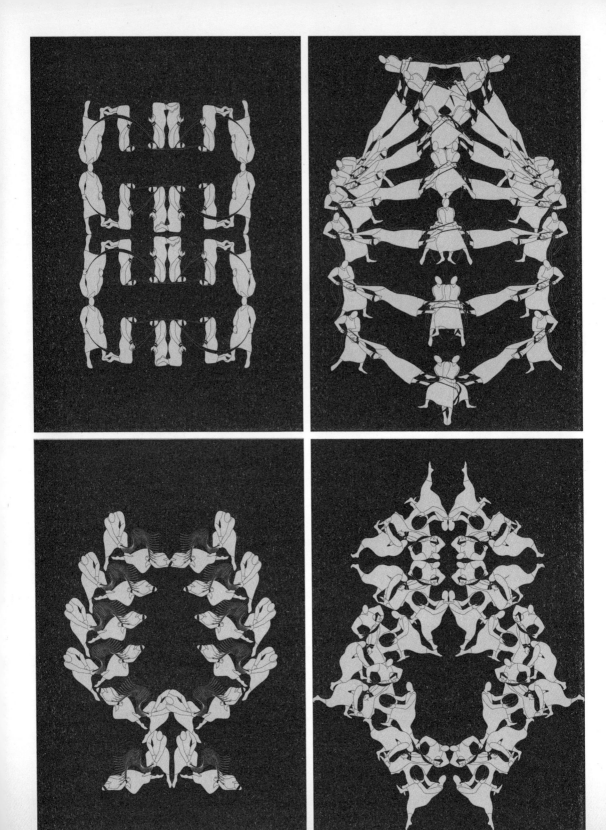

5.

5. *A Thousand and One Days I*,
four from a series of eight digital
drawings, by Iranian artist Parastou
Forouhar. Germany 2007.

DIVIDED COUNTRIES AND CULTURES: SIGNS OF TENSION AND RESOLVE

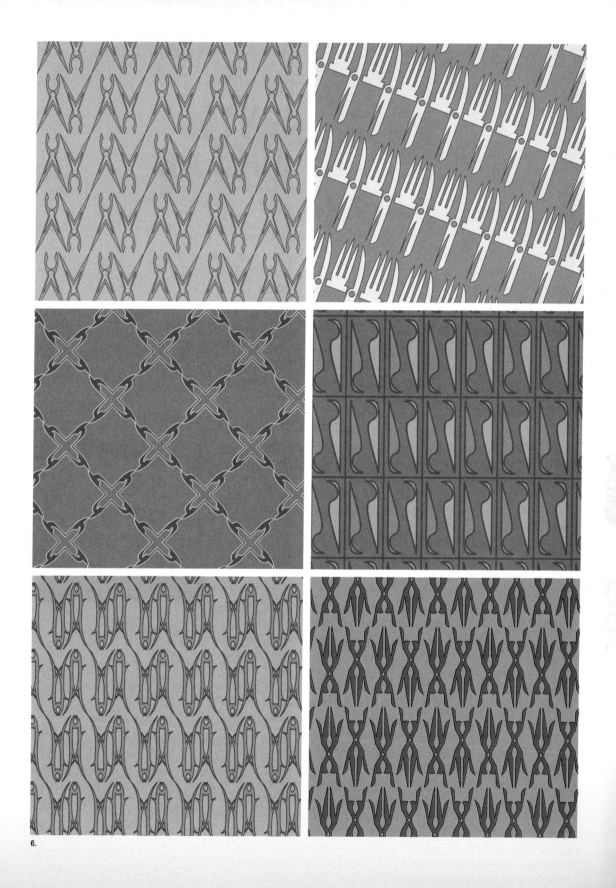

6.

6. *Guns*, from the *Eslimi* ('ornaments') series, digital prints on fabric, by Iranian artist Parastou Forouhar. Germany 2003–10.

HUMAN RIGHTS:
THE FIGHT GOES ON

By 2014 nearly twenty countries had legalized same-sex marriage; two of the most recent countries to pass legislation were Britain and France. Opposition was most fierce in France, emanating from the conservative right as well as hard-right neo-Nazis. Approval of the law however also brought celebration. The news was welcomed by *Libération* newspaper with a front page of artwork by Pierre et Gilles – Pierre Commoy, photographer and Gilles Blanchard, painter – who presented a life-size portrayal of the two figurines normally standing on top of the wedding cake. The face in the picture on the wall behind them, smiling benevolently, is that of French President François Hollande who would finally sign the legislation into law.

Pierre et Gilles are known for their exotic hand-painted photographs: portraits of celebrities, fashion, pop and gay icons, from Andy Warhol and Jean-Paul Gaultier to Catherine Deneuve and Madonna. Their subjects are usually depicted in a fantasy-laden, dream world coloured with eroticism. Their work is often inspired by, or borrows elements from, religion, popular or gay culture, and has at times courted controversy. As a well-known gay couple themselves, the use of their art by *Libération* would have added special delight to the occasion.[33]

The retro style postcard shown here, sporting a heroic image of a 1940s US airman and a shocking quote, was published in 2004 by *New Internationalist* magazine and acts as a reminder that the US military has, over the years, been one of the most intractable institutions in its dealings with homosexuality. The quote on the card is attributed to Leonard Matlovich, a United States Air Force sergeant who was discharged after coming out as gay in 1975. Homosexuality remained forbidden in the US military until President Clinton introduced the problematic 'Don't Ask, Don't Tell' policy in 1993. It was intended as an attempt to end the ban on gay servicemen and women by more-or-less telling them to keep their sexuality a secret, but in the end the legislation seemed to actually increase discrimination as more homosexuals were harassed or discharged from the armed forces than ever before. The 'Don't Ask, Don't Tell' policy was finally repealed in 2011 by President Obama, allowing openly gay and lesbian personnel to serve in the US military.[34]

The Air Force pinned a medal on me for killing a man and discharged me for making love to one.

1.

1. Postcard published by *New Internationalist* magazine on the failings of the US military in dealing with homosexuality. UK 2004.

2. Front page of *Libération* newspaper, 23 April 2013, with artwork by Pierre et Gilles. France 2013.

Within the image:

◆ 1,60 EURO. PREMIÈRE ÉDITION N°9936   MARDI 23 AVRIL 2013   WWW.LIBÉRATION.FR

Libération

SPECIAL
PIERRE ET GILLES

~ *Vive les Mariés* ~

PIERRE ET GILLES 2013

IMPRIMÉ EN FRANCE / PRINTED IN FRANCE Allemagne 2,50 €, Andorre 1,60 €, Autriche 2,80 €, Belgique 1,70 €, Canada 4,50 $, Danemark 27 Kr, DOM 2,40 €, Espagne 2,30 €, États-Unis 5 $, Finlande 2,70 €, Grande-Bretagne 1,80 £, Grèce 2,70 € Irlande 2,40 €, Israël 20 ILS, Italie 2,30 €, Luxembourg 1,70 €, Maroc 17 Dh, Norvège 27 Kr, Pays-Bas 2,30 €, Portugal (cont.) 2,40 €, Slovénie 2,70 €, Suède 24 Kr, Suisse 3,20 FS, TOM 430 CFP, Tunisie 2,40 DT, Zone CFA 2 000CFA.

2.

HUMAN RIGHTS: THE FIGHT GOES ON

179

Feminism lives on in the twenty-first century. British artist Sarah Maple's brand of shocking humour appears in a form of in-your-face feminism, often combined with an interrogation of modern-day issues relating to her mixed cultural background – her mother is Muslim and her father Christian. Much of her work to date has involved dressing up, facing the camera (real or imagined) and delivering her message with the use of props, usually aiming to get a reaction out of the viewer. And she normally does – although she has in the past experienced angry reactions from people of faith who fail to see the humour in her work.[35]

Menstruate with Pride (2012) is a painting of Maple in a white dress stained with menstrual blood, making the raised-fist gesture of political defiance while the crowd around her backs away in horror. Another of Maple's swipes at gender politics shows her three-stage, fast-track transformation from hijab-wearing woman with penis envy, through sexy underwear, to corporate takeover. Her work can be ruthlessly funny or shocking or both, and any cultural or gender barrier or taboo is a potential target.

3. *Signs*, digital print by artist Sarah Maple. UK 2007.

4. *Menstruate with Pride*, painting by artist Sarah Maple. UK 2010–11.

5. *I Heart Orgasms*, painting by artist Sarah Maple. UK 2008.

3.

4.

5.

Multidisciplinary artist Eca Eps' photo-series *Naked in Africa* (2013) is reminiscent of feminist protests of the 1970s, when women turned their bodies into political tools by writing slogans on them. Remarkably, some of the messages on the women's bodies have remained the same in the twenty-first century. For despite the serene beauty and stillness of the bodies in Eps' photographs, the typographic statements show that women today face many of the same challenges as they have always faced: subjugation and violence, the constraints of religion, conflicting attitudes to abortion and the still on-going practice of female genital mutilation or FGM – the harmful traditional practice involving the partial or total removal of the female genitalia. Often blamed on cultural, religious or social factors and widely regarded as being restricted to countries in Africa and the Middle East, FGM is alarmingly present in the UK today. The NHS estimates 20,000 girls under the age of fifteen are presently at risk each year.[36]

But Eca Eps' women show strength and resolve: they are up to the challenges. Their posture is confident, and their statements (or thoughts) are quietly but assuredly defiant.

6. *#BringBackOurGirls*, drawing by artist María María Acha-Kutscher expressing solidarity with the worldwide campaign protesting the kidnapping of more than 200 schoolgirls from Chibok village in northern Nigeria by the terrorist group Boko Haram. Mexico 2014.

7. Photographs from the series *Naked in Africa* by artist and photographer Eca Eps which eloquently express twenty-first century women's issues. UK 2013.

6.

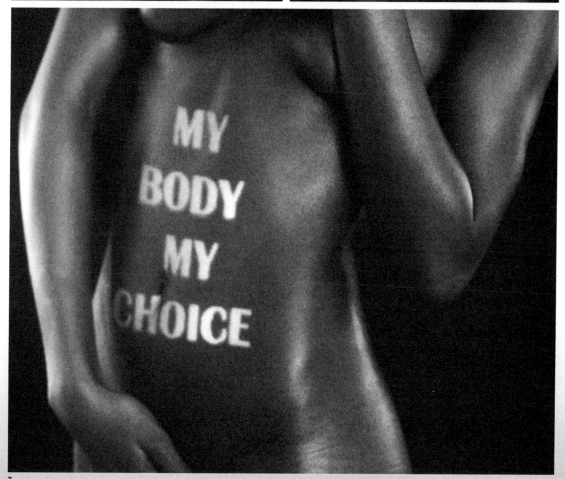

7.

CARTOONS, TERROR AND 'JE SUIS CHARLIE'

The French have long excelled at caricature. The early 1800s saw the rise of satirical cartoons and periodicals, highlighted by Charles Philipon's classic cartoon of King Louis-Philippe I's head transforming into an over-ripe pear (*poire* being French slang for simpleton or fool). After persistent anti-authoritarian cartooning, new censorship laws were introduced and satirical artists' graphic wit was limited to society figures. Nevertheless their comic papers still thrived. Thus a grand tradition of scabrous satire is embedded in the French psyche and is a regular component of much modern media.[37]

By the late 1890s France had fully embraced republicanism and its central tenets of *liberté, égalité* and *fraternité*. In 1905 these values were extended to include the principle of secularism – the separation of church and state – thus allowing freedom of speech for all. So it is within this cultural mind set and satirical tradition that the weekly magazine *Charlie Hebdo* was founded in 1969 (originally named *Hara-Kiri,* it took on its present name a year later). *Charlie Hebdo* made its reputation by outrageously mocking religious and political authority. In 2006, it published Danish cartoons caricaturing the prophet Muhammad (a highly controversial move since certain Islamic texts explicitly forbid any visual representation of the prophet). Despite accusations of racism and a lawsuit brought by the Grand Mosque of Paris, *Charlie Hebdo* forged ahead arguing that France's freedom of speech and separation of church and state gave it the right to criticize any religion.[38]

The magazine continued to lampoon radical Islam and, in November 2011, published a special edition purporting to be edited by the prophet Muhammad who was also caricatured on the cover. The magazine's Paris offices were firebombed as a result. Further cartoons of Muhammad were published despite death threats and government appeals for restraint.[39] Then, on 7 January 2015, two radical Islamist gunmen entered the magazine's offices and killed twelve and injured others on the *Hebdo* team including office staff, cartoonists, writers and the editor, Stéphane Charbonnier.[40] By the evening of 7 January over 35,000 people had gathered in the Place de la République holding candles and chanting 'Charlie, Liberté'. Spontaneous rallies took place throughout France, with many attendees holding pencils or pens aloft in defiance. There was international outcry and similar demonstrations of support occurred in cities throughout the world. On 11 January a nation-wide 'Unity Rally' brought world leaders and two million people to crowd the Parisian streets in solidarity. Unity Rallies also occurred in other French cities.

1.

1. *Je suis Charlie* (I am Charlie), a poster/graphic of great immediacy; it was designed by Joachim Roncin after hearing the shocking news of the massacre, and instantly became a symbol of solidarity, defiance and the right to freedom of speech. It grew in power through the twittersphere, had a strong presence in marches and demonstrations, and has become a sad but lasting memorial to those who were killed. France 2015.

2. *The Survivors Issue* of French comic magazine *Charlie Hebdo*, back on sale a week after twelve people were killed in its offices, including its editor. Controversially, and true to form, the cover bears a cartoon of the Prophet Muhammed – this time, weeping and holding a 'Je suis Charlie' sign. Above him are the words 'All is forgiven': reported to be a message from the survivors to the terrorists. France 2015.

2.

In an act of solidarity with those marching against the *Hebdo* murders, JR produced a photographic image of the eyes of Stéphane Charbonnier (aka 'Charb'), editor and chief cartoonist of *Charlie Hebdo* magazine and one of the twelve killed. The image was divided across eight placards to be carried by marchers, as shown here in the Unity Rally held in Paris on Sunday 10 January. Smaller eye-strip placards of all twelve murdered *Charlie Hebdo* workers were also produced for individuals to carry, and appeared in a rally in Union Square in New York City.[41]

At the same time, a catchphrase had formed that would continue to resonate long after the attacks: *Je suis Charlie* (I am Charlie). #JeSuisCharlie became an instant internet meme and the slogan amassed over two million tweets by the evening of 7 January.[42] A week after the atrocity took place, *Charlie Hebdo* defiantly went on sale with a cover featuring a cartoon of a tearful prophet Muhammad holding a sign reading 'Je suis Charlie' with the words *'Tout est pardonné'* (All is forgiven) written above.[43]

The 'Je suis Charlie' commentary not only gave voice to the collective outcry of grief and anger following the attack, but also gave rise to numerous fierce debates. Does the right to freedom of speech automatically include the right to offend? Are some religions untouchable – and others fair game?[44] Are such attacks a response to perceived injustices taking place in the world, such as the wars in Iraq or Syria? 'Je suis Charlie' not only came to represent the mourning of those killed, but for many it also became a statement in defence of free speech. It may yet also trigger an urgently needed reflection upon what freedom of speech actually *means* in the twenty-first century; upon whether freedom of speech is the only issue at stake; and an examination of what other actions may have contributed to the anger of those attacking that freedom.

3. *Je Suis Charlie* solidarity graphic, by Jean Jullien. France 2015.

4. *He Drew First*, solidarity cartoon, by David Pope. Australia 2015.

5. *Liberté Crucifié*, solidarity illustration, by Tomi Ungerer, 2015.

3.

4.

6. *Ceci n'est pas une terroriste* (This is not a terrorist), illustration by Pénélope Bagieu which appeared in the magazine *les inrockuptibles* in the aftermath of the *Charlie Hebdo* massacre of 7 January. It alludes to fears in France and elsewhere of an anti-Muslim backlash. Knowing that she may well be viewed as a potential terrorist by some, the woman sighs 'eh merde' (oh, shit). France 2015.

7. In solidarity, JR and his studio produced a photographic image of the eyes of Stéphane Charbonnier (aka 'Charb'), editor and chief cartoonist of *Charlie Hebdo* magazine and one of the twelve killed in the attack on the *Hebdo* offices. The image was divided across eight placards to be carried by marchers, as shown here in one of the many Unity Rallies held in France on Sunday 10 January. France 2015.

5.

eh merde ...

Ceci n'est pas une terroriste.

Pénélope*

6.

7.

JR: MAGNIFYING THE WORLD

The artist JR often produces work that requires engagement with ordinary people – the invisibles, the everyday, the unnoticed. After photographing them or requesting portraits, he enlarges the images to monumental size, pasting the magnified pictures throughout the environment. The visual effect is astounding. Whether in the favelas of Rio or the streets of Los Angeles, buildings start to speak, gigantic eyes blink in different directions and huge smiles pop out of the dark. It's as if a whole layer of humanity, hidden in the depths of cities and slums, has suddenly surfaced to see the light – and finds it dazzling.

Engagement is key to JR's work. He has travelled the world, sometimes placing himself in difficult situations. By initiating straightforward discussion with those involved, he gains their trust and – through photography, enlarging and pasting – tells their story. He began to work in this way after the 2004 riots in the Paris suburbs, or *banlieues*, taking close-up shots (using a 28-milimetre lens) of young residents pulling faces and pasting them on the walls of the historic Marais district, giving the residents of the *banlieues* a human face. The next stage in what he now called his *28 Millimétres* project was *Face2Face* (2007) in Israel and the West Bank, where a mixture of Israelis and Palestinians were photographed close-up, and the photos pasted throughout Israel, the West Bank and on both sides of the Separation Wall (see page 157).[45]

Then in 2008, came *Women Are Heroes* (the third stage of *28 Millimétres*) examining the role women play in holding families and communities together around the world, despite tragedy and conflict. JR's first stop was the slums of Kibera in Kenya, where 2000 square metres (21,500 square feet) of rooftops were covered with his photographs of resident women's faces (the photographs were also printed on vinyl providing the added benefit of making the rooftops waterproof). A further stop that year was a visit to Morro da Providência, one of Rio de Janeiro's most dangerous favelas, after hearing a news report of the killing of three innocent young men caught up in the existing drug wars. The women he met there told a story, not of grief and despair, but of courage and dignity – and the desire for identity, as the infamous favela was literally being 'disappeared' off the map, despite its location near the centre of the city. This time, their story was told through photographs of their eyes, proud and immovable, which they helped JR to paste on the sides of their houses: all looking directly towards the centre of Rio – an emotive reminder of their existence.[46]

1. *28 Millimetres: Women Are Heroes*, project by the French artist JR. The photograph shows an overview of an 'action' in a Kibera slum. Kenya 2009.

2. *Inside Out Project: The Time Is Now, Yalla!*, photographic 'pasting' in Naplouse, Palestine. In 2011 JR and his team set up giant photobooths in Israel and Palestine; both communities visited the booths and received large-format photos that they could paste anywhere, on their own or in groups. The project title states that it is now time for the two-state solution, bringing peace and prosperity: 'Yalla' means 'let's go!'.

3 (overleaf). *28 Millimetres: Women Are Heroes*, project by the French artist JR. The photograph shows an action in the favela Morro da Providência in Rio de Janeiro. Brazil 2008.

1.

2.

JR won the TED Prize in 2011, and launched a new global participatory project entitled *Inside Out*, through which he encouraged people to send him their own portraits and a statement concerning a cause that they felt strongly about. The Inside Out Project would then help them to find a vehicle for communicating their statement or cause. The group project *The Time is Now, Yalla!* (2011) is represented on page 189 by a photo 'pasting' in Naplouse, Palestine, involving both Israelis and Palestinians. The project title calls for the two state solution, bringing peace and prosperity: 'Yalla' means 'let's go!'. [47]

MAN'S FOLLY, NATURE'S FURY: DISASTERS, WARNINGS AND HOPE

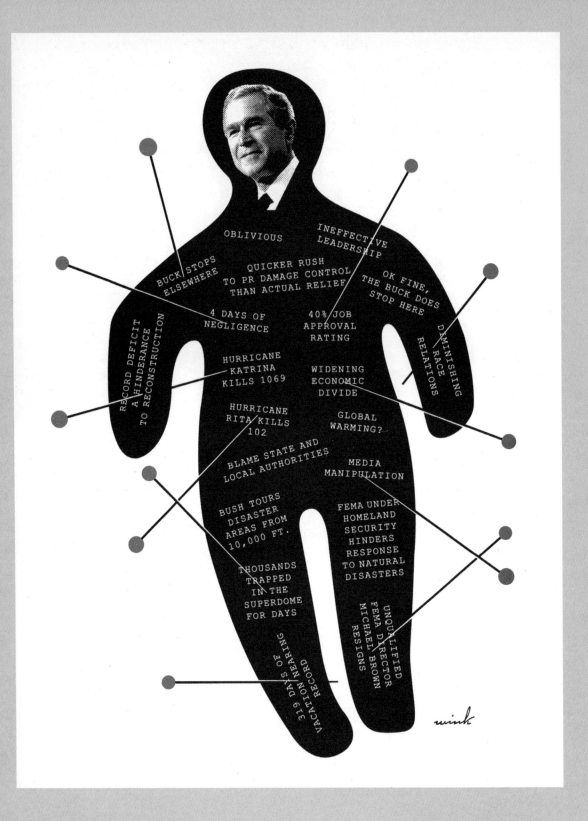

MAN'S FOLLY, NATURE'S FURY: DISASTERS, WARNINGS AND HOPE

As we entered the new millennium, twentieth-century fears and protests about environmental damage, pollution and nuclear power were slowly transformed into twenty-first-century visions of seemingly inevitable dystopian futures. Scientists continued to argue over the potential dangers of global warming and climate change and, as if to underline the pervading sense of doom, a devastating series of disasters struck. In 2004 the Asian tsunami killed 230,000 people in eighteen countries (with Indonesia, Sri Lanka, India and Thailand bearing the greatest losses). Hurricane Katrina ravaged the south coast of the US in 2005. An earthquake in Sichuan Province, China, in 2008 resulted in 87,000 dead and 18,000 missing.

In January 2010 the Haiti earthquake killed 220,000 and injured 300,000. Later that year, the Deepwater Horizon oil spill spewed over 200 million gallons of crude oil into the Gulf of Mexico. The next decade started with the Japanese earthquake and tsunami that caused the Fukushima nuclear accident of 2011, when the tsunami knocked out the power and cooling systems in three reactors. The earthquake itself caused over 19,000 deaths.[1]

Sometimes they created investigations aiming to expose injustice; or other worlds or spaces to retreat to. Sometimes they presented warnings of what might be lost if corporate interests or human disinterest went too far. Sometimes they produced messages of beauty and comfort within the heartbreak and wreckage.

The fashion designer Vivienne Westwood has lectured passionately on the dangers of global warming in colleges, online and in the media – and her politics shout out from her fashions on the catwalk. 'Climate Revolution', the name of her ongoing environmental campaign, has become a symbol of her in-your-face activism and determination to stop abuse and pollution of the environment.

This roll call of misfortune made arguments about global warming and climate change even fiercer, and amplified debates about the role of humankind as chief disrupter of natural processes and the ecosystem. Creative individuals, including artists and designers, played their part in such debates as well as in facing up to the disasters. They became observers and discoverers; recorders and documenters; critics and campaigners; visual activists, protesters and culture jammers; as well as sympathizers and supporters of humanitarian causes.

Modern urban living has not only robbed many wild animals of their habitats, it has also stripped humankind of its sense of space and integration with these animals. Perhaps that is why coming upon large renditions of animals in the city, through street art or performance, is so wonderful (especially creations by the Belgian street artist ROA). Maybe wild animals are missed far more than humanity will admit? In an effort to explore that question, the artist Marcus Coates has explored traditions of folk belief or

shamanism in the British Isles in order to seek out and communicate with animal spirits.

By practicing such traditions, and accessing the knowledge and understanding of different worlds, he hopes to find solutions to problems in the present. It's an intriguing mission: the search for new spiritualities and rituals to address current problems may be more than useful in a world where religion is more often a cause for conflict or discontent (see page 202).

KATRINA: DEVASTATION IN AMERICA

Hurricane Katrina hit the US south coast in the early morning on 29 August 2005, demolishing coastal Mississippi and nearly obliterating one of the country's best-known cities, New Orleans. Large sections of the city were supposed to be protected by levees that had been built along Lake Pontchartrain and the Mississippi River, thereby allowing construction and settlement on land well below the level of both lake and river. On 28 August eighty per cent of New Orleans residents had heeded the Mayor's call to evacuate the city. Those left behind were the city's most vulnerable, largely from poor black communities or the ill and the aged, unable to run or drive. Soon after the hurricane had landed the levees were breached and before the day was out eighty per cent of the city was submerged, some areas under 2.5 metres (8 feet) of water, with 80–100,000 residents left stranded. Some survivors fled for the Superdome football stadium, which sat on higher ground, while looting took place elsewhere. Rescuers – often ordinary people – dragged survivors from roofs and houses. The response from the Federal Emergency Management Agency (FEMA) and other agencies was slow and shameful. President George W. Bush and the National Guard finally

arrived on 12 September; Bush held a meeting with local officials on Air Force One. Soon after, the FEMA director lost his job and Bush's approval rating plummeted.[2]

Creative projects soon appeared, documenting the disaster and surrounding events and offering help and solidarity. Spike Lee's four-hour HBO documentary film *When the Levees Broke: A Requiem in Four Acts* (2006) was by far the most heartfelt, angry and comprehensive coverage of Katrina, the aftermath, rescue attempts and the high emotions of those involved. It also became an activist's statement against racism and an investigative search for accountability. Another revealing true story was that of Abdulrahman Zeitoun, a New Orleans building contractor originally from Syria who spent two days in his old canoe rescuing stranded neighbours. He was then arrested by the National Guard, accused of being a member of Al-Qaida, and was imprisoned for nearly a month until the charges were dropped. A book entitled *Zeitoun* (2009) chronicled his experiences, and exposed the failings of the Bush government to deal with the disaster, as well as the post-9/11 attitude of Americans towards Muslims at that time.[3]

The Hurricane Poster Project invited the design community to raise money for victims of Katrina by producing posters for sale; proceeds from the sales supported the work of the American Red Cross. (Three of the most popular posters are shown on pages 208–209.) In 2008, the street artist Banksy visited to observe the progress of the clean-up operation and painted a number of pieces in tribute to the people of New

Orleans. The book *Unfathomable City: A New Orleans Atlas*, by Rebecca Solnit and Rebecca Snedeker, appeared in 2013 presenting an imaginative and heavily researched view of changes taking place in New Orleans over time – migrating populations and so on – and particularly developments relating to Katrina. If wishing to know more about lawless actions during the disaster, particularly those carried out by the police, this is the place to look.

CONFRONTING THE ADDICTION TO OIL AND PETROCHEMICALS

It is believed that BP is destroying sea turtles and other wildlife during their clean-up efforts in the Gulf of Mexico.

The Deepwater Horizon oil spill of April 2010 remains one of the largest oil spills in world history to date. The BP-operated Deepwater Horizon oil rig exploded on 20 April, killing eleven platform workers. At the time of the explosion it was drilling 1,500 metres (5,000 feet) below sea level. The rig burned for thity-six hours before sinking on the morning of 22 April. An 8-kilometre (5-mile) slick formed and continued attempts to cap or plug the ruptured well failed. It poured crude oil into the Gulf of Mexico for eighty-seven days before finally being shut down. The environmental disaster was enormous: every Gulf state – Louisiana, Mississippi, Alabama, Florida and Texas – had been polluted. By August nearly 5,000 dead animals (mainly birds and sea turtles) had been collected. BP launched a

massive clean-up operation and compensation payments began to those who suffered loss of earnings in the Gulf fishing and tourist industries; in 2012 opportunities for claiming compensation payments were still being advertized on public billboards in Florida's coastal areas.[4]

Thousands of volunteers were engaged in clean-up activities along coastal communities. Graphic designers sprang into action condemning the mess: Jude Landry's poster of an oil monster gripping the Gulf states was a call to action as well as raising funds for the clean-up (see page 216). Anthony Burrill's screen-print poster, shown here, was made using ink mixed with oily-sand from the Gulf coast during the actual spill; a conceptual memento that, by its very texture, inspires political anger in the viewer. Meanwhile the website logomyway.com, specializing in logo competitions, allowed a large number of graphic designers and artists to vent their anger by manipulating BP's logo. The subversions were fascinating in their variety, referencing dead or dying animals, industry, cartoons and even iconic photographs from the Vietnam War. Protests and anti-BP t-shirts popped up particularly in New Orleans, a city still reeling from the shock of Hurricane Katrina in 2005.

A different kind of poisoning, located not far from Deepwater Horizon, has been addressed in the collaborative project *Petrochemical America* (2012). Richard Misrach's photographic record of the 'Chemical Corridor' (known locally as 'Cancer Alley') documents the physical and socio-economic toll taken by chemical production along a stretch of the Mississippi River from Baton Rouge to New Orleans. His collaborators, landscape architect Kate Orff and her team, have researched and mapped data from the region, producing an 'ecological atlas' representing and analysing the various changing ecologies of the region. Together the project, published as a book, reveals the impact of the petrochemical industry on the environment and humankind not only in the present, but also into the future.[5]

VISIONS OF THE FUTURE

Former US Vice President Al Gore's comprehensive introduction to the issues of global warming and climate change, entitled *An Inconvenient Truth*, appeared as a book and film in 2006. Various denials and challenges emanated from the science community, but Gore undeniably managed to popularize both issues to a broad, international audience. Since then the current and future challenge of climate change has been constantly present in twenty-first-century thinking and in the collective imagination.

That being said, in Britain the risk of the city of London flooding has never been considered far-fetched. Additionally its main flood defence, the Thames Barrier, has a life expectancy ending in 2030.[6] The twin concerns of climate change and rising sea levels, combined with an ageing Thames Barrier, has led numerous filmmakers, animators, designers and architects to dream of floating cities, buildings on stilts and high-tech futures as possible remedies of a flooded London (or other cities, for that matter). Yet the creative agency Squint/Opera has produced a different take on the premonition of a future flooded city, and exhibited five images entitled *Flooded London* in the 2008 London Festival of Architecture (see page 224). Set in 2090, when London has been overwhelmed by rising sea levels, they show a relaxed, peaceful utopia where people swim or fish from half-submerged London landmarks and spend time inventing makeshift submarines and other machinery from recycled, pre-flood materials.[7] And there may be a lesson here: sink the hectic, rat-race lifestyle and everyone could be happier – but should it really take a disaster to achieve it?

Raised in the heavily industrialized Pearl River Delta, Chinese artist Cao Fei focused her early work on satirizing consumerism or capturing the lives and fantasies of factory workers and ordinary people, wishing to escape their mundane lives. In 2007 she shifted to the realm of interactive media, in particular the online role-playing game,

Second Life. Taking on a virtual identity as the avatar 'China Tracy', she planned her own development entitled *RMB City* (2007–11) within the game, which grew to become a centre for new projects and artworks, financed or supported by collectors or institutions in the real world.[8] Keen to traverse the boundaries between the virtual world and the real, she moved on to *RMB City Opera* (2009), where avatars and virtual spaces appear with real actors in a stage performance. *RMB City* offers fun, interest and engagement, but a virtual identity in a virtual world also offers a sense of escape, whether from the mediocrity of everyday life or the rigidity of a society with its strict, interfering political system. It may also one day offer opportunities for escape from the real-world's environmental wreckage.

Canadian artist Kelly Richardson's large-scale, immersive installations also merge the real and the unreal, but in a very different way. Her use of photographic images and film footage, isolated sounds and highly calculated movements produce a brooding, uneasy ambiguity. Is the viewer gazing upon the lair of some horror lying beneath water and poisoning the landscape? Or is this a warning of things to come, as trees appear like holographic ghosts, clicking in and out of sight, as if missing but now returned to haunt humanity? All are conjurings of the effects of humanity and industrialization on the environment; and warnings to humankind of what may lie beneath as well as what may already be lost.

Page 194. *Voodoo*, poster for The Hurricane Poster Project showing outrage at the Bush Administration's inadequate response to the Katrina crisis. By designer and illustrator Richard Boynton of Wink design firm (Richard Boynton and Scott Thares). USA 2005.

Page 195. Left: *No Globe*, a subversive snow globe toy containing the cooling towers of a coal-fired power station which, when shaken, rains black ash. Created by Dorothy art collective. UK 2009.
Right: *Plastic Dog*, a series of electronic comic strips by Henning Wagenbreth, Germany 2004.

Page 196. Left: *Journey to the Lower World, Preparation with Beryl*, by artist Marcus Coates. UK 2004.
Right: *Hope*, poster for The Hurricane Poster Project, designed and illustrated by Wink. USA 2005.

Page 197. Left: *Is BP burning sea turtles alive?*, poster targeting BP's clean-up efforts after the Deepwater Horizon oil spill, designed and illustrated by Scott Laserow. USA 2010. Right: The process of making a poster relating to the BP Deepwater Horizon oil spill. Screenprinted by Anthony Burrill using ink made from oily sand taken from the Gulf shore after the spill. USA 2010.

Page 198. Video still from *Live in RMB City*, showing China Tracy (Cao Fei's avatar) travelling around the city with her baby son. China 2009.

Page 199. Toxic Contamination Wallpaper, by Francesco Simeti. Italy/USA 2000.

THE POLLUTED PRESENT: START A REVOLUTION

Vivienne Westwood, responsible for the 1970s styles of Britain's punk years, subsequently became Britain's leading fashion maverick – and has remained so to this day. Her fashion empire is world renowned and so is her political activism, especially her deep commitment to the environment. She has lectured on the threat of climate change online, in colleges and other venues and on television. Her website climaterevolution.co.uk is a conglomeration of articles, protests and campaigns relating to climate change, anti-fracking, preserving the rainforest and other issues including Greenpeace's Save the Arctic campaign. Forever a dynamic figure, she also feeds her ecological concerns into her high-profile fashion brand and her catwalk shows, as well as protesting in the street. Westwood is one of the few high-profile designers to so blatantly combine design with environmental activism.[9]

1. Vivienne Westwood and Climate Revolution. UK 2012. Photograph by Martin Parr.

1.

A SENSE OF LOSS

1.

Belgian street artist ROA focuses on painting animals, usually rendered in black and white and often very large in scale (the smaller the animal, the larger the painting seems to be). The paintings tower over people in the street, asserting their presence on walls in the urban environment and beyond. ROA keeps his subject matter local, always trying to paint the natural animal inhabitants of that particular area.[10] The paintings stress the relationship between humans and animals, reminding us that we should exist in the city together, sharing space. However the animals are often driven away or even killed. So in one sense the large-scale depictions are a sad tribute to animals that may have been pushed away in the name of urbanization and redevelopment. Yet because of their beauty and towering stature, the portraits may also be seen as assertive and defiant, acting as a reminder of what needs to be valued and protected.

There is also the possibility of finding new forms of spirituality for the modern world through ancient techniques. In 2008, ornithologist and artist Marcus Coates produced a film, *The Plover's Wing*, showing how he practises traditions of folklore and shamanism in order to communicate with animal spirits. Hence by accessing the knowledge and understanding of different worlds, he might find solutions for modern-day problems. In the film he demonstrates how he enters a trance-like state, which he calls 'becoming animal' (the physical embodiment of an animal), and journeys to the 'lower world' of animal spirits in order to seek answers from those he encounters.[11]

Coates travels to Israel and while there meets with the mayor of the city of Holon. When asked a question by the mayor about the Israeli-Palestinian conflict, he goes into a trance and makes his journey to the lower world. He describes seeing a green plover (a type of bird), feigning an injury to draw predators away from its nest. He interprets the bird's behaviour into advice that he reports back to the mayor, which is, in short, to 'identify with the victim's position'.[12]

However finding solutions is only part of the art. The idea of probing the spiritual boundaries of being human – or animal – or both, is an interesting one. Such explorations might lead to new ideas and understanding about what it is to be human, or aid us in integrating with the realm of nature once again – which may just help in the search for a better world.

1. *Firebird, Rhebok, Badger and Hare,* from the project *The Plover's Wing: A Meeting with the Mayor of Holon, Israel,* by artist Marcus Coates. UK 2008.

2. *Beaver,* by the Belgian street artist ROA, art located in London. UK 2009.

3. *The lenticular Rabbit – fleece perspective,* freehand spray can art by ROA, located in London. UK 2009. Photograph by RomanyWG.

4. *The Lenticular Rabbit – nerve system perspective,* freehand spray can art by ROA, located in London. UK 2009. Photograph by RomanyWG.

5. (overleaf) *The lenticular Rabbit – frontal view,* freehand spray can art by ROA, located in London. UK 2009. Photograph by RomanyWG.

2.

3.

4.

EXTENDING THE VISUAL HISTORY OF KATRINA

Hurricane Katrina was one of the greatest natural disasters that the US has ever known. It made landfall on coastal Mississippi on the morning of 29 August 2005. It then continued on its devastating path to demolish New Orleans, where the breaching of the levees resulted in eighty per cent of the city being left submerged (see page 196). The hurricane was a natural catastrophe that could not have been avoided, but further *man-made* disasters were soon to unfold in the city. They would be reflected on in a number of creative projects that were produced at the time or in years after.

A few examples are shown on pages 208 and 209 from the Hurricane Poster Project of 2005. The design community produced posters to be sold online, with proceeds going to the American Red Cross in support of the victims of Katrina. It was one of the graphic design community's great moments of solidarity and connectedness within the US, at a time when it's help was badly needed.[13]

1.

Laurie DeMartino's delicately rendered poster of teardrops was inspired by the words of a traumatized survivor who, unable to pull his wife to safety, was forced to surrender her to the sweeping floodwaters. John Foster's powerfully drawn image of an old woman with her poodle on her lap, sitting on her roof while alligators swim in predatorial circles beneath, projects feelings of fear and vulnerability. The quote at the top of the poster may appear small in size, but its implications are huge. 'George Bush doesn't care about black people' was a statement of disgust at the delayed government response, made by singer Kanye West, live on camera, at a benefit concert for hurricane relief.[14] It became famous at the time and continued to resonate for years after, recalling the notoriously late visit to the stricken city by President George W. Bush as well as the shamefully slow progress of FEMA, the Federal Emergency Management Agency. Similar feelings are expressed in Scott Laserow's poster, showing a jazz musician perched on top of a corner of the state of Louisiana, nearly under water. It conjures up images of a state, sinking slowly until almost submerged: a meaningful visual metaphor for the distress and devastation that ensued while FEMA dragged its heels for months.

1 and 2. Street art in New Orleans by Banksy, created three years after Hurricane Katrina, including the popular *Umbrella Girl*. USA 2008.

2.

Three years after Katrina, the UK street artist Banksy visited New Orleans to see how the clean-up operation was progressing and created more than a dozen works in tribute to the people of New Orleans. Scattered across the city, the images related to events that took place during the disaster as well as more recent issues linked to the recovery process. One of the best known pieces is *New Orleans Umbrella Girl* whose umbrella fails to protect her, as rain falls inside the umbrella while outside it remains dry: reputedly a reference to the breaching of the levees and their failure to do their job and protect people. Another painting shows a child flying a refrigerator (instead of a kite), possibly alluding to refrigerators – which contain potential contaminants – lining the streets after the flood, waiting for collection by the authorities.[15]

4.

3. Poster for The Hurricane Poster Project, designed and illustrated by John Foster (Bad People Good Things). Incorporated within the poster is Kanye West's famous statement to the media 'George Bush doesn't care about black people'. USA 2005.

4. Poster for The Hurricane Poster Project, designed and illustrated by Scott Laserow. USA 2005.

5. Poster for The Hurricane Poster Project, designed and illustrated by Laurie DeMartino. USA 2005.

3.

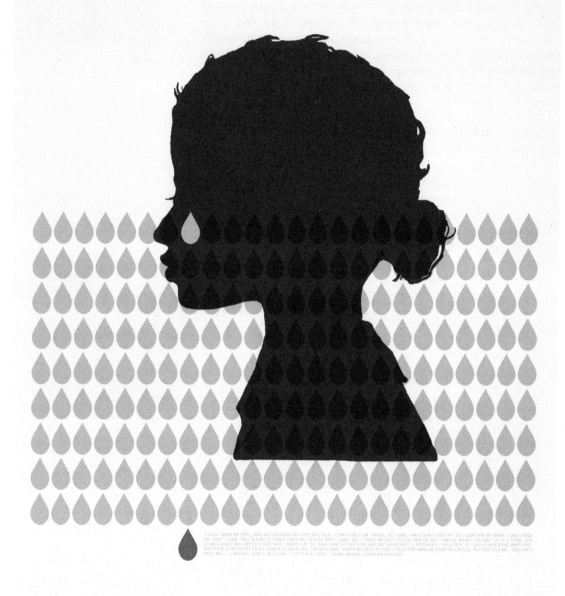

Another interesting aspect of the collection of images is their ability to survive, or not, as a visual history. As time went by, Umbrella Girl alone was covered with plexiglas (perspex); then defaced with red spray paint; then cleaned; then rescued from an attempt by four robbers to remove her intact, attacking the wall with power drills. Other images didn't fair so well. Some were plastered over accidently by people not realizing the value of what lay beneath; and some were intentionally painted over by people possibly not wishing to remember the events. Still other images were on parts of buildings now demolished. Nevertheless the fate of the Banksy images still draws visitors to New Orleans and fascinating accounts of the images' survival or demise assure their place in the city's collective memory and exist as visual histories that can still be located online.[16]

Further accounts of and reflections on the Katrina disaster appeared in 2013 in the book *Unfathomable City: A New Orleans Atlas* (by Rebecca Solnit and Rebecca Snedeker). It pays tribute to the history, culture, people and survival of the city. Its imaginative use of maps speaks volumes about the location of levee breaching, flood-water depths and violence in the city in the aftermath of Katrina (particularly on the part of the police, see the 'Snakes' on page 213), the presence of the oil industry along the Louisiana gulf coast, and the location of the BP oil spill that would follow. All of the forms of documentation and activism mentioned are important: they ensure that far into the future, the record of events that occurred during and after Katrina will not be forgotten.

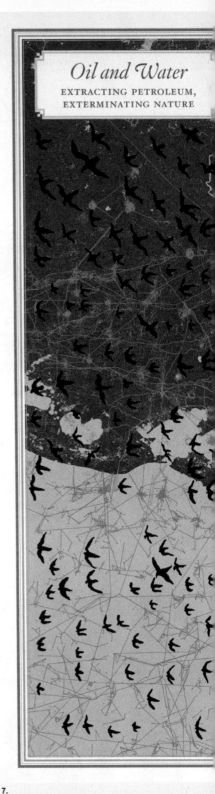

7.

6.

6–7 and 8 (overleaf). Cover illustration and inside spreads of *Unfathomable City: A New Orleans Atlas* by Rebecca Solnit and Rebecca Snedeker. USA 2013.

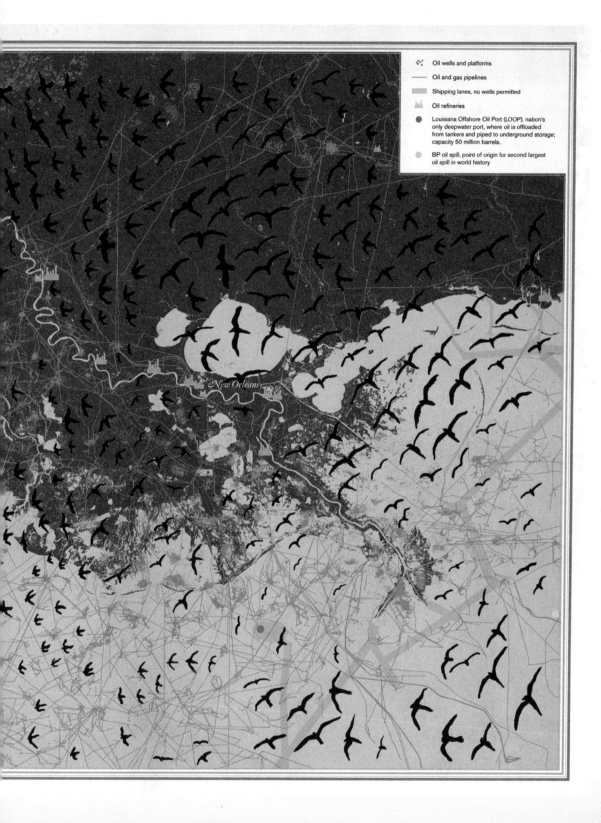

Oil wells and platforms

Oil and gas pipelines

Shipping lanes, no wells permitted

Oil refineries

Louisiana Offshore Oil Port (LOOP), nation's only deepwater port, where oil is offloaded from tankers and piped to underground storage; capacity 50 million barrels.

BP oil spill, point of origin for second largest oil spill in world history

New Orleans

Lake Pontchartrain

Robert E. Lee Blvd

Pontchartrain Blvd

Lakeview

2

New Orleans

17th Street Canal

Orleans Avenue Canal

London Avenue Canal

Paris Ave

Elysian Fields Ave

Franklin Ave

4

Gentilly

METAIRIE

1

Canal Blvd

3

St Bernard Ave

Gentilly Blvd

9

8

Almonaster Ave

Metairie Rd

Esplanade Ave

10

Orleans Ave

Bayou St. John

N Claiborne Ave
N Robertson St

11

Bienville St

N Broad St

Treme

Marigny

Bywater

St Cla

S Carrollton Ave

Mid City

Canal St

N Claiborne Ave

Governor Nicholls St

7

46

Earhart Blvd

Tulane Ave

15

N Rampart St

16

French Quarter

9

8

S Claiborne Ave

3
4

10

Central Business District

13

19
20
21

19
20
21

25

26
18

20
21

Algiers Point

22

Carrollton

12

Broadway St

Tchoupitoulas St

Superdome

11

12

5

Morial Convention Center

22

14

17

24
23

Newton St

2

1

2

St Charles Ave

14

Jackson Ave

16

Franklin Ave

13

Garden District

15

River

GRETNA

Uptown

Napoleon Ave

Louisiana Ave

Magazine St

Tchoupitoulas St

Mississippi

River Rd

4th St

16

HARVEY

Snakes and Ladders
WHAT ROSE UP, WHAT FELL DOWN
DURING HURRICANE KATRINA

LADDERS: ACTS OF RESCUE AND SOLIDARITY

1 "Cajun Navy" launches hundreds of rescue boats; U.S. Fish and Wildlife brings 60 boats, rescues 21,000 people

2 Michael Prevost rescues "the roof people of Lakeview" by canoe

3 St. Bernard Projects: Donnell Herrington and cousin rescue more than 100 by boat

4 St. Raphael School: 300 people take refuge

5 Lake Charles Cajun Navy rescues 1,000, mostly senior citizens

6 Mary Queen of Vietnam Church anchors the Vietnamese American community

7 Cajun Navy launches rescue boats

8 George W. Carver Elementary School: 100 people take refuge

9 One man with a boat rescues 300 people

10 Mama D and the Soul Patrol care for their community

11 Woman with a pirogue (flat-bottom boat) rescues elderly people near La Maison Bleu Guest House

12 Sierra Club runs environmental justice programs

13 Five punks evacuate with 62-year-old neighbor

14 Memorial Medical Center: doctors and nurses stay

15 Charity Hospital: doctors and nurses stay

16 Hotel guests form a mutual-aid community

17 Police rescues Keith Bernard Sr. and neighbor

18 Holy Cross Neighborhood Association organizes locals

19 WWL radio: Garland Robinette keeps broadcasting

20 Harrah's Casino: Cajun Navy stages rescues

21 Hundreds of tourists form mutual-aid community

22 Morial Convention Center: witness on site reports that "looters" brought provisions for old people and babies; police officer Dumaine Carter serves and protects

23 Common Ground Health Clinic arises

24 Anarchist street medics tend to people door to door

25 Coast Guard "Operation Dunkirk" evacuation point

26 Malik Rahim's home: Common Ground is born—"solidarity not charity"

27 Donnell Herrington, bleeding profusely (see Snakes 19), is rescued by strangers, who take him to West Jefferson Medical Center, where doctors save his life

28 William Tanner attempts to rescue wounded Henry Glover, who had been shot by police (see Snakes 25, 26, 27)

SNAKES: THE SABOTAGE OF SURVIVAL

1 Police beat two men, knock out one's teeth, rough up journalist

2 Israeli mercenaries hired to guard gated community

3 Prisoners abandoned in flooded Orleans Parish Prison

4 New Orleans Police Department headquarters: 249 officers go AWOL; order to "shoot looters" issued

5 Coroner's office botches autopsies and records

6 Danziger Bridge: seven police shoot six unarmed pedestrians, one in the back; two die and four are injured, including a mother whose forearm is blown off and a teenager disabled for life

7 Police shoot Matt McDonald in the back

8 President George W. Bush stages photo-op in Jackson Square

9 Blackwater mercenaries go rogue

10 Police shoot unarmed man, who survives

11 Hundreds prevented from evacuating the Superdome; national media spreads false rumors about rapes and murders there

12 Mayor Ray Nagin cowers in Hyatt Regency, spreads false rumors

13 Cadillac dealership plundered by police

14 Morial Convention Center: police shoot and kill Danny Brumfield in front of his family; Homeland Security Secretary Michael Chertoff tells NPR, "Actually I have not heard a report of thousands of people in the convention center who don't have food and water"

15 Walmart Supercenter: MSNBC reporter insults a child on national news; mainstream media demonize survivors

16 Crescent City Connection: transit and Gretna police and Jefferson Parish sheriffs turn back stranded people at gunpoint, block bridge exits, use racial slurs

17 Heavily armed vigilantes terrorize and shoot African Americans

18 Vigilante kills a man at Daigle's Grocery

19 Algiers vigilante shoots rescuer Donnell Herrington in the back and neck; buckshot also hits his cousin and his friend (see Ladders 3, 27)

20 While distributing food, Common Ground cofounder Scott Crow is forced to lie face down at gunpoint, threatened with death by police

21 Police, vigilantes initiate armed stand-offs with African American residents

22 African American man shot, his body left to rot in the sun

23 Jamil Joyner shoots police officer Kevin Thomas in the head

24 Officer David Warren, armed with high-powered rifle, shoots at citizen, misses

25 Officer Warren fatally shoots Henry Glover

26 Police compound at Paul B. Habans Elementary School: officers beat William Tanner and Henry Glover's brother, steal Tanner's car, let Glover bleed to death in back seat of car

27 Levee: police torch William Tanner's car with Henry Glover's body inside

Levee break and direction of water flow

Height of water

■ 10+ feet
■ 8–10 feet
■ 6–8 feet
■ 4–6 feet
▒ 2–4 feet
░ 0–2 feet

DEEPWATER HORIZON OIL SPILL: VENTING THE ANGER

Only five years after the disaster of Hurricane Katrina, BP's Deepwater Horizon oil rig situated in the Gulf of Mexico exploded on 20 April 2010 creating the biggest oil spill in US-controlled waters to date. An 8-kilometre (5-mile) oil slick formed, and the ruptured well poured crude oil into the Gulf of Mexico for eighty-seven days, releasing an estimated 4.9 million barrels of crude into those waters. The leaked oil landed along Louisiana's coastline first and within weeks, the other Gulf States – Mississippi, Alabama, Florida and Texas – had been polluted.[17]

US President Barack Obama made BP responsible for the clean up; by July 2010 BP had already spent US $3.5 billion (£2.9 billion) on their own clean-up operation. In addition 170 Coast Guard vessels and thousands of volunteers were involved in local community clean-up activities. However, the environmental damage was extensive; so was the impact on the economic life of the Gulf communities as shrimp and oyster fishing and tourist charter-boat fishing industries were shut down. The legal action and compensation claims were far above any estimates (and are still ongoing).[18]

The psychological impact was hefty too. BP became a hate figure, and the oil industry, already a target for activism, came under heavy protest. Logomyway.com, a website that generated competitions for designing logos, became the base for a competition to redesign BP's logo – a culture-jamming exercise if ever there was one. Contributors vented their hatred and anger through an incredible number of logo manifestations that referenced everything from graphic clichés (such as the fish skeleton) to an iconic photograph of the shooting of a Vietcong soldier during the Vietnam War.

Other artists took a calmer but equally powerful path, creating memorable posters to raise awareness and funds for the clean-up. Jude Landry's *Octopus Vulgaris* (2010) shown here, depicts a monstrous octopus, reminiscent of science-fiction films, entangling all the Gulf States in an oily slime. Anthony Burrill's poster, *Oil & Water Do Not Mix* (2010), offers a visual metaphor for the traumatic effects of industrial pollution on the natural world. It is screenprinted using ink made from oily sand taken from the Gulf shore after the spill.

1. A selection of the many redesigns of BP's logo on the competition website logomyway.com, USA 2010.

BAD PLANNING
big problems

*biosphere poisoners

be prepared

bpolluted

broken promise.

2. *Octopus Vulgaris*, poster created by Jude Landry to raise awareness and funds for the Gulf of Mexico oil spill clean-up. Also a comment on the fragility of the Gulf States' economies and their dangerous dependence on feeding the USA's oil needs. USA 2010.

3. Poster for an anti-BP walking tour and protest in the Central Business District (CBD) of New Orleans. USA 2010. Photograph by Sara Andersdotter.

4. Poster by Anthony Burrill relating to the BP Deepwater Horizon oil spill. Screenprinted using ink made from oily sand taken from the Gulf shore after the spill. Co-produced with Happiness Brussels agency; proceeds benefited the non-profit Coalition to Restore Coastal Louisiana. USA 2010.

2.

3.

OIL & WATER DO NOT MIX

GULF OF MEXICO 2010

4.

CONFRONTING A TOXIC NIGHTMARE

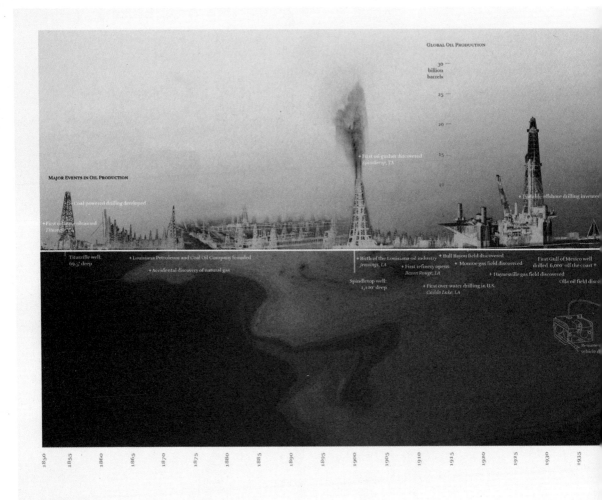

Labels within image:
GLOBAL OIL PRODUCTION
30 billion barrels
25
20
15
10

MAJOR EVENTS IN OIL PRODUCTION

+ First oil gusher discovered
Spindletop, TX

Coal powered drilling developed

+ Portable offshore drilling invented

+ First oil well obtained
Titusville, PA

Titusville well
69.5' deep

+ Louisiana Petroleum and Coal Oil Company founded

+ Accidental discovery of natural gas

+ Birth of the Louisiana oil industry
Jennings, LA

+ First refinery opens
Baton Rouge, LA

Spindletop well:
1,100' deep

+ First over water drilling in U.S.
Caddo Lake, LA

Bull Bayou field discovered

+ Monroe gas field discovered

+ Haynesville gas field discovered

First Gulf of Mexico well
drilled 6,000' off the coast +

Olla oil field disco

Remote
vehicle d

1850 1855 1860 1865 1870 1875 1880 1885 1890 1895 1900 1905 1910 1915 1920 1925 1930 1935

2.

Petrochemical America is a collaboration between photographer Richard Misrach and landscape architect Kate Orff. On an assignment from the High Museum, Atlanta, to photograph the American South in 1998, Misrach came across the area known as 'Cancer Alley' in Louisiana. He spent a year photographing this stretch of the Mississippi River between Baton Rouge and New Orleans and the historic route that runs alongside it, the River Road. The area contains over 100 industrial plants, producing a quarter of America's petrochemicals. The corridor also contains a large number of communities existing within what is considered to be a highly toxic environment: referred to by the industry as the 'Chemical Corridor', and by the public as 'Cancer Alley'.[19]

1. *Playground and Shell Refinery, Norco, Louisiana, 1998.* Photograph by Richard Misrack.

2. *Depths of Addiction.* Architectural drawings and narrative cartography within Kate Orff's *Ecological Atlas,* from the project *Petrochemical America,* USA 2012.

1.

2008

Total global oil extraction
31.1 billion barrels

Unconventional oil
7.4 billion barrels

Conventional oil
23.6 billion barrels

+ Horizontal drilling developed

+ Tar sands oil extraction
Alberta, Canada

+ Semi-submersible platform invented

+ bigolar seismic technology used to find oil

+ Alaska pipeline completed

"If we refuse to take into account the full
cost of our fossil fuel addiction—if we
don't factor in the environmental costs
and national security costs and true
economic costs—we will have missed our
best chance to seize a clean energy future."
President Barack Obama

Projected oil production

+ **Deepwater Horizon oil spill**
United States
1.2 billion barrels

+ Remote operated vehicles used for drilling

Hydraulic fracturing first used in commercial oil production

108

Depths of Addiction

Since Spindletop, extraction technology has advanced at pace
with demand. Today, we are drilling farther from shore in the
deepest, coldest water, "fracking" for natural gas in vital water-
sheds and parklands, strip-mining for oil in tar sands, and
exploding mountaintops for coal. Oil production on Louisiana
lands peaked in the 1970s. America's forty-year decline in
oil production, coupled with climbing demand, creates a
technological and political paradox. The increasing vertical
and horizontal distances from far-off oil fields to American
gas tanks means that we are expending more energy to make
energy. For example, the Perdido Oil platform, located nearly
two hundred miles from the Gulf of Mexico's shore, drills at a
depth of nearly ten thousand feet, costing $3 billion to build.
The projected decline of global oil production forces a reex-
amination of returns on investment and the viability of current
economic, political, and environmental paradigms.

[125]

3.

4.

5.

3. (previous page) *Swamp and Pipeline, Geismar, Louisiana, 1998.* Photograph by Richard Misrack.

4. (previous page) *Helicopter returning from Deepwater Horizon Spill, Venice, Louisiana, 2010.* Photograph by Richard Misrack.

5. 'The Ecology of Waste', architectural drawings and narrative cartography within Kate Orff's *Ecological Atlas*, from the project Petrochemical America. USA 2012.

MAN'S FOLLY, NATURE'S FURY: DISASTERS, WARNINGS AND HOPE

Gas release into air

on Dioxide

Atmosphere

Deposition on settlement

Asbestos

Ethylene Oxide

Surface water   Settlement

Particulates

Soil

Uptake of toxins through soil

Inhalation of dust

Ingestion of milk and meat

Uptake of drinking water supply from the Mississippi River

Surface water

Runoff into surface water

Bioaccumulation of toxins

Ingestion of aquatic animals

Aquatic animals

Hexachlorobenzene

Dioxins

Hexachlorobenzene

PACs

Mercury

PCBs

Benzene

Formaldehyde

Ethylene Oxide

Atrazine

The Ecology of Waste

Complex ecological and metabolic pathways integrate waste into all living and nonliving things, including plants and wildlife, humans and domesticated animals, air, water, and soil. In some cases, such as air releases, disposed waste is dispersed into the wider landscape and de facto stored in multiple sets of lungs and in the atmosphere. In other cases, substances become more concentrated and dangerous as they move up the food chain, since they build up in fatty tissue. For example, mercury and PCBs increase in concentration in birds like bald eagles, since they consume fish, accumulating much higher levels of mercury over their lifetime than are stored in any one individual fish. As top carnivores, humans accumulate chemicals and metals from diverse sources like milk, meat, fish, fruit, and vegetables. Waste ecosystems affect our ability to live fully and healthfully within our surroundings.

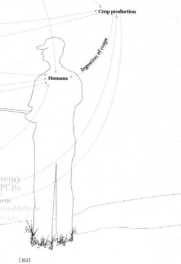

Crop production

Ingestion of crops

Humans

[153]

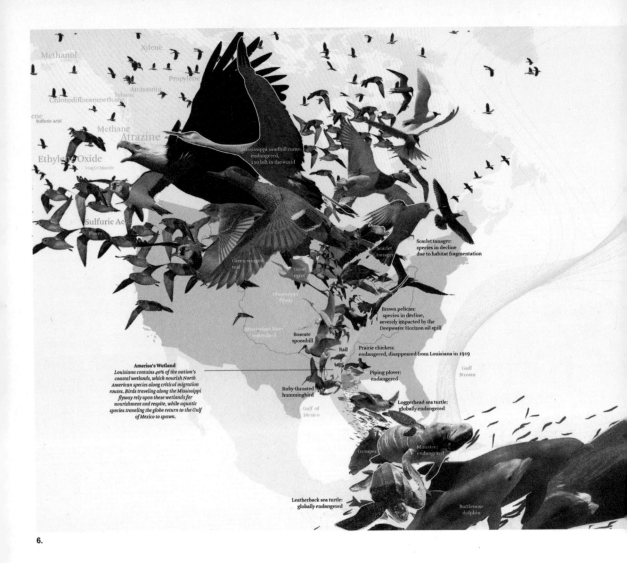

6.

Twelve years later Misrach was asked to revisit that particular collection of photographs for the purpose of exhibition and publication in 2012. On re-examination he began to wonder if conditions in the area had changed. He enlisted the help of Manhattan-based landscape architect Kate Orff, whose own specialism was interpreting and regenerating contaminated, neglected landscapes. In March 2010, Misrach, Orff and associates from her firm SCAPE, travelled to Louisiana and spent weeks interviewing people along the Corridor. Orff planned out a sequence of the photographs, plus maps, graphs and so on to create a visual narrative, which in turn influenced Misrach's re-photographing of the area. Their collaborative process of working and reworking resulted in the content of the 2012 publication, showing Misrach's photographs alongside revealing, contextualizing captions in part one, and Orff's 'Ecological Atlas' in part two.[20]

Misrach's photographs tell a tale of rural contamination and hazardous waste sites, ruined and demolished communities, as well as homes, schools and playgrounds existing just yards away from industrial infrastructure. They are distinct in their message of alarm and outrage; there may be legendary fields of mist or steamy bayous, but it is clear that they are poisonous not pretty.

6. 'Life and Livelihoods at Risk', architectural drawings and narrative cartography within Kate Orff's 'Ecological Atlas', from the project Petrochemical America. USA 2012.

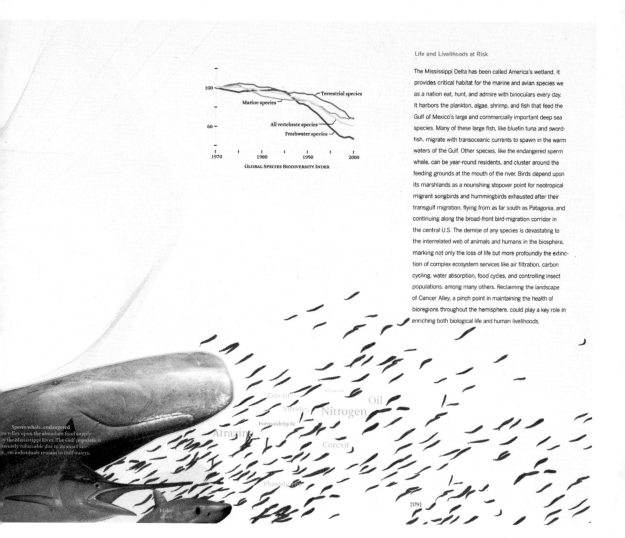

The Mississippi Delta has been called America's wetland. It provides critical habitat for the marine and avian species we as a nation eat, hunt, and admire with binoculars every day. It harbors the plankton, algae, shrimp, and fish that feed the Gulf of Mexico's large and commercially important deep sea species. Many of these large fish, like bluefin tuna and sword-fish, migrate with transoceanic currents to spawn in the warm waters of the Gulf. Other species, like the endangered sperm whale, can be year-round residents, and cluster around the feeding grounds at the mouth of the river. Birds depend upon its marshlands as a nourishing stopover point for neotropical migrant songbirds and hummingbirds exhausted after their transgulf migration, flying from as far south as Patagonia, and continuing along the broad-front bird-migration corridor in the central U.S. The demise of any species is devastating to the interrelated web of animals and humans in the biosphere, marking not only the loss of life but more profoundly the extinc-tion of complex ecosystem services like air filtration, carbon cycling, water absorption, food cycles, and controlling insect populations, among many others. Reclaiming the landscape of Cancer Alley, a pinch point in maintaining the health of bioregions throughout the hemisphere, could play a key role in enriching both biological life and human livelihoods.

GLOBAL SPECIES BIODIVERSITY INDEX

In the 'Ecological Atlas', architectural drawings (incorporating illustration, imaginative projection and additional data) expand on Misrach's photographs to produce a form of narrative cartography that charts links between the industrial sites, their neighbourhoods and environments. Three techniques are used to aid this narrative: 'maps' for orientation; 'data narratives' for analyzing and revealing associated industrial or ecological processes; and 'eco-portraits' for synthesis, where data and observations converge into an overall ecology or process view. [21]

Finally, encased in a pocket in the back cover of *Petrochemical America*, is the companion booklet *Glossary of Terms and Solutions for a Post-Petrochemical Culture*: a call to action enabling a shift away from America's collective addiction to petrochemicals. It takes the form of a listing of possibilities, day-to-day changes and life/work adjustments that is slightly reminiscent of the 1970s *Whole Earth Catalog*, but which speaks to a new generation. It is also inter-esting that the conclusive statement to this listing, as well as the entire project, sidesteps the 'absence of government efficacy' and heads straight for the accumulation of individual endeavours and public-private partnerships as agents of change and transformation – and consequently, a hope for the future.[22]

AFTER THE FLOOD

1.

Creative agency Squint/Opera exhibited five images entitled *Flooded London* in the 2008 *London Festival of Architecture*. They tell a story set in the year 2090 and it's clear a catastrophe happened a while in the past. London has been overtaken by rising sea levels, and there are very few people around. The survivors seem settled into a way of life that is inventive and low-tech, and the pace is calm. The hysteria of business-driven city life (symbolized, for example, by the City of London) is either submerged or a wreck; two women are fishing off an open-office level of a Canary Wharf high-rise.[23]

Other people are in a former London gallery or museum, engaged in making new things from pre-flood materials, and show satisfaction at having built a low-tech machine that will power a light bulb. The spirit of invention stretches to the suburbs: in a street of terraced houses, the road has become overgrown by plants, long since free from cars, as well as most of the houses. One house appears loved and inhabited, its garden bordered with topiary hedges. A man works on a homemade submarine and the end of the street has become a slipway, from which to launch it. This is no horrible, dystopian future, but a tribute to survival, invention and the human ability to 'carry on' and make the best of things. (If viewed satirically, some might even say the bankers, city-types and lovers of the rat race got what they deserved.)[24]

2.

1–4. *Flooded London*, five images that foresee the future, produced by creative agency Squint/Opera for an exhibition at the 2008 *London Festival of Architecture*. UK 2008.

3.

4.

THE GREAT ESCAPE: GO VIRTUAL

1.

Chinese artist Cao Fei grew up in the Pearl River Delta; a region of heavy industrialization driven by globalization. She was therefore surrounded by clashes between urban and rural lifestyles and values in an area of dense population and rapidly growing factories. Little wonder then, that her creative work often explores the fantasies and desires of people wanting to break out of their mundane lives.[25]

Her fascination with fantasy and role-play, as well as cultural contradictions, took her into interactive-media projects, especially the online role-playing game, *Second Life*, for which she constructed her avatar, China Tracy. In 2008 she planned and developed the island city named *RMB City* within *Second Life*; the city's title is derived from the Chinese currency *renminbi*.[26] *RMB City* itself is an inchoate mass of stereotypes and symbols of China's past and present – a panda floats in midair, a statue of Mao is half-submerged in the harbour, the rusty wreckage of the National Stadium (the 'Bird's Nest') surrounds the People's Park. It's a virtual universe where participants live through personalized avatars and is financed by real-world collectors and art institutions. It has also become a platform for the creation of new projects and artworks by other artists. Cao Fei produced further extensions in film, such as *Live in RMB City* (2009), in which China Tracy and her baby son explore the buildings and meet different characters in *RMB City*, while she tells her son about virtual and real life and death. And her *RMB City Opera* (2009) uses both *Second Life* avatars and spaces, alongside real-world actors in a live stage performance. It is a series of episodes between a young man and woman. On stage they log on to *RMB City*, switch avatars frequently (at times becoming superheroes), dance and sing, while the projection of the avatars coincides with real performers on stage.[27]

Cao Fei's interest is in living in parallel worlds – the real and the virtual – and informing connections between the two. After all, a virtual world of freedom offers interesting possibilities for escape, especially to those living in a real-world country where government and social restrictions can be limiting and environmental destruction is increasing.

1. Detail of a video still from *Live in RMB City*, showing China Tracy (Cao Fei's avatar) with her baby son. China 2009.

2–4. Different views of *RMB City*, an online virtual world where users socialize using self-styled avatars. Planned and developed in the role-playing game *Second Life* by artist Cao Fei. China 2008.

2.

3.

4.

THE GREAT ESCAPE: GO VIRTUAL

WARNINGS OF THE FUTURE

Canadian artist Kelly Richardson's installation *Leviathan* (2011) is an immersive experience that uses three enormous screens to draw the viewer into a dark swamp of trees that look deeply foreboding, while a very slight breeze makes an occasional branch flicker, suggesting the briefest sign of life. The trees sit in a vast mass of liquid that shifts and rolls with a slow, flowing movement; there is an eerie, threatening light from beneath, perhaps radiation or some strange life form or disease is brewing. The sound emanating from this scene is a low, monotonous hum: is it the product of a malevolent poisoning? Or a mythical evil come to haunt the present, or a post-apocalyptic future?[28]

Leviathan is actually not a fictional landscape. It originated from documentary film footage shot by Richardson on Caddo Lake, outside the town of Uncertain, Texas, where oil was first drilled underwater. The bald cypress trees are not really dead, but adaptable – their root structure is underwater and they grow without leaves. But rather than deal in blatant narratives about oil or pollution, Richardson constructs ambiguities – which can be far more frightening – and allows viewers to create their own readings.[29]

Her installation *The Erudition* (2010), created on the same monumental scale, is even more chilling. A visualization reminiscent of science fiction, it presents a landscape – whether earthly or alien is unknown – that seems barren (yet natural), but for the interference of ghostly images of trees. They flicker and dodge erratically, in and out of sight, to the sound of strange electrical clicking or fizzing noises; and they never seem to appear in the same place twice. The sky is vast, the colours are cold and the trees appear to be phantoms. Is this a post-apocalyptic landscape on earth? Or another planet in the distant future, where trees only exist virtually and are suffering a malfunction?[30]

Both installations treat Richardson's ongoing concern about the effects of industrialization on the environment. And because this concern is delivered through dark imaginings, ambiguities and associations, it becomes difficult for the viewer to just walk away. The immersive experience has a mesmeric effect and viewers can conjure their own powerful vision about what the future may hold.

1. *Leviathan*, three-screen, high definition video installation with stereo sound, 14.5 × 2.7 metres (48 × 9 feet). By artist Kelly Richardson. Canada 2011.

2 (overleaf). *The Erudition*, three-screen, high definition video installation with stereo sound, 14.5 × 2.7 metres (48 × 9 feet). By artist Kelly Richardson. Canada 2010.

MAN'S FOLLY, NATURE'S FURY: DISASTERS, WARNINGS AND HOPE

1.

ENDNOTES

Graphic Highlights of the Digital Age: The Visual Legacy of the 1990s

1 Liz McQuiston, *Graphic Agitation: Social and Political Graphics since the Sixties*, London, 1993, pp. 96–7
2 John Passmore, *Tanks Hero Is Executed, Evening Standard*, 23 June 1989
3 Interview with Dr Sara Andersdotter, Installation Artist and Lecturer, London, September 2014
4 Richard Vine, *New China, New Art*, London and New York, 2011, pp. 12–15, 20–6
5 Liz McQuiston, *Graphic Agitation 2: Social and Political Graphics in the Digital Age*, London, 2004, pp. 32–3, 38–9
6 Ibid., pp. 33–6, 44–55
7 Ibid., pp. 84–95
8 Ibid., pp. 120–3, 132–9
9 Ibid., pp. 123–7,140–71

Discontent and Uprisings: Economic and Political Unrest

1 Interview with Jeremy Barr, Professor of Broadcasting and Convergent Media, Ravensbourne, September 2014
2 *The Economist Pocket World in Figures: 2012 Edition*, London 2011, pp. 142–3
3 Symon Hill, *Digital Revolutions: Activism in the Internet Age*, Oxford 2013, pp. 22–3 and 74–5
4 Kurt Andersen, *The Protester, Time*, vol. 178, no. 25, 26 December 2011 – 2 January 2012, p. 70, and Hill 2013, pp. 66–8.
5 Much of the material mentioned is included or expanded upon in the book *Syria Speaks: Art and Culture from the Frontline*, a bitter document of Syria after the bombing started. Malu Halasa, Zaher Omareen and Nawara Mahfoud, *Syria Speaks: Art and Culture from the Frontline*, London 2014, pp. vii–xv.
6 Nahid Siamdoust, 'Power of the People', *Time: The Year in Review 2009*, New York 2009, pp. 58–9. And Symon Hill, *Digital Revolutions*, pp. 35–7.
7 Juan Luis Sánchez, 'Spain: The Formidable Voices of the Plazas', *Index On Censorship*, vol. 42, no. 1, March 2013, pp. 8–11
8 Limor Shifman, *Memes in Digital Culture*, Cambridge MA 2014, p. 50–3
9 Laura Barnett, 'Kara Walker's Art: Shadows of Slavery', www.theguardian.com, 10 October 2013
10 Sophie Mayer, 'Pussy Riot: A Punk Prayer', *Sight and Sound*, August 2013, pp. 68–9, and 'Pussy Riot: The Story so Far', www.bbc.co.uk, 23 December 2013
11 Yaman Kayabali, 'Protest Art in Real Time', *Creative Review*, August 2013, pp. 66–8
12 Dave Zirin, *Brazil's Dance with the Devil: The World Cup, the Olympics, and the Fight for Democracy*, Chicago, IL 2014, pp. 205–14
13 Interview with Andrew Barr, Writer and Broadcaster, September 2014
14 Ai Weiwei (edited and translated by Lee Ambrozy), *Ai Weiwei's Blog: Writings, Interviews, and Digital Rants 2006–2009*, Cambridge MA 2011, p. 267

15 Leo Lewis, 'It's Impossible to Out-Think the Authorities, They Make the Rules', *The Times Saturday Review*, 20 September 2014, pp. 4–5
16 Toby Manhire (ed.), *The Arab Spring: Rebellion, Revolution and a New World Order*, London, 2012, pp. 13–48, and Mia Gröndahl, *Tahrir Square: The Heart of the Egyptian Revolution*, Cairo, 2011, pp. 5–6
17 Gröndahl, ibid., pp. 105, 132
18 Mia Gröndahl, *Revolution Graffiti: Street Art of the New Egypt*, London, 2013, p. 153
19 Ibid., p. 1
20 Ibid., pp. 29, 49
21 Ibid., p. 133
22 Ibid., p. 166–71
23 Ibid., p. 173–91
24 Malu Halasa, Zaher Omareen and Nawara Mahfoud, *Syria Speaks: Art and Culture from the Frontline*, London, 2014, pp. vii–xv. The ongoing situation in Syria makes it difficult to gain access to many artists and their works, and as such we are extremely indebted to two major sources for their efforts in disseminating the pieces included here. The first is the exhibition and accompanying publication *Culture in Defiance: Continuing Traditions of Satire, Art and the Struggle for Freedom in Syria*, held in Amsterdam and London, 2012–13. The second is the book *Syria Speaks: Art and Culture from the Frontline*, edited by Malu Halasa, Zaher Omareen and Nawara Mahfoud, which showcases the work of over fifty artists and writers who are challenging the culture of violence in Syria.
25 Aram Tahhan, 'Words Against Bullets: Syrian Political Posters' in *Culture in Defiance: Continuing Traditions of Satire, Art and the Struggle for Freedom in Syria* (exhibition publication), Amsterdam, 2012, pp. 33–7
26 Malu Halasa, 'Painting the Revolution' in ibid., pp. 16–19
27 Halasa et al 2014, pp. xiii, 241
28 Charlotte Bank, 'Alshaab Alsori Aref Tarekh: The Art of Persuasion' in *Syria Speaks: Art and Culture from the Frontline*, London, 2014, pp. 66–77, 78–83
29 Symon Hill, *Digital Revolutions: Activism in the Internet Age*, Oxford 2013, pp. 30–3
30 'Upheaval in Iran' and Nahid Siamdoust, 'Power of the People' in *Time: The Year in Review 2009*, New York, 2009, pp. 52–9
31 Ibid.
32 Symon Hill 2013, pp. 85–7
33 Ophelia Noor, 'In Pictures: Spain's Graphic Voices', www.owni.eu, 8 June 2011
34 Ben Chu, 'The Greek Patient Returns for More Help', *The Independent*, 21 August 2012, p. 55
35 Alexandra Saliba, 'The Good of Small Things', *New Internationalist*, January/February 2013, pp. 52–6, and John Carlin, 'Get Us Out of Here', *The Independent Magazine*, 30 March 2013, pp. 20–9
36 Mattathias Schwartz, 'Pre-Occupied: The Origins and Future of Occupy Wall Street', *The New Yorker*, 28 November 2011, pp. 28–35
37 *The Occupied Wall Street Journal*, www.occupiedmedia.us, and Limor Shifman,

Memes in Digital Culture, Cambridge, MA, 2014, pp. 50–3
38 Carole Kismaric and Marvin Heiferman, *Growing Up with Dick and Jane: Learning and Living the American Dream*, San Francisco, CA, 1996, p. 21
39 Laura Barnett, 'Kara Walker's Art: Shadows of Slavery', www.theguardian.com, 10 October 2013, and Eleanor Heartney, Helaine Posner, Nancy Princenthal, Sue Scott, *The Reckoning: Women Artists of the New Millennium*, London and New York, 2013, pp. 224–8
40 Introduction by Anna Zobnina in Emely Neu (curator) and Jade French (ed.), *Let's Start a Pussy Riot*, London, 2013, pp. 14–16
41 Marc Bennetts, *Kicking the Kremlin: Russia's New Dissidents and the Battle to Topple Putin*, London, 2014, p. 137
42 'Pussy Riot: The Story So Far', www.bbc.co.uk, 23 December 2013
43 'Russian Curators Prosecuted for Showcasing Banned Art: Media Round-Up', www.artradarjournal.com, 2 August 2010
44 Glyn Williams, Brian, 'The Brides of Allah: The Terror threat of Black-Widow Suicide Bombers to the Winter Olympics', www.huffingtonpost.com, 30 March 2015
45 Ibid., Taryn Jones, 'The Blue Noses', www.artinrussia.org, 19 October 2012, and Elea Baucheron and Diane Routex, *The Museum of Scandals: Art that Shocked the World*, London and New York, 2013, pp. 128–9
46 *Time: The Year in Review 2013*, New York, 2013, pp. 54–5
47 Yaman Kayabali, 'Protest Art in Real Time', *Creative Review*, August 2013, pp. 66–8
48 Kaya Genç 'The Standing man of Taksim Square: A Latterday Bartleby', www.theguardian.com, 20 June 2013, and Luke Harding, 'Turkey's Protesters Proclaim Themselves the True Heirs of Their Nation's Founding Father', www.theguardian.com, 8 June 2013
49 Dave Zirin, *Brazil's Dance with the Devil: The World Cup, the Olympics and the Fight for Democracy*, Chicago, IL, 2014, pp. 11–23
50 Ibid., pp. 205–10
51 Justin McGuirk, 'Brazil's Two Biennales', *Creative Review*, August 2013, pp. 60–3
52 Taken from the author's notes collected from television news reports at the time, as well as people in the street.
53 Lee Moran, 'Day of "Global Revolution" Comes to London as Thousands of Demonstrators Take Over the City', www.dailymail.co.uk, 15 October 2011
54 Interview with Jeremy Barr, Professor of Broadcasting and Convergent Media, Ravensbourne, September 2014.
55 Mark Sinclair, 'An Ongoing Occupation', www.creativereview.co.uk, 5 November 2012
56 Richard Vine, *New China, New Art*, London and New York, 2011, p. 14
57 Ai Weiwei (edited and translated by Lee Ambrozy), *Ai Weiwei's Blog: Writings, Interviews, and Digital Rants 2006–2009*, Cambridge,

MA, 2011, pp. 219–23, 267. See www.aiweiwei.com
58 Ibid.
59 Victoria L. Valentine, '"According to What?": Ai Weiwei Survey Opens at Hirshhorn', www.artsobserver.com, 25 October 2012
60 http://www.saatchigallery.com/artists/qiu_jie. htm?section_name=china_art. And http://www.independent. co.uk/arts-entertainment/art/ features/sheng-qi-cutting-off-my-finger-was-my-proudest-moment-8375534.html
61 Stephen Vines, 'A Lease No One Thought Would Run Out', www.independent.co.uk, 3 Jan 1997
62 Tania Branigan, 'Protests Swell for Umbrella Revolution in Hong Kong', *The Guardian*, 30 September 2014, pp. 1 and 3
63 Ying Chan, 'People Power: The People Have Found Their Voice', *The Guardian: G2 magazine*, 30 September 2014, pp. 7–8
64 Jon Henley, 'People Power: Protesting with Brollies at the Ready', *The Guardian: G2 magazine*, 30 September 2014, pp. 8–9
65 Joyce Lau, 'Art Spawned by Protest; Now to Make It Live On', *The New York Times International*, 16 November 2014, p. 12
66 Kevin Chan, 'Protesters' Camp is Torn Down by Police', *i – The Independent*, 12 December 2014, p. 27

The 360° Frontier: Wars in Afghanistan and Iraq

1 Sean Loughlin, 'Rumsfeld on looting in Iraq: "Stuff happens"', www.cnn.com, 12 April 2003
2 'The End of a Misguided Mission', *The Independent on Sunday*, 22 May 2011, p. 41, and Suzanne Goldenberg, 'Bush Allies Admit War Blunders', *The Guardian*, 6 October 2004, p. 1
3 Fred Halliday, *Shocked and Awed: How the War on Terror and Jihad Have Changed the English Language*, London and New York, 2011, p. 12
4 Ibid., p. 104
5 Ibid., pp. 72 and 81–2
6 Ibid., pp. 261–2
7 Terry H. Anderson, *Bush's Wars*, New York and Oxford, 2011, pp. 112–6
8 'The Butler Report' (Special Section), *The Independent*, 15 July 2004, pp. viii–ix
9 Terry H. Anderson, *Bush's Wars*, New York and Oxford, 2011, pp. 132–6
10 Halliday 2011, p. 119
11 Riverbend, *Baghdad Burning: Girl Blog from Iraq*, London 2006. (Introduction by James Ridgeway, pp.xii-xviii.)
12 Salam Pax, *The Baghdad Blog*, London 2003
13 Stephen F. Eisenman, *The Abu Ghraib Effect*, London, 2007, pp. 9 and 19
14 'The End of a Misguided Mission', *The Independent on Sunday*, 22 May 2011, p. 41
15 Ibid.
16 Medea Benjamin, *Drone Warfare: Killing by Remote Control*, London and New York, 2013, p. 6.
17 Ibid, pp. 31–44
18 Stop the War Coalition, www.stopwar.org.uk

19 Sybille Prou and King Adz, *Blek le Rat: Getting Through the Walls*, London, 2012, pp. 7–8, 12, 105–6

20 Terry H. Anderson, *Bush's Wars*, New York and Oxford, 2011, p. 177–8

21 Stephen F. Eisenman, *The Abu Ghraib Effect*, London, 2007, p. 19

22 Anjani Trivedi, 'The Abu Ghraib Prison Pictures – Joe Darby (2004)', www.time.com, 10 June 2013

23 Eisenman 2007, p. 29, and Anderson 2011, p. 177–8

24 Peter Beaumont, 'Iraq Inspires Surge of Protest Art', *The Observer*, 9 Sept 2007, p. 41, and Juan Forero, 'Great Crime at Abu Ghraib Enrages and Inspires an Artist', *The New York Times*, 7 May 2005

25 Introduction by Craig R. Whitney to Steven Strasser (ed.), *The Abu Ghraib Investigations: The Official Reports of the Independent Panel and the Pentagon on the Shocking Prisoner Abuse in Iraq*, New York, 2004, pp.vii–xxiii

26 Jerome Taylor, 'War on Terror Boardgame Branded Criminal by Police', *The Independent*, 9 August 2008, p. 25

27 Ibid.

28 Medea Benjamin, *Drone Warfare: Killing by Remote Control*, London and New York, 2013, pp. 5–10.

29 Dorothy art collective, *The Guantanamo Bay Collection*, www.wearedorothy.com

30 Fred Halliday, *Shocked and Awed: How the War on Terror and Jihad Have Changed the English Language*, London, 2011, p. 90

31 Ibid., pp. 88–9

32 Martin Herbert, 'Fighting Talk', *Tate Etc.*, Issue 19, Summer 2010, pp. 106–7

33 Lizzie Carey-Thomas, 'Air Craft', *Fiona Banner: Harrier and Jaguar* (Tate exhibition brochure), London, 2010, pp. 3–4

34 Halliday 2011, p. 111

35 Dorothy art collective, *Casualties of War*, www.wearedorothy.com

36 Adrian Searle, 'Last Post: Steve McQueen's Tribute to Britain's War Dead Features Stamps Bearing the Soldiers' Faces. Why Wouldn't the MoD Help Him?', 12 March 2007, www.theguardian.com

38 'Queen and Country: A Project by Steve McQueen', www.artfund.org

39 Anderson 2011, pp. 218, 221–4

40 Medea 2013, pp. 7, 19

41 Foreword by Carol Rosenberg in Janet Hamlin, *Sketching Guantanamo: Court Sketches of the Military Tribunals 2006–2013*, Seattle, 2013, p. 8

42 Ibid., pp. 14–15

43 Ibid.

44 Afterword by Karen J. Greenberg, ibid., p. 171

45 Anderson 2011, pp. 142–5

46 The University of Chicago: The Oriental Institute, 'Michael Rakowitz: The Invisible Enemy Should Not Exist', www.uchicago.edu

47 Michael Rakowitz, *The Invisible Enemy Should Not Exist*, www.michaelrakowitz.com

48 Kelly Nosari, 'Rachel Khedoori', www.dailyserving.com, 28 July 2010, and 'Rachel Khedoori', www.hauserwirth.com

49 Annie Buckley, 'Rachel Khedoori', www.artinamericamagazine.com, 13 November 2009

50 David Nott interviewed by Eddie Mair for *PM*, BBC Radio 4. The interview is archived in two parts by www.audioboom.com

51 Chris Sharratt, 'RA Summer Exhibition: Bob and Roberta Smith's Syria Painting', www.a-n.co.uk, 6 June 2014

Divided Countries and Cultures: Signs of Tension and Resolve

1 Fred Halliday, *Shocked and Awed: How the War on Terror and Jihad Have Changed the English Language*, London, 2011, pp. 204–5

2 William Parry, *Against the Wall: The Art of Resistance in Palestine*, London, 2010, pp. 9–10

3 Andrew Salmon, *To the Last Round: The Epic British Stand on the Imjin River, Korea 1951*, London, 2010, pp. 13–22

4 Bruce Cumings, *North Korea: Another Country*, New York, 2004, p. 3

5 'Banners, Bayonets and Basketball' by Koen De Ceuster in David Heather and Koen De Ceuster, *North Korean Posters: The David Heather Collection*, London and New York, 2008, pp. 9–10

6 Ibid., pp. 10–11

7 Peter Gottschalk and Gabriel Greenberg, *Islamophobia: Making Muslims the Enemy*, Lanham, MD, 2008, pp. 3–7

8 'French Scarf Ban Comes into Force', www.news.bbc.co.uk, 2 September 2004

9 Angelique Chrisafis, 'France's Headscarf War: "It's an Attack on Freedom"', www.theguardian. com, 22 July 2013

10 Angelique Chrisafis, 'Veiled Attacks', *The Guardian*, 11 November 2010, pp. 4–7

11 'Art, Death and Language' by Lutz Becker in Rose Issa (ed.), *Parastou Forouhar: Art, Life and Death in Iran*, London, 2010, p. 19

12 Robert Aldrich (ed.), *Gay Life and Culture: A World History*, London, 2006, pp. 360–3, and 'Gay Marriage Around the World', www.pewforum.org, 2 September 2014

13 John Lichfield, '"A Breeze of Joy": French Gay Marriage Law Clears Last Hurdle', *The Independent*, 24 April 2013, p. 32

14 Terri Judd, 'Russian Politician Brands Stephen Fry "Sick" in Anti-Gay Rant', *The Independent*, 12 August 2013, p. 8, and Philip Hensher, 'Don't Pressurise Ms Balding. Just Get Boycotting', *The Independent*, 12 August 2013, p. 17

15 Aryn Baker, 'The Fighter: Malala Yousafzai', *Time*, vol. 180, no. 27, 31 December 2012 – 7 January 2013, pp. 96–107

16 'India "Gang-Rape": Student, Friend Attacked on Delhi Bus', www.bbc.co.uk, 17 December 2012

17 Rose Troup Buchanan, 'Boko Haram seizes town f kidnapped school-girls after government troops"run away"', www.independent.co.uk, 15 November 2014

18 William Parry, *Against the Wall: The Art of Resistance in Palestine*, London, 2010, pp. 9–12

19 Ibid.

20 'Face2Face', www.jr-art.net

21 Larissa Sansour, 'The Post-Apocalyptic Present', *Art and Conflict*, London, 2014, pp. 56–60, and www.larissasansour.com

22 Ibid.

23 A.J.P. Taylor, *English History 1914–1945*, Harmondsworth, 1985, pp. 107, 499–500

24 Yossi Lemel, 'Memories of the Holocaust', www.youtube.com, uploaded on Jan 25, 2010

25 Ibid.

26 Ibid.

27 'Banners, Bayonets and Basketball' by Koen De Ceuster in David Heather and Koen De Ceuster, *North Korean Posters: The David Heather Collection*, London and New York, 2008, pp. 9–11, 16

28 Ibid., pp.12–14

29 'A Photo Project' by Klaus Klemp in Dieter Leistner, *Korea/Korea: A Photo Project by Dieter Leistner*, Berlin, 2013, pp. 7–9

30 Angelique Chrisafis, 'Veiled Attacks', *The Guardian*, 11 November 2010, pp. 4–7

31 Foreword by Rose Issa, p. 6, and 'A Cultural Predicament' by Russell Harris, p. 10, in Rose Issa (ed.), *Parastou Forouhar: Art, Life and Death in Iran*, London 2010

32 'Art, Death and Language' by Lutz Becker in ibid., pp. 18–9

33 Natasha Fraser-Cavassoni, 'Pierre et Gilles', *V Magazine*, V82, www.vmagazine.com

34 Karen McVeigh and Paul Harris, 'US Military Lifts Ban on Openly Gay Troops', www.theguardian.com, 20 Sept 2011

35 Alice Jones, 'Sarah Maple: "I'm Not the New Tracey Emin"', www.independent.co.uk, 29 November 2014

36 NHS Choices – Female Genital Mutilation, www.nhs.uk/conditions/female-genital-mutilation, and World Health Organisation, *Fact Sheet No. 241*, www.who.int/mediacentre/factsheets/fs241

37 Ann Gould (ed.), *Masters of Caricature: from Hogarth and Gillray to Scarfe and Levine*, London, 1981, pp. 70–1. Introduction by William Feaver (p. 11) and Steven Heller and Gail Anderson, *Graphic Wit: The Art of Humor in Design*, New York, 1991, pp. 16–17

38 Adam Sherwin, 'Banned and Resurrected but Always in the Grand Tradition of Gallic Satire', *The Independent*, 8 January 2015, pp. 10–11. And John Lichfield, 'They Burst into the Offices, Opened Fire, and Cried "Vengeance"', *The Independent*, 8 January 2015, pp. 6–7

39 Adam Sherwin, 'Banned and resurrected' pp. 10–11 and Kim Willsher, Julian Borger and Jon Henley, *The Guardian*, 8 January 2015, pp. 1 and 3

40 John Lichfield, 'They Burst into the Offices', pp. 6–7

41 Blog.ted.com/stephane-charbonnier-eyes-courtesy-of-ted-prize-winner-jr

42 Alexander Topping and Kim Willsher, 'Je suis Charlie: An Outpouring of Grief and Defiance', *The Guardian*, 8 January 2015, pp. 24–5

43 Ruadhán Mac Cormaic, 'Charlie Hebdo Back on Paris News Stands', *The Irish Times*, 14 January 2015, p. 8

44 Mehdi Hasan, 'As a Muslim I'm Fed Up with the Hypocrisy of Free-speech Fundamentalists', *New Statesman*, 16–22 January 2015, p. 40

45 Elizabeth Day, 'The Street Art of JR', www.theguardian.com, 7 March 2010

46 Ibid.

47 www.insideoutproject.net

Man's Folly, Nature's Fury: Disasters, Warnings and Hope

1 'Tsunami 2004 Facts and Figures', www.tsunami2004.net, 21 May 2013; 'The May 12, 2008 Deadly Sichuan Earthquake: A Recap – 3 Years Later', www.earthquake-report.com, 10 May 2011; 'Haiti Earthquake – Our Response', www.oxfam.org; The Ocean Portal Team, 'Gulf Oil Spill', www.ocean.si.edu; and World Nuclear Association, 'Fukushima Accident', www.world-nuclear.org, December 2014 (updated)

2 The Editors of Time, 'Special Report: Hurricane Season. Ordeal in New Orleans', *TIME: The Year in Review 2005*, New York, 2005, pp. 14–19, and 'Bush Arrives for New Orleans Tour', www.cnn.com, 12 September 2005

3 Ed Pilkington, 'The Amazing True Story of Zeitoun', *The Guardian* (G2 section), 12 March 2010, pp. 8–11

4 Alice-Azania Jarvis, 'Disaster by Numbers', *The Independent*, 14 September 2010, pp. 12–13, and David Usborne, 'BP, the Gulf Oil Spill and 87 Days that Changed the World' and Michael McCarthy, 'This Disaster Teaches that Technology is Not Infallible', *The Independent*, 17 July 2010, pp. 6–7

5 Richard Misrach, *Petrochemical America*, www.fraenkelgallery.com

6 'The Geography of Science – Flood in London: A Mission Impossible?', Royal Geographical Society, www.rgs.org

7 Marcus Fairs, 'Flooded London by Squint/Opera', www.dezeen.com, 18 June 2008

8 'Cao Fei' by Eleanor Heartney in Eleanor Heartney et al, *The Reckoning: Women Artists of the New Millennium*, London and New York 2013, pp. 87–9

9 Vanessa Thorpe, 'Vivienne Westwood: Climate Change, Not Fashion, is Now my Priority', www.theguardian.com, 8 February 2014

10 'Roa Street Artist Biography', www.stencilrevolution.com

11 'TateShots: Marcus Coates', www.tate.org.uk

12 Ibid.

13 Graphic Advocacy: International Posters for the Digital Age (2001-2012), an online exhibition curated by Elizabeth Resnick, Massachusetts College of Art and Design, http://graphicadvocacyposters.org/posters/

14 Spike Lee (dir.), *When the Levees Broke: A Requiem in Four Acts*, HBO documentary, 240min, 2006. (Act III)

15 Doug MacCash, 'Banksy fifth anniversary tour recalls 2008 New Orleans visit', *The Times-Picayune*, http://www.nola.com/arts/index.ssf/2013/08/fifth_anniversary_tour_recalls.html. And John S. Stokes

III, 'New Orleans – Banksy', Custom Puzzle Craft, http://www.custompuzzlecraft.com/Weather/banksy.html

16 Ibid.

17 Alice-Azania Jarvis, 'Disaster by Numbers', *The Independent*, 14 September 2010, pp. 12–13

18 Michael McCarthy, 'This Disaster Teaches that Technology is Not Infallible', *The Independent*, 17 July 2010, pp. 6–7, and Alice-Azania Jarvis, 'Disaster by Numbers', *The Independent*, 14 September 2010, pp. 12–3

19 Richard Misrach and Kate Orff, *Petrochemical America*, New York 2012, p. 17

20 Ibid.

21 Ibid., pp. 115–7

22 Ibid., p. 214

23 Marcus Fairs, 'Flooded London by Squint/Opera', www.dezeen.com, 18 June 2008, and 'Flooded London', www.squintopera.com

24 Ibid.

25 'Cao Fei' by Eleanor Heartney in Eleanor Heartney et al, *The Reckoning: Women Artists of the New Millennium*, London and New York, 2013. p. 87

26 Ibid, pp. 88–9

27 Ceren Erdem, 'RMB City: Spectatorship on the Boundaries of the Virtual and the Real', www.interventionsjournal.net, 26 January 2012

28 'Kelly Richardson: Future Anterior' by Alistair Robinson in Kelly Gordon et al, *The Last Frontier: Kelly Richardson*, Lethbridge, AB and Sunderland, 2013. pp. 20–4

29 Ibid.

30 Ibid., pp. 72–3

BIBLIOGRAPHY AND FURTHER READING

As it is assumed that many readers search websites and follow Twitter and other social media, this listing deals mainly with books, journals and films of interest.

Ai, Weiwei (2011) *Ai Weiwei's Blog: Writings, Interviews, and Digital Rants 2006-2009*, The MIT Press, Cambridge, MA.

Aldrich, Robert (ed.) (2006) *Gay Life and Culture: A World History*, Thames and Hudson, London.

Anderson, Terry H. (2011) *Bush's Wars*, Oxford University Press, New York, NY.

Art and Conflict, a research enquiry supported by the Arts and Humanities Research Council and the Royal College of Art, 2013–14. Essays by Jananne Al-Ani, Bernadette Buckley, Michaela Crimmin, Malu Halasa, Jemima Montagu, Sarah Rifky, Larissa Sansour and Charles Tripp. Published by the Royal College of Art, 2014.

Benjamin, Medea (2013) *Drone Warfare: Killing by Remote Control*, Verso, London.

Bennetts, Marc (2014) *Kicking the Kremlin: Russia's new dissidents and the battle to topple Putin*, Oneworld Publications, London.

Burgin, Andrew (2011) *Stop The War: A Graphic History*, Francis Boutle Publishers/Stop The War Coalition, London. (A pictorial timeline of British protests relating to the wars in Afghanistan and Iraq.)

Cumings, Bruce (2004) *North Korea: Another Country*, The New Press, New York, NY.

Delisle, Guy (2006) *Pyongyang: A journey in North Korea*, Jonathan Cape, London.

Eddie Mair's 2013 interview with surgeon David Nott (in two parts):

Part One: https://audioboom.com/boos/1823489-you-would-be-squelching-around-with-blood-on-the-floor

Part Two: https://audioboom.com/boos/1824604-my-experience-working-in-a-secret-syrian-hospital From *The PM Programme* with Eddie Mair, broadcast on BBC Radio 4.

Eisenman, Stephen F. (2007) *The Abu Ghraib Effect*, Reaktion Books, London.

Gordon, Kelly et al (2013) *The Last Frontier: Kelly Richardson*, Southern Alberta Art Gallery, Lethbridge, Alberta and Northern Gallery for Contemporary Art, Sunderland.

Gottschalk, Peter and Greenberg, Gabriel (2008) *Islamophobia: Making Muslims the Enemy*, Rowman and Littlefield Publishers Inc, Lanham, MD.

Gröndahl, Mia (2013) *Revolution Graffiti: Street Art of the New Egypt*, Thames and Hudson, London.

Gröndahl, Mia (2011) *Tahrir Square: The Heart of the Egyptian Revolution*, The American University in Cairo Press, Cairo.

Halasa, Malu (2014) et al, *Syria Speaks: Art and Culture from the Frontline*, Saqi Books, London.

Halliday, Fred (2011) *Shocked and Awed: How the War on Terror and Jihad Have Changed the English Language*, I.B. Tauris, London.

Hamlin, Janet (2013) *Sketching Guantanamo: Court Sketches of the Military Tribunals 2006-2013*, Fantagraphics Books, Seattle, WA.

Heartney, Eleanor et al (2013) *The Reckoning: Women Artists of the New Millenium*, Prestel, Munich.

Heather, David and De Ceuster, Koen (2008) *North Korean Posters: The David Heather Collection*, Prestel, Munich.

Hill, Symon (2013) *Digital Revolutions: Activism in the Internet Age*, New Internationalist Publications, Oxford (UK).

Iraq and Afghanistan Veterans of War, iava.org.

Issa, Rose (ed.) (2010) *Parastou Forouhar: Art, Life and Death in Iran*, Saqi Books.

Jiang, Jiehong (2008) *The Revolution Continues: New Art from China*, Jonathan Cape/Saatchi Gallery, London.

Johnson, Oliver (2013) 'War on the Ru-net: Voina's "Dick Captured by the FSB" as a Networked Performance', *Third Text*, No 124, Vol 27 Issue 5, September.

Kismaric, Carole and Heiferman, Marvin (1996), *Growing Up with Dick and Jane: Learning and Living the American Dream*, Collins Publishers, San Francisco, CA.

Klayman, Alison (2012) *Ai Weiwei: Never Sorry*, Expressions United Media/Muse Film and Television/Never Sorry, 91min, USA.

Lappé, Anthony (2007) *Shooting War*, Weidenfeld & Nicolson, London. (Illustrated by Dan Goldman).

Ledwidge, Frank (2013) *Investment in Blood: The True Cost of Britain's Afghan War*, Yale University Press, New Haven, CT.

Lee, Spike (2006) *When The Levees Broke: A Requiem in Four Acts*, HBO Documentary Films/ 40 Acres & A Mule Filmworks, 240min, USA.

Leistner, Dieter (2013) *Korea/Korea: A Photo Project by Dieter Leistner*, Gestalten, Berlin.

Lerner, Mike and Pozdorovkin, Maxim (2013) *Pussy Riot: A Punk Prayer*, Roast Beef Productions, 88min, Russia/UK.

Lewisohn, Cedar (2008) *Street Art: The Graffiti Revolution*, Tate Publishing, London.

Manco, Tristan et al (2010) *Graffiti Brasil*, Thames and Hudson, London.

Manhire, Toby (ed.) (2012) *The Arab Spring: Rebellion, Revolution and a New World Order*, Guardian Books, London.

McQuiston, Liz (2004) *Graphic Agitation Two*, Phaidon Press, London.

Misrach, Richard and Orff, Kate (2012) *Petrochemical America*, Aperture, New York, NY.

Neu, Emely and French, Jade (2013) *Let's Start a Pussy Riot*, Rough Trade, London.

Palmer, Kathleen (2011) *Women War Artists*, Tate Publishing/Imperial War Museum, London.

Parry, William (2010) *Against the Wall: The Art of Resistance in Palestine*, Pluto Press, London.

Pax, Salam (2003) *The Baghdad Blog*, Atlantic Books/The Guardian, London.

Prou, Sybille and Adz, King (2012) *Blek Le Rat: Getting Through the Walls*, Thames and Hudson, London.

Riverbend (2006) *Baghdad Burning: Girl Blog from Iraq*, Marion Boyars, London.

Sacco, Joe (2009) *Footnotes in Gaza*, Jonathan Cape, London.

Shifman, Limor (2014) *Memes in Digital Culture*, The MIT Press, Cambridge, MA.

Solnit, Rebecca and Snedeker, Rebecca (2013) *Unfathomable City: A New Orleans Atlas*, University of California Press, Berkeley.

Strasser, Steven (ed.) (2004) *The Abu Ghraib Investigations: The Official Reports of the Independent Panel and the Pentagon on the Shocking Prisoner Abuse in Iraq*, PublicAffairs/Perseus Books, New York, NY.

Stiglitz, Joseph E. and Bilmes, Linda J. (2008) *The Three Trillion Dollar War: The True Cost of the Iraq Conflict*, Allen Lane/Penguin Books, London.

Sturdee, Nick (2011) 'Russia's Robin Hood', *Index on Censorship: The Art Issue*, Vol 40 No 3.

Vine, Richard (2011) *New China, New Art*, Prestel, Munich.

Zirin, Dave (2014) *Brazil's Dance with the Devil: The World Cup, the Olympics, and the Fight for Democracy*, Haymarket Books, Chicago, IL.

Wallis, Clarrie (2007) 'State Britain', *State Britain: Mark Wallinger* (exhibition catalogue), Tate Publishing, London. Fold-out pamphlet.

237

Phaidon Press Limited
Regent's Wharf
All Saints Street
London N1 9PA

Phaidon Press Inc.
65 Bleecker Street
New York, NY 10012

www.phaidon.com

First published 2015
© 2015 Phaidon Press Limited

ISBN 978 0 7148 6970 4

A CIP catalogue record for
this book is available from
the British Library.

Commissioning Editor:
Emilia Terragni

Project Editor:
Adam Jackman

Production Controller:
Leonie Kellman

Design:
TwoPoints.Net/
Studio Chehade

Printed in Romania

DEDICATION

To Jeremy

ACKNOWLEDGEMENTS

The author wishes to
give special thanks to the
following for consultation
and generous assistance
in the making of this book:
Dr Sara Andersdotter, London;
Andrew Barr, Pathhead,
Scotland; Professor Jeremy
Barr, London; Marc and
Debbie Haynes, London;
Adam Jackman, London;
Richard Manning, London;
Virginia McLeod, London;
Luz, Alex and Anthony;
McQuiston, Bradenton USA;
Annalaura Palma, London;
Emilia Terragni, London;
Ana Vicente, London;
Verdi Yahooda, London

PUBLISHER'S NOTE

This work is intended as
a survey of contemporary
political and social agitation
via graphics in the twenty-
first century. The publishers
wish to make it clear that
the views expressed in the
images contained in this
publication are not their own
but those of the individuals
and organizations that created
them. The publishers do not
consider that these views are
necessarily justified, truthful
or accurate.

The materials included
demonstrate the utilization
of graphic art by individuals
and bodies with differing
aims. Those employing
graphic means to spread
their views are of varying
repute, and range from
governments through to
alleged terrorist organizations
and include, amongst others,
various pressure groups
and commercial institutions.
The book depicts the many
graphic methods used and
portrays the lengths to which
people will go in order to
communicate their views to
the public. The inclusion of
such work is for the purpose
of criticism and review of the
use of the graphic medium
and in no way indicates that
the publishers agree with the
sentiments expressed therein,
nor that the targets of the
illustrations are deserving of
such treatment.